GROWTH IN THE AMERICAN SOUTH

Growth
in the American South

CHANGING REGIONAL EMPLOYMENT
AND WAGE PATTERNS
IN THE 1960s AND 1970s

Robert J. Newman

New York University Press
New York and London
1984

Copyright © 1984 by New York University
All rights reserved

Library of Congress Cataloging in Publication Data

Newman, Robert J., 1947–
  Growth in the American South.

  A revision and expansion of thesis (Ph. D.)—University of California, Los Angeles, 1980.
    Bibliography: p.
    Includes index.
    1. Labor and laboring classes—United States—1918–   . 2. Labor mobility—United States—History—20th century. 3. Migration, Internal—United States—History—20th century. 4. Wages—United States—Regional disparities—History—20th century. 5. Labor supply—Sunbelt States—History—20th century.
6. Wages—Sunbelt States—History—20th century.
7. United States—Economic conditions—1945–   —Regional disparities. I. Title.
HD8072.5.N49   1983   331.12′5′0975   83-12204
ISBN 0-8147-5757-X

Manufactured in the United States of America

Clothbound editions of New York University Press books are Smyth-sewn and printed on permanent and acid-free paper.

TO JACQUE AND STACY

Contents

Contents

List of Tables

List of Figures

Acknowledgments

THE BASIS OF this study was my Ph.D. dissertation submitted to the Department of Economics, University of California, Los Angeles, in 1980. I wish to express sincere thanks to my thesis adviser, Finis Welch, for initially suggesting the topic and for his advice and direction throughout the preparation of the dissertation. Beyond his direct input, he instilled in me a special appreciation for the art of bridging the gap between theory and estimation. The other members of my thesis committee, Robert Cotterman, Walter Fogel, and James Smith, were also helpful in their criticisms and suggestions. However, it is difficult to express the full extent of my debt and gratitude to my de facto advisor, Michael Ward at the Rand Corporation. The quality demands he imposed, along with his constant advice and encouragement, were more than a student had any right to expect. I am further indebted to John Antel, Lee Lillard, and John Lunn for valuable comments along the way.

Substantial revision and expansion of the dissertation for publication in its present form was accomplished at Miami University in Oxford, Ohio. I wish to thank my colleague William J. Moore for first urging me to undertake this task. In addition, he read the manuscript before final revision and provided numerous comments and suggestions that improved the plan and exposition of the book. I am also grateful to Don Bellante at Auburn University for reading a copy of the final manuscript.

The financial support of the Foundation for Research in Economics and Education at UCLA, the University of British Columbia Humanities and Social Sciences Committee, and the Department of Economics at Miami University was indispensable and sincerely appreciated. Alice Cox deserves considerable gratitude for her careful typing of the many versions of the manuscript.

Acknowledgment is made to the editors of *The Review of Eco-*

nomics and Statistics (North-Holland Publishing Company) and the *Southern Economic Journal* for permission to utilize portions of previously published articles.

Finally, I owe a deep personal appreciation to my entire family, in particular to my wife, Jacque, and my daughter, Stacy, for their unfaltering encouragement and support throughout the long period consumed by this study.

Chapter 1

Introduction

"Go South Young Man, Go South"—Apocrypha

ONE CHARACTERISTIC SHARED by almost all countries is the existence of significant regional inequalities in income and wealth within the national economy. Without fear of contradiction, we can identify one salient historical feature of national economic growth and development: it seldom proceeds uniformly across regions. In fact, growth, at least in the early stages, tends to be concentrated in certain areas. This uneven growth tendency produces a pattern of regions within the national economy, each of which can be identified by a different level of economic prosperity. Even the most advanced countries include at least one so-called backward region that has failed to keep pace with the rising income levels of other regions. Examples include the Maritime Provinces in Canada, the Mezzogiorno or southern half of Italy, and the far north in Sweden. In the United States, the South has generally been considered the backward region, which has been reflected in its lower per capita income and its smaller and less diversified industrial base.

For at least the last two decades, however, the South has been one of the fastest-growing regions in the United States. During this period we have witnessed considerable shifts in the location of industrial activity, and overall the redistribution of industry employment has been from the non-South to the South. This movement of industry and jobs to the South and the concomitant revitalization of the region has generated a substantial amount of public attention, so much so that it is now popularly referred to as the Sunbelt phenomenon.[1] Although "Sunbelt" has favorable climatic connotations, the term is universally considered a code word for the emergence of many southern states and urban areas as the new frontier of U.S. economic development. The term also evokes emotional reactions. For example, the rhetoric surrounding this issue often suggests to some a coming of the second war between the states, whereas others may argue that the diverging fortunes of the South and the non-South are a measure of the North's fall from economic grace.

Another equally impressive manifestation of this phenomenon has been a significant narrowing of the traditional South/non-South earnings differentials. It is well known that average wages in the South have been lower than average wages in the rest of the nation, at least since the turn of the century. Little empirical work has been undertaken to explain the origin of these differentials, but a fairly substantial body of literature has evolved that documents and attempts to account for their existence. However, while we have some knowledge of the dynamic patterns in regional wage differentials over the first half of the twentieth century, little is known about these patterns over the last two decades. This fact is due to a change in research focus that occurred in the 1960s. While earlier studies were concerned primarily with secular trends in earnings differentials, recent studies have been more concerned with accounting for the existence of South/non-South wage differences at a single point in time. Unfortunately, because of the differences between these studies in data sources, variable definitions, standardization techniques, and degree of aggregation, intertemporal comparisons are difficult and confusing.

PURPOSE OF STUDY

The purpose of this study is twofold: (1) to document the extent and magnitude of these two interrelated dimensions of the Sunbelt phenomenon and (2) to explore alternative explanations for the observed patterns in the data. The first major task of this study is to empirically examine forces that may have acted to accelerate the migration of industry to the South. Though numerous explanations have been advanced (ranging from warmer climate to cheap labor), three have persistently aroused an impressive level of debate. Unfortunately, they have received considerably more attention at the hands of polemicists than of empiricists.

First, many have argued that a significant portion of the regional redistribution of industry can be attributed to differentials in state and local taxing policies. By far the most frequently mentioned of these has been the state corporate income tax. These rates vary widely across states; more important, there has been a dramatic change in the interregional structure of corporate taxes over the last few decades. Beginning in the early 1950s the average tax rate in the South began to decline relative to that in the non-South. Between 1950 and 1978 the average state corporate income tax rate in the South declined from 185 percent above, to 13 percent below, the average in all states.

A second explanation alleges that states in the South have begun to exhibit a more favorable business climate. Although it is difficult to directly measure a state's business climate, one important manifestation of that climate is its position with respect to collective bargaining via the legal division of power between union and management in the collective-bargaining process. It is hypothesized that firms will view legal obstacles to union organization and bargaining power as a positive signal of a state's probusiness environment. Constructing legal obstacles was clearly an overriding consideration for proponents of state right-to-work (RTW) laws. There is little doubt that the intent of this legislation was to make unions less secure and to slow down or even halt their rate of growth. Of the nineteen RTW states, ten are located in the South. As we shall show, however, this issue cannot solely be considered a uniquely southern phenomenon. The empirical results reported in Chapter 5 contradict the widely held notion that RTW laws epitomize the institutional and social characteristics of the South.

Finally, a great deal of attention has been given to the role of unions in this southern migration. The general presumption is that in highly organized states, typically those in the North, unions have been successful in imposing higher-than-average wage costs on employers. Unions may have also imposed rigid work rules that have their impact on the firm's overhead costs. Movement to the South, accordingly, is seen as a flight from high-union states.

In order to determine whether these arguments have validity, we transform them into empirically testable hypotheses and subject them to the data. Answers to two questions are sought: (1) Have these factors been important in determining the direction and magnitude of interstate migration of industry? (2) Are there systematic reasons for differences between industries in the degree to which these factors affect migration decisions?

The second major task of this study is to document the dynamic patterns in South/non-South wage differentials over the last two decades. In addition, an attempt is made to distinguish between competing hypotheses concerning the movement in these differentials. For example, is there some evidence that might suggest that rapid employment growth in the South and changes in regional wage differentials are related? To set the stage for the analysis of recent changes in South/non-South earnings differentials, we first place the issue in historical context. Utilizing data from a variety of sources, we attempt to piece together an overall picture of the secular patterns in these differentials prior to the 1950s. Attention then turns to a more rigorous analysis of the dynamic patterns of regional wage differentials over the last two decades.

SCOPE OF STUDY

This study covers the years 1957–79 for industry migration and 1959–78 for regional wage differentials.[2] These years roughly correspond to the period normally associated with the Sunbelt phenomenon. The basic area unit of analysis is the state, and for much of the analysis states are grouped in accordance with the regional and divisional classifications designated by the U.S. Bureau of the Census (see Table 2.3). The redistribution of industry is measured in terms of changes in total employment by various two-digit industry groups. Wage differentials between regions are measured by average weekly wage rates.

For industry redistribution, we examine *comparative* changes in employment between states and regions. Our point of reference is that rate of growth in industry employment that occurred at the national level. If a state grew more rapidly than the United States for a particular industry, we say that state experienced a *relative gain*. On the other hand, if a state grew less rapidly than the United States, we say that state experienced a *relative loss*.

In the analysis of South/non-South earnings differentials, we examine the change in wage ratios between an initial year and a terminal year. We then decompose the observed change in the ratio into a component attributable to actual wage changes and a component attributable to changes in the composition of the labor force between regions. This allows us to distinguish between competing hypotheses that might be offered as explanations of the recent convergence in South/non-South wage differentials.

MAJOR CONCLUSIONS

With the exception of only one industry examined in this study, growth rates in southern states exceeded the corresponding growth rates in the non-South by a considerable margin. In terms of industry redistribution, the South experienced an overall relative gain of approximately 1,709,000 employees in the manufacturing sector between 1957 and 1979. In the nonmanufacturing sector, the South's relative gain amounted to 3,482,000 employees. Outside manufacturing, the largest of these relative gains occurred in wholesale and retail trade; roughly 815,900 employees. These relative gains had the effect of substantially increasing the South's share in total manufacturing and nonmanufacturing employment.

Empirical results lend considerable support to the arguments that corporate tax rate differentials between states, the extent of unionization, as well as a favorable business climate have been major factors accounting for a portion of the redistribution of industry to the South. Evidence also reveals considerable variation in the coefficient estimates across industries, but that this variation is systematically related to capital intensity and to the rate at which an industry is expanding or contracting capacity. That is, relatively capital-intensive industries are more sensitive to changes in tax rate differentials and less sensitive to labor cost differentials than are relatively labor-intensive industries. Second, rapidly expanding industries are more sensitive to these changing differentials than are slower-growing or declining industries.

During the period between 1959 and 1978 there has been a significant narrowing of traditional South/non-South wage differentials. The data suggest that wages for male workers in the South rose vis-à-vis their counterparts in the non-South. Decomposing the change in the average wage ratio between regions (for each of five age groups) into a component attributable to composition effects and a component attributable to wage effects reveals that the improvement in the relative wages for southern male workers has been primarily due to wage effects. That is, we observed no significant alteration in the composition of the southern labor force that could have accounted for the observed convergence in average wages, either between or within cohorts. The results from this decomposition imply that wage convergence between the South and the non-South during the 1960s and

1970s was most likely due to the acceleration of industry migration to southern states. The hypothesis is that these increases in demand for labor in the South exerted upward pressure on wages because of short-run inelasticities of labor supply.

NOTES

1. Throughout this study we use the words Sunbelt and South interchangeably. Though these two terms are not strictly synonymous, the South represents such a large subset of the Sunbelt that making a distinction between the two terms becomes important only at the margin.

2. Reasons for selecting specific years are discussed in appropriate sections of succeeding chapters.

Part I
Interregional Employment Patterns, 1957–1979

Chapter 2

Extent and Direction
of Regional Gains and Losses

METHODS OF MEASURING RELATIVE GAINS
AND LOSSES

NUMEROUS MEASURES HAVE been employed in previous studies to compare differential growth patterns across regions and states. These would include *changes* in the value of shipments, value added, number and size of facilities, and employment. In this study we have chosen to measure locational change in terms of changes in total employment, including both wage and salaried workers. This measure is desirable for two reasons. First, in most policy discussions concerning regional growth disparities, especially by government officials and labor leaders, the primary focus is on changes in employment. Second, changes in employment reflect changes in labor demand more closely than other measures and is important to our understanding of the changes that have occurred in regional wage differentials.

The unit of analysis in this study is the state. While an analysis based on countries or metropolitan areas might contribute a little more to our understanding of locational change, data limitations prevent us from pursuing the analysis at that level of disaggregation. The emphasis is on the redistribution of industry between states and regions as measured by *comparative changes* in industry growth. Our point of reference will be the rate of growth that occurs at the national level. Gains and losses will be evaluated in terms of a state's growth rate relative to the U.S. average.

In measuring relative gains and losses, we do not distinguish between growth that occurs because of the physical movement of plants between locations and differential growth rates of firms that remain in a given location. Therefore, it is not clear whether an industry expands in one state relative to another because of the migration of facilities or as a result of the expansion of existing facilities within that state. However, while this may be an interesting issue, it is not a crucial distinction for our purposes.

This study examines industry migration over the last two decades. Specifically, we cover the period between 1957 and 1979. These two years were chosen as the initial and terminal dates for measuring relative gains and losses between states in order to satisfy two conditions. First, we want a measure of comparative growth during an interval of sufficient length such that the change between initial and terminal dates is independent of cyclical movements within the interval. Using such a measure minimizes the effects of purely random or transient changes in employment. Second, by measuring changes between similar phases of the business cycle, we can eliminate most of this cyclical influence. The resulting trend indicators would then be consistent with any magnitude of cyclical amplitude.[1]

The particular measure used to gauge the extent of industry redistribution between areas involves a comparison of actual employment in 1979 for each region or state with a hypothetical figure showing the amount of employment predicted for that area based on U.S. growth. The prediction imputes the national growth rate to each state. The resulting figure represents the predicted level of employment, assuming that employment within a state had grown at the national rate. It is calculated in the following manner:

$$AD = E_{si}^1 - E_{si}^0 \left(\overline{E}_i^1 / \overline{E}_i^0 \right)$$

where E_{si}^1 denotes total employment in state s, industry i, for 1979; E_{si}^0 represents the same in 1957; and $\overline{E}_i^1$ and $\overline{E}_i^0$ represent the associated employment levels in each industry for the United States.[2] This measure has two objectives. First, we desire a specification that yields measures that are conceptually simple, easily interpreted, and readily compared with previous studies. Second, we attempt to distinguish between growth-induced change that occurs because of national trends in industry expansion or contraction and growth-induced change that occurs as a result of factors associated with a particular state. A positive (negative) number represents a relative gain (loss) in employment. The difference between actual and hypothetical employment in 1979 is assumed to reflect the importance of state-specific or region-

SOUTH/NON-SOUTH DIFFERENTIALS IN GROWTH OF INDUSTRY EMPLOYMENT
FOR SELECTED INDUSTRY GROUPS, 1957-79
(employment and AD expressed in thousands of employees)

| | Employment 1957 | | Employment 1979 | | Percent Δ in Employment | | AD: |
	South	Non-South	South	Non-South	South	Non-South	South
MANUFACTURING:							
Textile Mill Products	603.2	394.1	662.7	203.7	9.9	-48.3	+138.7
Apparel & Other Textile Products	303.9	891.4	595.0	641.6	95.8	-28.0	+280.6
Lumber & Wood Products	257.6	349.8	286.7	391.0	11.3	11.8	- .7
Furniture & Fixtures	119.0	239.4	219.9	233.9	84.8	- 2.3	+ 69.2
Paper & Allied Products	127.6	413.4	205.1	459.8	60.7	11.2	+ 48.3
Printing & Publishing	142.9	719.4	292.7	910.3	104.8	26.5	+ 93.3
Chemicals & Allied Products	279.5	502.6	439.0	633.7	57.1	26.1	+ 55.6
Rubber & Misc. Plastics	21.8	297.9	60.1	453.1	175.7	52.1	+ 25.1
Leather & Leather Products	38.0	277.5	49.7	144.7	30.8	-47.9	+ 26.2
Stone, Glass, & Clay Products	138.6	413.9	224.7	436.1	62.1	5.4	+ 58.9
Primary Metals	202.1	1127.1	253.6	954.7	25.5	-15.3	+ 69.9
Fabricated Metals	123.3	985.5	337.5	1284.9	173.7	30.4	+157.1
Machinery, ex. Electric	117.4	1394.0	471.7	1901.8	301.8	36.4	+287.3
Electric, Electronic Equipment	104.3	1216.2	472.9	1524.5	353.4	25.3	+315.2
Transportation Equipment	253.6	1468.7	377.8	1612.7	49.0	9.8	+ 84.7
MINING	399.3	387.3	545.6	386.5	18.5	- 0.2	+724.4
CONTRACT CONSTRUCTION	860.0	2005.0	1780.0	2698.0	56.3	34.5	+435.8
WHOLESALE & RETAIL TRADE	3202.0	8332.0	9624.0	13772.0	102.8	65.3	+815.9
FINANCE, INSURANCE, & REAL ESTATE	542.0	1841.0	1433.0	3490.0	106.6	89.6	+313.3
SERVICES	1532.0	4614.0	4890.0	12127.0	219.2	162.8	+648.2
GOVERNMENT	2324.0	5070.0	5618.0	10524.0	141.7	107.6	+544.5

Source: Calculated from data in U.S. Department of Labor, Bureau of Labor Statistics, Employment and Earnings, States and Areas, 1939-78, 1979, and Supplement to Employment and Earnings, States and Areas, 1977-79.

Definitions: $AD = E^1 - E^0 (\overline{E}^1/\overline{E}^0)$.

where E^1 = total employment in the South for a particular industry in 1979.

E^0 = total employment in the South for a particular industry in 1957.

$\overline{E}^1$ & $\overline{E}^0$ = U.S. employment for each industry for 1973 and 1957, respectively.

specific factors in producing a divergence between actual employment and that expected on the basis of national trends.

SOUTH/NON-SOUTH RELATIVE GAINS AND LOSSES

The extent to which employment growth rates differed between the South and the non-South during the past two decades is revealed in Table 2.1, which documents these differentials and also provides our measure of the resulting distribution of industry among these two regions.[3] Columns 1–4 contain the total employment for each industry in 1957 and 1979.[4] The numbers in columns 5 and 6 are the simple percentage growth rates over the period in question. The numbers in the last column are the calculated redistributive measure (AD) for the South.[5]

The shifts in industry employment between the two regions have been quite dramatic over the last two decades. Overall, there has been a very pronounced movement of industry employment toward the South. Although this movement to the South has been documented by Fuchs (1962) for the years between 1929 and 1954, there appears to have been a decided acceleration in the migratory process during the 1960s.[6]

In the manufacturing sector the non-South experienced a *relative* loss in employment for every industry except lumber and wood products. In five of these industries—textiles, apparel, furniture, leather, and primary metals—the non-South witnessed an *absolute* reduction in employment. For example, total employment in the apparel industry fell by roughly 250,000 employees. This represents a 28 percent decrease in labor employed within this industry outside the South. As a result, our redistributive measure reveals that the South experienced a relative gain in apparels of approximately 280,000 employees. For all five industries the loss in total employment for the non-South exceeded 750,000.

With only one exception (lumber and wood products), the growth rates for manufacturing industries in the South exceeded the growth rates in the non-South by a substantial margin.[7] For example, in machinery products, a traditionally high-wage, capital-intensive industry, employment in Southern states quadrupled between 1957 and 1979. The redistributive measure indicates a relative gain for the South of 287,000 employees. Impressive gains were also made in fabricated metals, and electronic equipment. For manufacturing as a whole, the South had a relative gain of about 1,709,000 employees between 1957 and 1979.

The same general pattern of southern migration is present for the six nonmanufacturing industries. In all cases the relative gains have been decidedly in favor of the South. The largest gain occurred in wholesale and retail trade, followed closely by mining. In the latter case, however, the South's relative gain can be attributed largely to the non-South's complete absence of growth. In both regions the largest gains were made in the service sector, reflecting the overall trend toward an increasing share of total output originating in this

TABLE 2.2

TOTAL EMPLOYMENT IN THE SOUTH AS A PERCENT
OF U.S. EMPLOYMENT

Industry	Percent Share		
	1957	1979	Δ
Textile Mill Products	60	76	+16
Apparel Products	25	48	+23
Lumber and Wood Products	42	42	0
Furniture and Fixtures	33	48	+13
Paper and Allied Products	24	31	+ 7
Printing and Publishing	17	24	+ 7
Chemicals and Allied Products	36	41	+ 5
Rubber and Misc. Plastics	7	12	+ 5
Leather and Leather Products	12	26	+14
Stone, Glass, and Clay	25	34	+ 9
Primary Metals	15	21	+ 6
Fabricated Metals	11	21	+11
Machinery, ex. Electric	8	20	+12
Electric, Electronic Equipment	8	24	+16
Transportation Equipment	15	19	+ 4
Mining	51	59	+ 8
Construction	30	40	+10
Wholesale and Retail Trade	28	41	+13
Finance, Insurance, and Real Estate	23	29	+ 6
Services	25	29	+ 4
Government	31	34	+ 3

Source: Calculated from data in U.S. Department of Labor, Bureau of
         Labor Statistics, Employment and Earnings, States and Areas
         1939-78, 1979 and Supplement to Employment and Earnings, States
         and Areas 1977-79.

sector of the economy. For the nonmanufacturing sector, the South experienced a relative gain of about 3,482,000 employees.

The resulting relative gains and losses had the overall effect of increasing the South's share in total manufacturing and nonmanufacturing employment. These gains are depicted in Table 2.2, where we compare the South's share of total U.S. employment for each industry in 1957 and 1979. With the exception of lumber and wood products, states in the South increased their share of total employment in every industry. Several of these gains are rather substantial and, in turn, provide convincing evidence with respect to the magnitude of the Sunbelt phenomenon. Also, these data support Fuch's earlier conclusions that: (1) most industries, especially manufacturing, are now more geographically scattered; (2) most areas are now less dependent on a single industry group for employment; and (3) the interregional differences in industrial structure have been substantially eroded, that is, regions have become more equal in their industrial makeup.

DIVISIONAL GAINS AND LOSSES

Although the preceding section documents the extent to which the South gained relative to the non-South, a considerable amount of variation exists within each region. On average, the non-South experienced a rather sizable relative loss in almost every industry, but this was not the case for every area outside the South. As one might expect, states in the West had higher growth rates than states in the Northeast. Also, some southern states grew at a slower rate than the national average and hence witnessed some relative losses. To get some idea of this within-region variation, the redistributive measure (AD) is calculated for each of the nine census divisions outlined in Table 2.3. These calculations are displayed in Table 2.4 along with total employment for each industry in 1957 (E^0) and 1979 (E^1). In the remainder of this section, we discuss in detail the redistribution of each industry across divisions.

Textile Mill Products. Between 1957 and 1979 total textile employment in the United States actually declined. Total employment at the end of this period was about 87 percent of what it was in 1957. The only states to experience any appreciable gains in employment were located in the South Atlantic and Pacific divisions.

TABLE 2.3

UNITED STATES CENSUS DIVISIONS

Non-South:

New England (NE)	Mountain (MT)	West North Central (WNC)
Maine	Montana	Minnesota
New Hampshire	Idaho	Iowa
Vermont	Wyoming	Missouri
Massachusetts	Colorado	North Dakota
Rhode Island	New Mexico	South Dakota
Connecticut	Arizona	Nebraska
Middle Atlantic (MA)	Utah	Kansas
New York	Nevada	
New Jersey	Pacific (PAC)	
Pennsylvania	Washington	
East North Central (ENC)	Oregon	
Ohio	California	
Indiana		
Illinois		
Michigan		
Wisconsin		

South:

South Atlantic (SA)	East South Central (ESC)
Delaware	Kentucky
Maryland	Tennessee
D.C.	Alabama
Virginia	Mississippi
West Virginia	West South Central (WSC)
North Carolina	Arkansas
South Carolina	Louisiana
Georgia	Oklahoma
Florida	Texas

Source: U.S. Bureau of the Census.

The largest relative gain occurred in the South Atlantic division, where the share of textile employment increased by approximately 130,500 employees. This represents 87 percent of the total relative loss in the North (NE, MA, ENC, and WNC). Overall, the migration pattern in textiles continues to be primarily out of the Northeast and into the South Atlantic states, which represents no dramatic change from earlier decades of this century.

Apparel Products. The migration pattern for apparels closely parallels that of textiles. Unlike the redistribution of textiles, however, relatively large gains were also made outside the South

TABLE 2.4

INTERDIVISIONAL DIFFERENTIALS IN GROWTH OF EMPLOYMENT
FOR SELECTED INDUSTRY GROUPS, 1957-79
(AD and employment expressed in thousands)

		NE	MA	ENC	WNC	SA	ESC	WSC	MT	PAC
MANUFACTURING:										
Textile Mill Products	AD	- 56.70	- 57.16	- 35.26	- 0.96	+130.47	+ 12.31	- 4.11	--	+ 11.41
	EO	137.9	190.0	56.7	1.8	503.4	83.1	16.7	--	7.7
	E1	63.1	107.9	14.0	0.6	567.8	84.5	10.4	--	18.1
Apparel & Other Textile Prods.	AD	- 28.01	-241.51	- 62.28	8.03	+146.52	+ 85.20	+ 48.87	--	+ 53.53
	EO	90.0	590.7	106.5	44.3	152.7	101.2	50.0	--	59.9
	E1	65.1	369.6	47.9	37.8	304.5	189.9	100.6	--	115.5
Lumber & Wood Products	AD	- 9.75	- 1.57	- 6.74	- 6.96	- 5.76	- 1.62	+ 6.67	+12.59	+ 13.15
	EO	35.0	41.2	64.3	16.1	112.0	79.7	65.9	21.7	171.5
	E1	29.3	44.4	65.0	11.0	119.2	87.3	80.2	36.8	204.5
Furniture & Fixtures	AD	- 7.87	- 36.54	- 38.91	3.74	+ 42.69	+ 19.35	+ 7.18	--	+ 17.82
	EO	16.4	71.9	105.6	9.9	77.8	22.7	18.5	--	35.6
	E1	12.9	54.5	94.8	8.8	141.2	48.1	30.6	--	62.9
Paper & Allied Products	AD	- 18.01	- 36.39	- 19.22	22.07	+ 19.68	+ 17.64	+ 10.96	--	+ 1.88
	EO	56.4	136.2	148.1	23.7	68.2	29.1	30.3	--	49.0
	E1	51.3	131.0	162.8	51.2	103.5	53.4	48.2	--	62.1
Printing & Publishing	AD	- 2.28	- 94.47	- 57.80	+ 12.67	+ 49.21	+ 15.58	+ 28.55	+15.51	+ 33.02
	EO	61.2	268.2	228.3	72.2	71.1	29.4	42.4	11.1	78.4
	E1	83.1	279.7	260.7	113.4	148.4	56.6	87.7	31.0	142.4
Chemicals & Allied Prods.	AD	+ 3.55	- 51.71	- 18.84	- 0.36	+ 18.14	+ 4.04	+ 33.47	+ 5.58	+ 6.13
	EO	12.5	230.4	172.9	35.7	147.1	68.8	63.6	2.2	48.9
	E1	20.7	264.3	218.3	48.6	219.9	98.4	120.7	8.6	73.2
Rubber & Misc. Plastics	AD	- 42.92	+ 2.12	- 19.24	--	- 3.44	+ 28.54	--	--	+ 31.46
	EO	60.5	68.2	141.5	--	10.8	11.0	--	--	22.7
	E1	54.2	111.6	207.9	--	13.9	46.2	--	--	67.9
Leather & Leather Prods.	AD	- 11.05	- 13.29	- 9.03	1.57	- 0.61	+ 17.09	+ 9.80	--	+ 8.66
	EO	86.1	110.5	34.3	40.2	14.3	16.4	7.3	--	6.4
	E1	42.0	54.8	12.1	23.2	8.2	27.2	14.3	--	12.6
Stone, Glass, & Clay	AD	+ 0.43	- 46.20	- 34.02	7.77	+ 21.21	+ 11.67	+ 26.05	+14.50	+ 14.13
	EO	18.2	156.6	146.0	41.7	73.4	28.2	37.0	4.1	47.3
	E1	22.2	141.1	140.6	42.1	109.0	45.4	70.3	19.4	70.7
Primary Metals	AD	- 9.92	-103.52	+ 18.93	11.33	+ 21.45	+ 14.71	+ 33.72	- 2.33	+ 15.62
	EO	66.9	428.5	511.6	28.9	87.4	77.1	37.6	18.4	72.8
	E1	50.9	286.0	484.0	37.6	100.9	84.8	67.9	14.4	81.8
Fabricated Metals	AD	- 19.06	-147.58	- 63.41	29.58	+ 71.50	+ 5.83	+ 79.76	+ 3.12	+ 40.27
	EO	102.9	281.7	446.9	52.5	44.7	33.4	45.2	4.5	97.0
	E1	131.5	264.6	590.5	106.4	136.9	54.7	145.9	9.7	182.2

TABLE 2.4 (continued)

		NE	MA	ENC	WNC	SA	ESC	WSC	MT	PAC
Machinery, ex. Electric	$\dot{AD}$	− 54.54	− 191.36	− 222.54	+ 45.77	+ 104.36	+ 38.00	+ 144.97	+ 9.11	+ 126.23
	E^0	161.2	370.2	671.0	94.2	41.8	34.0	41.6	14.0	83.4
	E^1	198.6	390.0	831.2	193.7	170.0	91.4	210.3	31.1	257.2
Electric, Electronic Equip.	$\dot{AD}$	+ 12.30	− 267.91	− 243.20	+ 46.69	+ 144.56	+ 37.37	+ 133.27	+ 9.10	+ 149.42
	E^0	138.5	429.0	486.6	38.3	49.3	44.2	10.8	4.3	120.1
	E^1	197.1	380.7	492.5	107.6	219.1	104.2	149.6	15.6	331.0
Transportation Equip.	$\dot{AD}$	− 6.85	+ 96.37	+ 19.70	+ 14.15	+ 18.50	+ 50.08	+ 16.13	−−	− 26.44
	E^0	110.8	248.3	648.6	115.9	116.9	36.1	100.6	−−	345.1
	E^1	121.2	190.6	769.3	148.1	153.6	91.8	132.4	−−	372.4
MINNING	$\dot{AD}$	− 6.96	− 646.26	− 113.67	− 183.95	− 308.33	+ 572.36	+ 460.38	+ 284.43	− 57.98
	E^0	1.6	103.4	84.7	58.9	122.9	29.0	247.4	98.7	40.0
	E^1	1.2	57.9	89.0	51.4	114.8	91.6	339.2	145.4	41.6
CONTRACT CONSTRUCTION	$\dot{AD}$	+ 87.78	− 312.89	− 240.23	− 4.24	+ 159.59	+ 74.12	+ 202.11	+ 126.31	+ 83.01
	E^0	179.0	538.0	599.0	226.0	443.0	133.0	284.0	122.0	341.0
	E^1	192.0	528.0	696.0	349.0	852.0	282.0	646.0	317.0	616.0
WHOLESALE & RETAIL TRADE	$\dot{AD}$	− 76.08	− 1176.78	− 403.99	− 78.60	+ 503.99	+ 72.77	+ 239.10	+ 338.41	+ 581.18
	E^0	706.0	2469.0	2416.0	1033.0	1525.0	585.0	1092.0	407.0	1301.0
	E^1	1160.0	3146.0	3826.0	1730.0	3174.0	1097.0	2151.0	1051.0	2859.0
FINANCE, INSURANCE, & REAL ESTATE	$\dot{AD}$	− 51.60	− 427.20	− 105.98	− 22.39	+ 174.95	+ 27.94	+ 110.40	+ 102.72	+ 191.15
	E^0	176.0	686.0	455.0	188.0	274.0	92.0	176.0	65.0	271.0
	E^1	312.0	990.0	834.0	366.0	741.0	218.0	474.0	237.0	751.0
SERVICES	$\dot{AD}$	− 15.82	− 1036.80	− 338.23	− 35.40	+ 458.87	+ 53.89	+ 135.45	+ 298.02	+ 480.02
	E^0	416.0	1519.0	1223.0	487.0	765.0	272.0	495.0	225.0	744.0
	E^1	1136.0	3169.0	3048.0	1313.0	2577.0	807.0	1506.0	921.0	2540.0
GOVERNMENT	$\dot{AD}$	− 102.93	− 453.71	− 119.59	− 112.73	+ 366.17	+ 54.33	+ 123.93	+ 136.81	+ 107.72
	E^0	431.0	1380.0	1292.0	632.0	1195.0	446.0	683.0	356.0	979.0
	E^1	838.0	2559.0	2701.0	1267.0	2975.0	1028.0	1615.0	914.0	2245.0

Source: Calculated from data in U.S. Department of Labor, Bureau of Labor Statistics, Employment and Earnings, States and Areas, 1939-78, 1979 and Supplement to Employment and Earnings, States and Areas 1977-79.

Definitions: $AD = E^1 - E^0(\bar{E}^1/\bar{E}^0)$.

Where E^1 = Total employment within region iii 1979.

E^0 = total employment within region in 1959.

$\bar{E}^1$ & $\bar{E}^0$ = total U.S. employment in 1979 and 1959, respectively.

Atlantic division. For example, the Pacific division had a relative gain of nearly 54,000 employees. Nevertheless, states in the South Atlantic division received about 43 percent of the North's relative loss of 340,000 employees. Notice that absolute levels of employment declined rather dramatically in every division of the North, while employment almost doubled in every other division. These employment gains and losses had the effect of significantly altering the distributional share of employment for the South. At the beginning of this period the South's share of total employment in apparels was 25 percent. By 1979 this share had risen to 48 percent.

Lumber and Wood Products. Total U.S. employment in lumber increased by 11 percent over the last two decades. With the exception of the states in the New England and West North Central divisions, absolute employment increased. But, in terms of redistribution (or share), only the three western divisions experienced relative gains. As might be expected, most of the modest growth that occurred in this industry can be attributed to the expansion in the Northwest region (MT and PAC). For the South, relative losses in the South Atlantic and East South Central divisions slightly outweighed gains in the West South Central states. The net effect was a relatively insignificant loss in the South of about 700 employees. As a result, the South's share of total U.S. employment remained unchanged between 1957 and 1979, about 42 percent.

Furniture and Fixtures. The furniture industry grew about 27 percent nationally, with the largest relative gain occurring in the South Atlantic. In this division employment rose from just under 78,000 to over 140,000, which translates into a growth rate of roughly 80 percent. At the same time, absolute levels of employment were falling throughout the North, so that the South's share rose from 33 percent in 1957 to 48 percent in 1979.

Paper and Allied Products. The largest relative gain in the paper industry occurred in the West North Central division, and the largest absolute gain in employment occurred in the South Atlantic. Some substantial relative gains also occurred in the East South Central and West South Central divisions. As in each of the previously mentioned industries, the migration pattern for paper was decidedly out of the

Northeast. The South's share increased by 7 percentage points over this period.

Printing and Publishing. Total employment in the printing and publishing industry increased in every division, but relative losses were exclusively in the Northeast. This was especially true for the three states in the Middle Atlantic division, where relative losses exceeded 94,000 employees. Over 50 percent of the offsetting relative gains can be attributed to employment growth in the South Atlantic; approximately 50,000 employees. This growth contributed substantially to the South's 7 percentage point increase in share.

Chemicals and Allied Products. The chemical and related products industry expanded by about 37 percent between 1957 and 1979. Most of this growth occurred in the South Atlantic and West South Central divisions. These two divisions accounted for a relative gain of just over 50,000 employees. Notice that states in New England experienced a relative gain of 3,500 employees. This was one of only three manufacturing industries for which New England did *not* have a relative loss in employment. The South's share of total U.S. employment increased modestly from 36 to 41 percent.

Rubber and Miscellaneous Plastics. During this period rubber and plastics was the fastest-growing industry in our sample. Employment grew by 60 percent.[8] The redistribution of this industry was primarily toward two divisions, the East South Central and the Pacific. Also, a modest relative gain occurred in the Middle Atlantic states. However, owing to the paucity of published data for several states, we cannot say anything about relative growth rates for the West South Central, West North Central, and Mountain divisions. Nevertheless, it is unlikely that our qualitative conclusions about the redistribution of this industry would change with the acquisition of these data.

Leather and Leather Products. This particular industry was actually contracting over the period in question. By 1979 total employment in leather and leather products was only about 62 percent of its level at the beginning of the period. What little expansion there was occurred in the East South Central, West South Central, and

Pacific divisions. States in the South accounted for 76 percent of this relative gain. The result was a 14 percentage point gain in its share of total employment.

Stone, Glass, and Clay. This industry grew at a modest rate of 20 percent between 1957 and 1979. While most divisions in the North experienced reductions in employment, every other division witnesses employment expansion. The largest absolute gains were in the South Atlantic and West South Central divisions. However, the largest relative gain was experienced by states in the West South Central division; roughly 26,000 employees.

Primary Metals. Total employment in 1979 was approximately 90 percent of its level in 1957. With the exception of the West North Central division, employment in the North declined by about 186,000. Notice that even though employment actually fell by 27,600 in the East North Central division, its decline was below the national average. As a result, it had a relative *gain* of 19,000 employees. The West South Central division had both the largest relative *and* absolute gain; 33,700 and 30,000 employees, respectively. As a result, the South's share of total employment rose from 15 to 21 percent.

Fabricated Metals. Some rather dramatic gains occurred in two divisions. In the West South Central division, employment increased by over 100,000, or 222 percent. States in the South Atlantic division experienced employment gains of 92,000, a 206 percent growth rate. The resulting relative gain in each of these divisions in the South was over 70,000 employees. The most impressive relative loss occurred in the Middle Atlantic; roughly 147,500 employees. Altogether, the South's share of the total relative gains was 63 percent.

Machinery Products. Machinery products experienced the second-highest growth rate, 57 percent. The regional shifts in this industry were quite impressive. The addition of new capacity in this industry was occurring most rapidly in three divisions, SA, WSC, and PAC. The loser in this regional migration was the Northeast, where relative losses exceeded 468,000 employees.

Electronic Equipment. The regional shifts in this industry were much the same as those occurring in machinery products. National expansion was about 51 percent, and relative gains were most dramatic for the SA, WSC, and PAC divisions. However, all the relative losses of 511,000 employees occurred in just two divisions, the Middle Atlantic and the East North Central. The New England division experienced a relative gain of 12,300 employees.

Transportation Equipment. The most notable feature of regional redistribution that occurred in transportation equipment was the relative loss experienced by the Far West, or the Pacific division (PAC). This industry includes aircraft and parts (in terms of total employment, it is second only to motor vehicles and equipment in this two-digit classification). Historically, this has been one of the nation's largest employers of skilled labor. Throughout the period in question, the West was losing its relative share of this industry to the South. This was especially noticeable during the period 1968–71, when the West Coast experienced a rather severe depression in the aircraft industry. While massive layoffs were being carried out in California and Washington, rapid employment gains in several southern states were acting to shift the regional distribution of this industry in favor of the South.

Mining. In terms of total employment, mining was the slowest-growing industry in the nonmanufacturing sector. Total employment fell in the non-South, with the largest absolute loss occurring in the Middle Atlantic states. The South Atlantic division also experienced substantial losses, both absolutely and relatively. These losses were more than compensated for, however, by the significant gains in the other two southern divisions.

Contract Construction. The growth of contract construction in the South is not surprising, considering the significant expansion of plant capacity that occurred during this period. Also, this growth followed closely the changes in the regional distribution of total U.S. population. For at least a century prior to the 1960s, the dominant pattern was one of heavy out-migration from the South. The South's changeover from a net out-migration to a net in-migration region is especially noticeable in the late 1960s. This pattern of net in-migration increased substantially during the 1970s, making the South the fastest-growing region in the United States.[9] These demographic patterns would obviously be expected to show up in net new construction. For example, throughout the last two decades new housing starts in the South exceeded new housing starts in every other region.[10] This would at least partly account for the South's relative gain of approximately 435,800 employees during this same period.

Wholesale and Retail Trade. Total employment in wholesale and retail trade in the South increased by 103 percent, whereas the growth rate in the non-South was 65 percent. Growth in this industry will also closely correspond to demographic shifts across regions. The largest relative gains in the South occurred in the South Atlantic and West South Central divisions. Overall, the South's relative gain exceeded 800,000 employees.

Finance, Insurance, and Real Estate. Of the 300,000 relative gain in employment experienced by the South, 95 percent occurred in the South Atlantic and West South Central divisions. The largest relative gain occurred in the Pacific division, but in terms of absolute gains, this division did not exceed the South Atlantic division by any appreciable amount. In the South Atlantic division, employment increased by 467,000; in the Pacific division, employment rose by 480,000. Some impressive gains were also made in the Mountain states. Employment in these states increased by 264 percent, or roughly 172,000 employees.

Service. The increasing importance of the service sector can be readily seen in the changing distribution of employment between sectors. In 1957 approximately 12 percent of total U.S. non-agricultural employees worked in the service sector. By 1979 this figure had increased to about 19 percent. Like contract construction and wholesale and retail trade, the growth in service-related activities will closely follow the regional redistribution of income and population. While employment increased substantially in every division, the largest relative gains were experienced outside the North.

Government. Even though government employment doubled in nearly every division of the North, this region experienced substantial relative losses. As might be expected, the largest gains, both absolute and relative, occurred in the South Atlantic division. In 1957 government employment accounted for about 14 percent of total nonagricultural employment. By 1979 employment in this sector was 17 percent of total U.S. nonagricultural employment. A large part of this growth occurred at the federal level. The District of Columbia would, therefore, have contributed a substantial share of the South Atlantic division's relative gain of 366,000 employees.

SUMMARY

Without question, the South has experienced substantial relative gains in industry employment over the last two decades. The movement of industry employment, inter alia, has been one important manifestation of what is now popularly referred to as the Sunbelt phenomenon. With the exception of only one two-digit industry (lumber and wood products), growth rates in southern states exceeded the corresponding growth rates in the non-South by a considerable margin.

In terms of industry redistribution, the South experienced an overall relative gain of approximately 1,709,000 employees in the manufacturing sector between 1957 and 1979. In the nonmanufacturing sector (excluding agriculture), the South's relative gain amounted to 3,482,000 employees. The largest of these relative gains occurred in wholesale and retail trade; roughly 815,900 employees. These relative gains had the effect of substantially increasing the South's share in total manufacturing and nonmanufacturing employment.

These migration patterns and the resulting redistribution of industry employment raise a few interesting and important questions. Why do industries move? Why are they moving to the South, and why did this movement accelerate in the early 1960s? In the next few chapters we direct our attention to these questions. However, rather than providing a complete list of the multitude of factors that can affect industry migration decisions, we will instead focus our attention on three heretofore empirically neglected but highly controversial explanations. We do this because the effects of other variables have been well established in previous empirical work. We begin first with some general considerations and then narrow our focus to the effects on migration patterns of changes in interstate differentials in corporate taxes, unionization rates, and business climate.

NOTES

1. At this writing, 1979 was the most recent year employment data were available.

2. This technique for measuring relative gains and losses is identical to that used by Fuchs (1962).

3. In this study the South is defined as three census divisions: South Atlantic, East South Central, and West South Central. See Table 2.3 for a list of the specific states.

4. Data on two-digit manufacturing and nonmanufacturing employment for each state, excluding Alaska and Hawaii, are taken from *Employment and Earnings,* published by the U.S. Bureau of Labor Statistics. Because of the paucity of employment data at the state level, two manufacturing industries are excluded. These are petroleum and coal products, and instruments and related products. In addition, food and kindred products and tobacco products are excluded because of their ties to specific areas.

5. Only AD for the South is presented, since its gain (loss) is the non-South's loss (gain); that is, the symmetry condition means that $AD_s + AD_{ns} = 0$ by definition.

6. See app. E in Fuchs (1962) for comparison. Though Fuchs uses a slightly different industry classification scheme, some rough comparisons are nevertheless possible.

7. It must be pointed out that part of this apparent disparity in growth rates can be attributable to a lower base in the South; that is, states with initially low employment levels may have exaggerated growth rates. Nevertheless, the absolute increases are substantial; hence, we cannot explain the higher growth rates in the South by this argument alone.

8. This industry group had one of the lowest initial levels of employment, which means that it had a higher chance of incurring a relatively large growth rate.

9. See Greenwood (1982) and Long and Hansen (1975).

10. U.S Bureau of the Census, *Construction Reports,* series C20.

Chapter 3

The Relocation Decision

A CONSIDERABLE AMOUNT of attention, at both the theoretical and the empirical level, has been devoted to the migration decision of individuals. The movement of individuals between locations in response to differences in economic opportunities has been well documented, and it is generally agreed that the direction of this movement is consistent with predictions of economic theory.[1] As indicated in the previous chapter, we have also witnessed considerable shifts in the location of industrial activity over the last two decades.[2] While in general we expect firms to respond to changes in locational advantages in the same manner as individuals, there are important differences between the two. For individuals, location amenities can play an important role in their decision calculus. Individual motives and propensities to move are strongly influenced by habit and past association. Most people may come to prefer their existing environment because they have grown accustomed to it. Put another way, they have invested heavily in location-specific human capital. In addition, with time in residence comes the formation of neighborhood kinship and family ties. These factors interact to create inertia in the migration response of individuals to differentials in income potential between alternative locations. It also means that individuals may be willing to sacrifice potential income to remain in their present location.

However, this is not the case for business firms. Ignoring differentials in locational advantages can result in bankruptcy rather than in the mere reduction in potential income. Thus, for firms, locational amenities play a far less important role in determining the kinds of location adjustments that are made following some change in interlocation costs of production. Inertia in the migration response of firms and industries results from the location-specific nature of capital. Most forms of physical capital are fixed in place and, consequently, are prohibitively expensive to move. Hence, the most profitable action for any firm may be to phase out production in the present location over time as physical capital deteriorates or becomes completely obsolete.

In this chapter we deal with two general points: (1) the sources of locational change and (2) the way in which an individual firm or industry migrates. With respect to point (2), we outline a simple migration decision that suggests that a firm's most profitable response to changing locational advantages may involve "waiting" at its present location for some period of time. In essence, the firm is faced with selecting an optimal migration date that in general is not immediate.

SOURCES OF LOCATION CHANGE

We can think of the causes for the migration of industry between states and regions as originating from one of two sources. The first can be loosely described as structural. This would include forces that cause overall employment to increase faster in some regions even in the absence of a change in the interregional costs of production. For example, two growth-inducing forces directly related to the rate at which a particular industry expands are the income elasticity of demand for its output and the rate of technological change. As real income rises, the desired composition of total output, at given relative prices, changes because of differences between industries in the income elasticity of demand. Since states and regions differ in the composition of their output, such changes will stimulate growth in some regions more than in others. These differential growth patterns may occur even within a two-digit industry group. This would occur if within each group there exists some variation in income elasticity of demand between three- and four-digit industry groups *and* if the distribution of industry composition within each two-digit group varies between regions. Even if two regions had the same level of employment in, say, transportation equipment, they may have a substantially different employment distribution within this aggregate grouping.

Technological change may also lead to regional growth disparities. Technical advance usually proceeds unevenly across industries. This process has the effect of altering relative prices, and to the extent that technological change occurs in industries with high price elasticities, output and employment for these industries will increase at above average rates.[3] In addition, change in technology may alter the costs of producing in one region relative to another. As a result, new plant capacity and production may expand in areas other than those in which they are presently located. For example, waterwheels are the first device used on a considerable scale for the conversion of nonhuman energy. As long as energy was nontransportable, industries tended to concentrate at waterpower sites. With the development of transportable energy sources, the location patterns changed. Such was the case in the early development of textile manufacturing in New England.[4]

A second source of locational change is an alteration in relative costs of production between regions arising from some change at a given location. In this study we abstract from structural influences and concentrate instead on the location-specific changes that have altered the relative costs of production between regions. Specifically, the objective is to determine the location effects of changes in interstate differentials of certain economic characteristics (e.g., tax policies) that directly or indirectly affect input prices. How these changes affect the firm's decision to migrate is the focus of the following section.

MIGRATION RESPONSE OF FIRMS AND INDUSTRIES

There are basically two ways in which regional movement of economic activity can occur. Shifts in the location of any specific industry are essentially a combination of geographic differentials in the rate of plant expansion in existing locations and the actual relocation of plant and equipment. Industries may differ significantly in the weights given to each type of movement. For those industries in which branch plants are important, the predominant part of movement will likely come from opening and closing of plants, which entail the actual relocation of factors of production.

The relocation of industry does not necessarily mean the migration of all factors of production. Certainly, land does not move; capital and labor may or may not move. Resources may remain in old locations, shift occupations, or pass in and out of other productive uses. For certain resources there are limits to which they can participate in an actual move. In addition to land, some forms of physical and human capital are completely immobile. They are involved in migration only to the extent that they are shifted into alternative uses in the same location. The way in which a particular productive factor can participate in location change will depend upon its spatial mobility and its adaptability to other uses (e.g., firm specific versus general capital).[5]

Consider the migration decision of an individual firm. It is assumed that firms are profit maximizers and are able to make rational (consistent) investment decisions following changes in locational characteristics.[6] The impetus to migrate is assumed to come from the changing cost of production between regions (or states) and the resultant impact on net revenue streams. A firm will migrate (replace its current facilities with capital facilities in another location) for purposes of obtaining benefits that arise as a result of cost savings from doing the same thing in a "cheaper" location. In response to a change in cost of production in one location relative to another, the firm will face two decisions: (1) migrate or stay put, and if it decides to migrate (2) when should this move be undertaken. The latter decision is essentially one of determining the optimal service life of the current location in face of an alternative that can yield the firm a higher net revenue stream. The fact that a new location may have a greater income than the one now occupied does not imply an immediate move. There are obstacles to mobility that impart some inertia to the migration process. As previously discussed, the main obstacle encountered by the firm is that its existing stock of capital is largely fixed in its present location. In addition, the move will involve expense, extra effort, and some disruption of existing trade contracts. Thus, the benefits afforded by the new location may be obtainable only in the long run. In this case, the optimal timing of the actual migration will be based on a comparison of *out-of-pocket* costs at the present location with *total* costs at the new location, less whatever might be realized from the sale of capital facilities at the current location. Note that the firm will ignore the cost of the existing investments, since capital outlays for sunk investments do not enter the future stream of income. Thus, they should not influence the migration decision. Hence, in the absence of the need for extensive renewal of existing capital facilities, the profit-maximizing path for the firm may entail continued operation of a location that may be "obsolete" on a total cost basis.

In general, the length of time before actual migration takes place will depend upon the durability of a firm's capital stock. To see this, let us first examine the case of a firm possessing an infinitely durable stock of capital that the firm already owns and has been operating in its present location for some period of time. Assume that production costs in some otherwise equally attractive location fall. Hence, the net revenue stream obtainable there exceeds the net revenue stream the firm is earning in its present location. We will assume that these two locations are mutually exclusive alternatives and that the firm cannot physically move its existing capital stock. As a result, the firm must decide whether it pays to replace its current location with the alternative (migrate). This will involve a comparison of the returns in each location. For its incumbent investment, the present value of the infinite net revenue stream is given by

$$V_p = \int_0^\infty R_p e^{-rt}\, dt = R_p/r \tag{3.1}$$

where R denotes a continuous uniform flow of net revenues, r is the market rate of interest, and the subscript p represents the present location. Following the reduction in production costs in the alternative location A, the firm must now weigh the potential gains from moving. The present value of the alternative is given by

$$V_A = \int_0^\infty R_A e^{-rt}\, dt - C_A = R_A/r - C_A \tag{3.2}$$

where C_A represents the cost of acquiring this new facility. Whether the firm opts to undertake a move will depend on whether the incremental annuity value is sufficient to cover the acquisition costs, that is,

$$R_p/r = V_p < V_A = R_A/r - C_A \tag{3.3}$$

or

$$(R_A - R_p)/r = d/r > C_A \tag{3.4}$$

Note again that the cost of the present investment does not affect the firm's decision. Since capital outlays for sunk investments do not enter the future stream of income, they should not influence the mi-

gration decision. Hence, the return to maintaining the present location is R_p/r because it requires no further capital outlays. On the other
hand, in order to obtain revenues from the alternative location, the
firm must buy into this stream at a cost of C_A. Only if the present
value of the difference in net revenue streams between the two locations is greater than the costs of buying into the alternative will migration occur. There is no question of timing; the firm either migrates
immediately (allowing appropriate time for the orderly disposition of
its assets), or it never migrates. If it chooses to migrate, there is no
incentive to remain in the present location for any additional period
of time. The decision rule can be rewritten in flow terms as follows:

$$d > rC_A \qquad\qquad (3.5)$$

Equation (3.5) states that, if the difference in net revenue streams is
greater than the annualized uniform equivalent of the present value
of the cost of acquiring the alternative location, it pays to migrate.

One way to view the infinite-life asset is to take the case of a
firm possessing assets whose productivity is closely tied to maintenance investments. In this situation, the firm has very little discretion
over its maintenance investments. In the more general case, however,
we can think of capital having a finite life. To illustrate, assume that
the firm has just completed an investment that is expected to yield a
constant net revenue stream for T years. Upon commencing operation, the firm discovers an alternative location that would yield a
higher net-revenue stream over the same length of time. Since the
returns from the present location can be obtained with no further outlays, however, it is more profitable to remain in its present location,
at least for some additional period of time. But, with time, the present value of the remaining stream of benefits falls. The firm will
migrate when the present value of the existing location is no longer
greater than the present value of the alternative (net of capital costs).
The optimal migration date (M_O) is illustrated in Figure 3.1. The
present-value curve for the existing location is V_p. Its negative slope
merely reflects a declining present value as the number of remaining
earnings periods decline.[7] The present-value curve for the alternative
location is V_A. It is horizontal because in each period the firm considers the alternative at its initial present value.

To generalize this decision, let $R_p(t)$ be the net revenue at time
t of a sunk investment in the present location p, and let $S_p(M_O)$ be its
salvage value as a function of the additional time the firm postpones

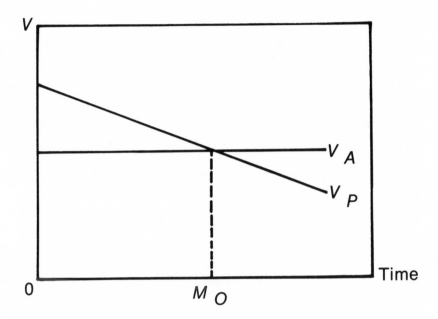

Figure 3.1

THE PRESENT VALUE OF PRESENT AND ALTERNATIVE LOCATIONS AND THE OPTIMAL MIGRATION DATE

the migration date.[8] We assume $S'_p(M_0) < 0$.[9] Let $R_A(t)$ be the net revenue the firm could earn with the same facility in the alternative location A. Further, let $R_A(t) > R_p(t)$ due to some change in the locational advantages. The cost of acquiring the alternative location is denoted by C_A. Keeping in mind that the firm's decision to migrate will be conditioned by a comparison of the net revenue streams, the problem is to choose an optimal migration date, M_0, such that the firm maximizes the following experssion:

$$V = \int_0^{M_O} R_p(t)e^{-rt}\, dt + S_p(M_0)e^{-rM_O}$$

$$+ e^{-rM_O}\left\{ \int_0^M R_A(t)e^{-rt}\, dt - C_A + S_A(M)e^{-rM} \right\} \qquad (3.6)$$

The integral within the brackets discounts the net revenue stream of the alternative location back to the point or date at which migration is undertaken, and the exponential term outside the brackets discounts this amount back to the present (the point at which the firm becomes aware of this alternative). By setting $\partial V/\partial M_O$ equal to zero, the optimal migration date can be written as

$$1/r\left[R_p(M_O) + S_p'(M_O)\right] - V_A = S_p(M_O) \tag{3.7}$$

where $V_A = \{\cdot\}$ above. This condition states that migration should occur when the net contribution to the present worth of the firm caused by remaining in the present location an additional period no longer exceeds the market value of the facilities in that location. For the sake of comparison later, we will simplify this expression by assuming that S_p and S_p' are negligible at the optimal migration date. Thus, we can rewrite (3.7) as

$$R_p(M_O) = rV_A \tag{3.8}$$

This equation states that, when the net revenue from the present location is equal to the annualized equivalent of the present value of the alternative location, it is time to migrate.

Intuitively, one would expect that less durable capital allows a firm to respond sooner to a change in profitable alternatives. We can incorporate this notion into the general decision rule in the following manner. Assume that durability is manifested in the earnings profile of a given stock of capital. Less durable capital deteriorates more rapidly, with a resultant increase in associated operating expense. To see what affect this has on M_O, we take a simple case by assuming that net revenues generated from a firm's capital decline linearly. Linear approximations are as follows:

$$\begin{aligned} R_p(t) &= R_p - \beta t \\ R_A(t) &= R_A - \beta t \end{aligned} \tag{3.9}$$

where β denotes the rate of decline in revenues attributable to deterioration of capital equipment. The parameter β serves as a convenient measure of the durability of capital. Substituting (3.9) into (3.6) and setting $\partial V/\partial M_O$ equal to zero yields the following expression for the optimal migration date:

$$M_O = 1/\beta \left\{ R_p(M_O) + S_p'(M_O) - r \left[S_p(M_O) + V_A\right] \right\} \tag{3.10}$$

Thus, the less durable a firm's capital stock (a higher value of β), the sooner the optimal migration date following a change in interregional costs of production.

In addition to direct outlays for capital in the alternative location, there may also exist costs that are associated solely with the act of moving from one location to another. These costs may arise as a result of a firm's previous commitments to its present location. For example, during any given short-run period a firm will be committed to a package of contracts, leases, and other less formal location-specific trade relations. Normally, getting out of these commitments in the short run will involve significant penalty costs. These previously entered into trade agreements will reduce a firm's flexibility by initially increasing the fixed costs of the alternative location. However, with sufficient time, a firm can take steps to reduce or eliminate these costs. Whether the optimal migration date is postponed in the presence of migration costs will depend on the number of such commitments and the speed at which they can be terminated without significant penalty costs. To see what effect consideration of migration costs might have on the optimal migration date, let the cost of moving to the alternative location be denoted by $C_A(M_O)$. Cost of acquisition will be composed of two components: (1) the actual capital outlay to obtain new facilities in the new location and (2) costs that vary inversely with the time in which the firm plans the move. This speed-of-adjustment concept implies that $C_A'(M_O) < 0$. Thus, the cost of the new location is a function of the additional time the actual migration is postponed.

Considering migration costs, the objective function (3.6) can be rewritten as

$$V = \int_0^M {}^OR_p(t)e^{-rt}\,dt + S_p(M_O)e^{-rM_0}$$

$$+ e^{-rM}{}_0\left\{\int_0^M R_A(t)e^{-rt}\,dt - C_A(M_O) + S_A(M)e^{-rM}\right\} \quad (3.11)$$

Upon maximization with respect to M_O, and assuming once again that S_p and S_p' are negligible at the period of migration, the optimal migration date can be expressed as follows:

$$R_p(M_O) = rV_A + C_A'(M_O); \quad C_A'(M_O) < 0 \quad (3.12)$$

Comparing this expression with the first-order condition (3.8), we see that the difference is the inclusion of the term $C_A'(M_O)$. This term represents the gain to be charged in favor of an additional year's

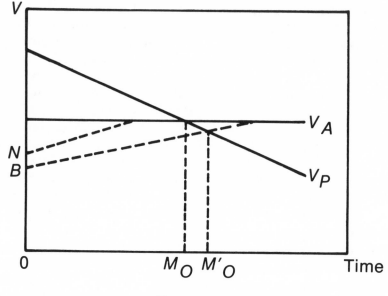

Figure 3.2

THE OPTIMAL MIGRATION DATE WITH MIGRATION COSTS

(period's) service from the present location. The decision to remain in the present location another period means that migration, if it takes place in the following period, can be undertaken at a lower cost. Hence, the introduction of location-specific trade relations can result in an optimal migration date that is pushed forward in time.

Two possibilities are illustrated in Figure 3.2. The first case is one in which migration costs are binding; that is, the rate at which migration costs decline with the planning horizon is sufficiently low to cause the optimal migration date to be postponed an additional period of time. This may be the case for firms with a relatively large number of location-specific agreements spread out over a fairly lengthy period. The effect of these trade relations is to make V_A less attractive initially (at period 0). As a result, the relevant alternative curve is now BV_A. In the absence of $C_A(M_0)$ the firm would migrate at M_0. With $C_A(M_0)$ the present location is preferred over the alternative for a longer period of time $(M_0' - M_0)$. The other possibility is denoted by NV_A. In this case, the presence of migration costs is nonbinding, and the optimal migration date remains unchanged. Therefore, depending on how quickly the firm can get out of its present commitments, the optimal migration date can either remain unchanged or be postponed for a period beyond M_O.

SUMMARY

In formulating a general statement of a firm's migration decision, we have focused primarily upon timing. The impetus to migrate comes from a change in the relative production cost at competing locations. In the extreme case, a firm possessing an infinitely durable stock of capital faces no timing problem. A firm will migrate *immediately* if the differentials in net earnings between the two locations exceeds the present value of the cost of acquiring facilities in the new location. Otherwise, the firm *never* migrates. In cases where capital has a finite life with varying degrees of durability, we introduce a problem of timing. Short of any drastic change in the structure of interlocation costs of production, a firm must determine the optimal point at which it is profitable to move, which in general will not be immediate. The present location may remain more attractive than the alternative ($V_p > V_A$) for some period of time even if net revenues in the alternative location are higher. This is because returns from the present location can be obtained with no further capital outlays. But, as time passes, the present value of the remaining stream of benefits in the present location falls. The firm will migrate when the present value of the existing location is no longer greater than the present value of the alternative (net of capital costs).

The length of time a firm remains in its present location will vary directly with the durability of its capital equipment, ceteris paribus. The less durable a firm's capital, the sooner the firm is allowed to respond to changes in net advantages between competing locations. Introducing migration costs that arise from penalty costs associated with breaking location-specific contractual trade relations may act to postpone the optimal migration date beyond the date selected in the absence of these costs. Whether this delay occurs will depend on how quickly these costs can be avoided by planning.

Finally, one additional consideration is worth mentioning. The length of time a firm remains in its present location prior to migration will depend on the *age* of its capital stock. For example, consider two firms identical in every respect except the age of their capital stock. One firm has just completed investment in its present location; the other firm has been operating in its present location for L years. Both are depicted in Figure 3.3. For both firms the optimal migration date is M_O, but note that the time remaining before migration differs between the two firms.[10] For any firm, the length of time remaining before migration will depend, other things equal, upon its position on the life-cycle profile of its current capital stock. For the first firm, migration will occur after $M_O - 0$ periods, whereas the second firm will remain in its present location only $M_O - L$. Hence, for existing firms, we expect to observe "older" firms migrating before "younger" firms in response to identical alternatives.

One interesting implication of this distinction is that, for any given change in interlocational costs that yields a migration response,

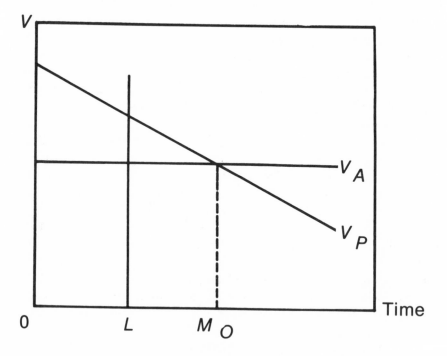

Figure 3.3

THE OPTIMAL MIGRATION DATE FOR TWO FIRMS
WITH DIFFERENT VINTAGES OF CAPITAL

the resulting migration of firms will take place sequentially. Rather than en masse migration, we expect to observe a migration "flow." The rate and pattern of this flow will depend upon the age distribution of existing capital within and between industries.

Finally, it should be pointed out that what we have outlined is a partial equilibrium migration decision for an individual firm. At the industry level, however, changes in location patterns are far less sluggish in adjustments to differential location advantages than at the individual firm level. To the extent that there exists a sufficient supply of potential entrants into the industry, the industry has the option of increasing the number of firms. Obviously, this increase at the extensive margin would occur at the new lower-cost locations. This supply of potential entrants can, in turn, hasten the migration response of existing firms within the industry, since the entry of new firms in the alternative location will alter the optimal migration date for each existing firm. That is, in order for existing firms to take advantage of "cheaper" locations, it is necessary for them to preempt potential entrants. The impact of this dichotomy between firm response and industry response will, in large part, depend upon the overall growth in demand for the industry's output. Nevertheless, these migration adjustments require time; for most cases, our model provides a fairly realistic description of the nature of industry migration.

NOTES

1. For an excellent survey of the theory and empirical work in this area see Greenwood (1982).

2. Changes in the location of industry prior to the 1960s is covered in several earlier studies. For example, see Fuchs (1962) and Perloff et al. (1960).

3. For example, assume that technological change occurs in only one industry. Assume further that we have Hicks neutral technological change. If we hold factor input constant and if productivity increases by 10 percent, the same factors can produce 10 percent more output. Demand for labor will fall, remain constant, or rise according to whether price elasticity is less than 1, equal to 1, or greater than 1. Hence, employment of labor rises following technological change only if the demand for output is elastic.

4. For a detailed discussion of this point see Hoover (1948).

5. A blast furnace will be of little use to other industries (aside from its scrap value), but the building in which it is housed may be of some use to non-steel-producing activities.

6. An alternative approach (hypothesis) is to view firms acting in a completely random manner, unable to consciously seek out the optimal location because of extreme uncertainty about their economic environment. Under this hypothesis, firms do not "adapt" to changes in the economic environment but are, instead, "adopted" by the environment. Those firms lucky enough to "fall" into an optimal location will succeed, and the unlucky ones will fail. However, both the conscious decision-making hypothesis and the random movement hypothesis yield observationally equivalent results. For a complete discussion of this viewpoint see Tiebout (1957).

7. The present value of an asset yielding a constant stream of returns falls with time because there are fewer remaining periods in which income is earned, that is,

$$\int_0^T R_t e^{-rt}\, dt > \int_0^{T-1} R_t e^{-rt}\, dt$$

8. The present analysis has its origin in models of capital replacement developed by Preinreich (1940), Smith (1961), and Terborgh (1944).

9. $S_p'(M_O) = \partial S_p(M_O)/\partial M_O$. In the analysis to follow derivatives are denoted by a prime.

10. It is important to note that we are drawing a distinction between age and calendar time. The optimal migration date (M_O) is fixed only in relation to the origin. The origin is constantly moving forward in calendar time. The value of M_O depends upon age of the capital stock, and the horizontal axis refers to time in terms of age and not calendar time. Thus, we can consider L in Figure 3.3 as representing the origin for the oldest firm.

Chapter 4

Explanations
for the Sunbelt Phenomenon

NUMEROUS EXPLANATIONS HAVE been advanced to account for the recent acceleration of industry migration to the South. They range from cheap southern labor to a more attractive tax and business climate in the South. However, three explanations have persistently evoked an impressive level of debate. These three explanations usually involve a "belief" that states in the South have a more favorable tax structure, lower levels of union activity, and a more attractive business climate.[1] Since we are examining the acceleration of southern migration, these explanations will have empirical validity only to the extent that these South/non-South differentials have *changed*.

The purpose of this chapter is to transform these explanations into empirically testable hypotheses by relating each to its anticipated effects on costs of production. In the next chapter we seek answers to two questions: (1) Have these three factors been important in determining the direction and magnitude of the interstate migration of industry? (2) Are there systematic reasons for differences between industries in the degree to which these factors affect migration decisions? Resolution of the first question will go a long way toward increasing our understanding of the role played by state and local governments in influencing regional disparities in economic growth. In the present debate, public officials in the North are pointing an accusing finger at the federal government for promoting the industrial migration to the South by unfairly channeling tax dollars to southern states. Providing an answer to the second question will allow us to more easily reconcile the ambiguous results from previous empirical work on industry location.

In the following discussion we outline the extent of South/non-South differentials in these three areas and develop the hypotheses to be tested in the next chapter. Also, we review the results from previous empirical work in this area.

STATE AND LOCAL TAXES

Probably no other single issue has received more attention than the role of state and local government taxing policies. At the local level, the most important source of revenue is the property tax. This tax varies substantially across cities and is obviously of some importance in firm location decisions. Normally, property taxes are assessed on assets such as land, structures, and physical machinery. As a result, these taxes would have their greatest impact on firms with a relatively high investment in real property. Since our unit of observation is the state, however, it is not clear how a meaningful property tax index can be constructed. Because most property taxes are levied at the local level, a statewide index would have to be formed by appropriately weighing each taxing jurisdiction to arrive at a composite measure for the state. Currently, no such measure exists.[2] Most attention, however, has been directed at the role of state corporate income taxes. Here data are available.

Historical Overview. As of 1978, forty-six states, including the District of Columbia, imposed a tax on corporate income. In all except thirteen states these taxes were applied with flat (proportional) rates.[3] These rates varied considerably across states, with a range of 1 percent in Arkansas to 12 percent in Minnesota.[4] Table 4.1 presents a chronology of adoption dates for state corporate income taxes. The asterisk denotes states in the South. States first began enacting such legislation in significant numbers during the second decade of this century. Hawaii was the first to have a tax on corporate income and was followed ten years later by Wisconsin. The first major wave of legislative activity in the South occurred during the 1920s. Of the eight states enacting a corporate tax during this period, six were in the South. By far the greatest number of enactments occurred during the decade of the Great Depression when a total of fifteen states joined the bandwagon. Legislative activity died down during the 1940s and 1950s, with the next surge of activity beginning in the 1960s.

TABLE 4.1

DATES OF ADOPTION OF STATE CORPORATE INCOME TAXES

Before 1921		1921-30		1931-40		1941-60		Since 1961	
Hawaii	1901	*Mississippi	1921	Idaho	1931	Rhode Island	1947	Indiana	1963
Wisconsin	1911	*North Carolina	1921	*Oklahoma	1931	Alaska	1949	*Wash., D.C.	1966
Connecticut	1915	*South Carolina	1922	Utah	1931	*Delaware	1957	Michigan	1967
*Virginia	1915	*Tennessee	1923	Vermont	1931	New Jersey	1958	Nebraska	1967
Missouri	1917	*Arkansas	1929	*Alabama	1933			*West Virginia	1967
Montana	1917	California	1929	Arizona	1933			Illinois	1967
New York	1919	Georgia	1929	Kansas	1933			Maine	1969
Massachusetts	1919	Oregon	1929	Minnesota	1933			New Hampshire	1970
North Dakota	1919			New Mexico	1933			*Florida	1972
				Iowa	1934			Ohio	1972
				*Louisiana	1934				
				Pennsylvania	1935				
				*Kentucky	1936				
				Colorado	1937				
				*Maryland	1937				
Total	9	Total	8	Total	15	Total	4	Total	10

Sources: State and Local Finances, Significant Features 1967 to 1970, Advisory Commission on Intergovernmental Relations, Washington, D.C. (Nov. 1969), and Book of the States, The Council of State Governments, Lexington, Ky. (1970-71, 1972-73, 1974-75, 1976-77, 1978-79, 1980-81, and 1982-83).

*States located in the South.

Not only were more states enacting corporate taxes, but existing taxes were being altered in several states. As a result, there have been significant changes in the relative tax position of states and regions over the last few decades.[5] Beginning in the early 1950s, the relative tax rate for several southern states, particularly those in the East South Central and West South Central divisions, began to decline sharply. On the other hand, relative tax rates for three divisions—New England, the East North Central, and the Middle Atlantic—began to rise in the early 1960s. By 1970 the relative tax index ranged from .60 in the West South Central divisions (down from 1.20 in 1950) to 1.37 in the Middle Atlantic division (up from 1.15 in 1950). The effect on the South's relative tax position can be seen in Table 4.2. Columns 1 and 2 contain the median corporate tax rate in the South and non-South, respectively. In 1950 the median tax rate in the South was 3.8 percent, while the median in the non-South was 2.0 percent. By 1970 the median in the non-South had risen to 5.6 percent as compared with 5.5 in southern states. Between 1950 and 1978 the South's relative position fell from 85 percent above, to 13 percent below, that of the non-South. This change in the regional tax structure is presented in the last column of Table 4.2.

These data are certainly consistent with the notion that the South has created a more favorable tax climate (at least with respect to corporate taxes). However, whether state corporate income tax

TABLE 4.2

MEDIAN CORPORATE TAX RATES BY REGION

Year	South	Non-South	South/Non-South
1950	3.8%	2.0%	1.85
1960	3.8%	3.5%	1.09
1970	5.5%	5.6%	.98
1978	5.9%	6.75%	.87

Sources: Facts and Figures on Government Finance, Tax Foundation, Inc., (1952-53) and The Book of the States, The Council of State Governments, Lexington, Ky. (1960-61, 1970-71, and 1978-79).

differentials affect the interstate and interregional movement of industrial activity has long been a controversial empirical question. The central question can be stated simply, as follows: Do state taxing policies *significantly* affect the mass of industry location decisions? There are two opposing viewpoints. One holds that low taxes have the effect of attracting business into the state. The second view takes the position that these differentials play no role in location decisions because state taxes represent only a small part of total costs.

Review of Previous Work. Despite the stylized facts presented above, there are a number of empirical studies that conclude that tax effects are of minor (statistically insignificant) importance in the mass of industry location decisions. There have been two types of empirical studies that examine industrial location changes. The first type is represented by the interview and survey questionnaire studies in which businessmen are asked to list the factors affecting their choice of location. The second type consists of quantitated models of business location. In earlier studies, one popular approach to the problem of identifying tax effects was to ask businessmen to list the factors affecting their choice of location. In some studies they were specifically asked about the effect of tax differentials on their choice of location. Generally, the former type of study found that nonmarket forces (e.g., personal considerations) played a dominant role in selecting a location. Economic influences were accorded a minor or secondary role. For example, Mueller and Morgan (1962) found that noneconomic reasons were more often cited by small firms. The most important determinant was the previous location of the owner. Larger, multiplant firms tended to search over a wide area before selecting their location. At least in the former case, economic factors, including area tax differentials, were not considered to be a major determinant of industry location patterns.

One possible interpretation of these results is that most firms do not pursue profit-maximizing objectives in the choice of their location. But are these results for small firms necessarily inconsistent with the profit-maximizing condition? Consider the decision sequence of a potential entrepreneur living in a particular community. The first decision is obviously to go into business for himself. Second, he is likely to search over a wide variety of activities that he is qualified to enter. Among these activities he is likely to choose one that is expected to be successful. But the expected payoff for each activity is not invariant to the local tax structure. Entering the selected activity is certainly not a violation of profit-maximizing behavior; his decision to enter a particular activity, of course, was subject to a location constraint. Should the activity prove to be successful and should he be asked to list those factors affecting his choice of location, he is sure to put personal considerations (his previous location) at the top of his list.[6] The observation that personality plays a much smaller part in the decision of a large, multiplant firm is not surprising, since large organizations are less likely to "care" about the noneconomic characteristics of the location.

In cases where the entrepreneur has been asked explicitly about tax influences, care should be exercised in drawing policy-related conclusions. To the extent that businessmen have an antitax bias, they are more apt to stress this factor when asked explicitly about taxes in hopes of influencing the results of the study. The emphasis placed on taxes by the respondent may be designed to affect the conclusions so that subsequent publication of the results could then be used to justify policies to lower taxes. Hence, the conclusions derived from these sorts of studies should be received with caution.

Within the quantitative group, a number of statistical studies appearing in the 1950s uniformly concluded that state differentials in taxes made no significant contribution to explanations of changes in industry location patterns.[7] However, the reliability of early studies on industry location and state and local tax effects is limited, since their conclusions were based upon simple correlations of tax levels and changes in value added or employment.[8]

More recent attempts to empirically model business location and investment decisions are exemplified by Carlton (1979), Hodge (1979), and Romans and Subrahmanyam (1979). Carlton's study represents the first attempt to empirically estimate a model of "new births" across cities utilizing a rather unique body of data provided by Dun & Bradstreet (DB). The DB tapes introduced a new and potentially rich source of data that allows researchers to address more detailed empirical questions. For example, for the first time analysts could separate changes in economic activity into births, moves, and contractions or expansions of existing firms. Carlton modeled new births as a Poisson process, since these are essentially infrequent and discrete events. The probability of a birth (establishment of a new firm) was postulated to be a function of the existing level of economic activity in a given SMSA (Standard Metropolitan Statistical Area).[9] Thus, the model related the number of births per SMSA to relevant economic variables, including energy costs, wage costs, agglomeration effects, business climate, property taxes, corporate income taxes, and individual income taxes. Three four-digit SIC (Standard Industrial Classification) industries were included in his sample: plastic products, electronic transmitting equipment, and electronic components. For all three industries examined, the tax variables failed to predict birth activity. Coefficients on both the state corporate income tax and the personal income tax failed to attain significance at conventional levels. But it is interesting to note that the coefficient on local property taxes was marginally significant and had such a wide confidence interval that it was impossible to rule out the possibility that property tax increases could cause large declines in new birth activity. Part of the reason for the poor performance of the corporate tax variable may be due to the limited number of industries included in Carlton's sample. It is not clear that other manufacturing industries would be as insensitive to tax rate differentials as are these particular industries. Hence, the small sample of industries limits our ability to generalize Carlton's results. In addition, the use of a contemporaneous tax rate as an explanatory variable may also account for his conclusion. Even though births presumably respond to current conditions, the correct definition of "current" may be open to debate. In many cases, the lead time between initial planning and actual start-up may be fairly substantial. This means that the observed birth may have been in gestation for some time, which, in turn, implies that the decision to conceive occurred in the past, when conditions may have been different from prevailing conditions at birth. Thus, to the extent that conception and birth do not occur simultaneously, a more appropriate empirical specification would include a lagged tax effect.

In Hodge's study, a formal model of a firm's regional investment decision was developed. The empirical estimation was designed to examine the forces that affect regional investment patterns in four different industries. They were the apparel, furniture, rubber and plastics, and the electronic industries. His results strengthened the conclusions of Carlton by firmly establishing the link between property taxes and local investment patterns. His results diverged from earlier studies, including Carlton's, in that he found state corporate taxes act to constrain the amount and type of investment that takes place within an area. However, state corporate taxes could be shown as significantly affecting investment patterns only within the furniture industry (an industry not examined by Carlton). Comparing his results with those of Carlton, Hodge pointed out that, whereas corporate tax rates may not have significantly affected choice of location, they have affected the amount of capital employed relative to the amount of labor employed. This conclusion implies that local taxes cause some distortion in the capital/labor ratio employed by industries and that they also affect the growth rates of established industries. One justification given by Hodge and others for the insignificance of state corporate taxes on location and investment decisions was the federal tax deduction argument. Corporations are allowed to deduct from gross income subject to federal taxation all payments on state corporate income taxes. While this may indeed mitigate their hypothesized effects, the deductibility allowance results in only an approximate *halving* of the burden of the state tax. As we will argue, this effect may be more important for some industries and less important for others. Nevertheless, Hodge's results leave us with a perplexing question: Why do taxes matter in one industry and not in the other three?

Romans and Subrahmanyam pursued two slightly different but equally interesting issues concerning the effects of state taxes on economic growth. The first tax issue had to do with the degree of progression in the tax structure. The hypothesis advanced by the authors was that businessmen, in their capacity both as entrepreneurs concerned with corporate taxes and as personal income tax payers, have incentives to locate in low tax progression states. This incentive is greater, the greater is the divergence between tax progression and benefit progression. Second, the authors dealt with the issue of transfer payments. To the extent that tax revenues are not used to finance the production of public goods and services but instead are used to finance transfer payments, the flow of benefits does not compensate for tax payments made by firms. Although a number of studies have suggested the divergence between tax payments and benefits received as one reason for the importance of considering the negative effects of state and local taxes, this represented the first serious attempt to empirically analyze this particular issue directly.

Their results indicated that, within regions, higher state transfer payments and tax progressions were associated with slower economic growth. This supported the hypothesis that high tax progression and the absorption of tax revenues into transfer payments drive out firms and higher-income individuals and perhaps attract lower-income individuals who benefit from low marginal tax rates and the receipt of tax expenditures. The resultant migration of firms and individuals leads to slower economic growth within the state.

Collectively, the most recent studies leave us with some ambiguity concerning the impact of state tax differentials on the migration patterns of industry in the United States. They do provide us with sufficient reason to question the conclusions from earlier empirical studies in this area, however. Furthermore, the contrast in results between the Carlton and Hodge studies raises an interesting question: Why does the impact of state corporate taxes on location patterns vary between industries?

Theoretical Considerations. Aside from the obvious objective of raising revenue, taxes at the state and local levels can be accorded three economically acceptable goals.[10] Formulation of a taxing policy would require taxes to be levied for the following reasons. First, taxes may be designed to approximate user charges paid for public services provided to industrial firms. User charges assume, however, that the taxed firm values those services enough to pay for them rather than do without them. Further, the government should provide them at a cost that does not exceed what the firm would have been willing to pay in the absence of the tax. Second, taxes may be designed to cover negative externalities associated with certain kinds of business activities (e.g., air and water pollution). Finally, taxes may be intended to extract location-specific rent accruing to firms located within the taxing jurisdiction. These rents arise whenever the advantages offered by a given location are sufficient to yield a return in excess of the returns obtainable at alternative locations, ceteris paribus. To the extent that taxes can be devised to accomplish any one of these goals, there is no a priori reason to expect any adverse consequences with respect to the efficiency of resource allocation.

It is extremely difficult, however, to move from the conceptual prescription to the practical formulation of such taxes. The principal difficulty involves the measurement of any one of these conceptual magnitudes. Given the current state of the art, no unambiguous monetary equivalent of location rent, negative externality, or public service provided is likely to serve as even a close approximation. With respect to the issue of user charges, it is difficult, if not impossible, to allocate benefits flowing from government expenditure to individual business firms. This reduces the ability of the taxing authorities to levy taxes that do not introduce some distortion in allocative efficiency. Legal constraints further complicate matters by requiring uniformity of treatment across firms even though benefits derived from government services may not be uniformly distributed. This is especially true at the state level in the application of corporate taxes. It is somewhat less of a problem at the local level for the application of property taxes.

There is also an implicit assumption that higher taxes make possible superior public services that directly benefit taxed firms.[11] While there may be a positive correlation between the tax rate and the quality and quantity of public services, the correlation is not perfect, and this is due to the nature of state and local spending patterns. The bulk of state and local spending is for services such as education and public welfare (transfer payments)—services that, at best, bring only indirect benefits to firms. This nonexhaustion of government expenditures on services provided to firms drives a wedge between tax payments and benefits received. Thus, even with a positive correlation, some spatial reallocation of resources will follow if tax rates differ between taxing jurisdictions.

The same can be said for attempts by local governments to charge firms the costs that they impose upon the community via negative externalities. To the extent that such taxes can be avoided by relocating, some change in the regional pattern of industrial location is likely. But, as Brazer (1961) has pointed out, this may improve rather than worsen the efficiency of resource allocation. Nevertheless, for the locality imposing these taxes, the result is a possible exodus of affected industries.

Finally, at a conceptual level, location-specific rent can be taxed heavily without causing a withdrawal of resources from the taxing jurisdiction. However, it is difficult for authorities to distinguish between firms that do and firms that do not earn location rents. Thus, following the imposition of a rent-extracting tax (if applied uniformly), all firms at the margin will definitely have an incentive to seek another location, whereas inframarginal firms will remain in their present location because they have the ability to absorb these taxes out of rents. While it may be possible to utilize local property taxes to extract rents, state corporate taxes are totally unsuited for this purpose. Hence, state taxes are unlikely to truly reflect either the value of services provided or the value to (some) firms of advantages derived from specific locations. How are the consequences of such an imperfectly structured tax system to be manifested in the long run?

First, one has to recognize an important feature of any reasonably competitive national economy; that is, there must be explicit recognition given to the mobility of resources *and* commodities between state and local taxing jurisdictions. As long as there exist no formal restrictions to mobility, returns to factors of production and product prices (net of transportation costs) must be uniform across jurisdictions. Any discrepancy in returns between areas will be followed by resource movement from low-return areas to high-return areas. If all resources were completely immobile, taxes exceeding the values discussed above could be shifted forward in the form of higher product prices or backward onto the suppliers of labor and capital. With incomplete mobility, the tax burden will be shifted to owners of the least mobile resource (i.e., land and some forms of capital), since all mobile resources can avoid taxes by relocating. It is this feature of the system that causes state and local taxes to adversely affect the spatial allocation of resources.[12]

We are now in a position to consider the allocative effects of the state corporate income taxes. In this study we treat the corporate income tax as a tax that strikes the earnings of capital. In practice this tax is a tax on accounting profits. But, in general, taxable accounting profits do not equal economic profits. The difference stems from the firm's inability to deduct from earnings the imputed returns to capital. Thus, a tax on "profit" will really amount to a tax on capital. If the firm were permitted to treat the full rental cost of capital as a cost of production, a tax on profits would be neutral.[13]

In the traditional treatment of tax incidence, the analysis is carried out for the federal corporate income tax, and the economy is divided into a corporate and a noncorporate sector.[14] Imposed within this environment, a corporate income tax necessarily creates a disequilibrium in the capital market, with the net rate of return to owners of capital in the untaxed sector being larger than the net rate of return to owners of capital in the taxed sector. This induces a flow of resources out of the corporate sector into the noncorporate sector. This movement continues until a new long-run equilibrium is reached in which the net rates of return to capital are once again equal *between sectors*. Conceptually, the imposition of a corporate income tax at the state level should cause the same disequilibrium effects. With state-to-state variation in tax rates, however, we add an additional dimension—geographic mobility. Owners of capital now have the added option of migrating between states.[15] The empirical implications suggested by this argument are straightforward. To the extent that an increase in the corporate tax rate within a state makes doing business in that state less profitable than doing the same thing in another state, then:

HYPOTHESIS 1: *Other things equal, improvements in a state's relative tax position will increase its attractiveness for industry expansion.*

This hypothesis merely states that, on average, industries should expand more rapidly in states that have recently lowered their tax *relative* to other states that are otherwise equally attractive to firms within industry. To the extent that the corporate income tax is a tax on the earnings of capital, however, we can translate this statement into the following hypothesis:

HYPOTHESIS 2: *Relatively capital-intensive industries are more sensitive to changes in interstate tax differentials than relatively labor-intensive industries.*

Hypothesis 2 follows from the fact that the sensitivity of costs to a change in the price of any particular input is directly related to the share of that input in total costs. To see this, let total costs be

$$C = \Sigma p_i x_i \tag{4.1}$$

where p_i denotes the price of input i and x represents quantities used of each input. For an increase in the price of input j the output constant change in C is given by

$$dC/dp_j = x_j \tag{4.2}$$

Since we are holding output constant, no distinction need be made between total costs and average costs. Hence, the elasticity of average costs with respect to an increase in the price of input j is

$$(dC/dp_j) \cdot (p_j/C) = p_j x_j/C = s_j \qquad (4.3)$$

where s_j denotes the share of input j in total costs. Thus, if the price of capital rises, capital-intensive firms are more adversely affected than are labor-intensive firms.

BUSINESS CLIMATE

A second explanation for the Sunbelt phenomenon alleges that states in the South have begun to exhibit a more favorable business climate. Presumably, a host of signals can be used by firms to gauge a state's attitude toward business. State government policy as expressed in statutory law and the attitudes and opinions of administering agencies may play an important role in the overall movement and consequent redistribution of industry between states. Whether the legal environment plays an independent role in influencing the patterns of industry growth is not clear-cut, since that environment is conditioned by the climate of public opinion and almost simultaneously influences public opinion. Nevertheless, some indicator of the prevailing government attitude toward business may shed some light on the role of policymakers in attracting or repelling industry growth. Although it is difficult to directly measure a state's business climate, one important manifestation of that climate is its position with respect to collective bargaining via the legal division of power between union and management in the collective-bargaining process. Legal obstacles to union organization and bargaining power will be viewed by firms as a positive signal of a probusiness environment. The creation of these legislative obstacles was clearly an overriding consideration in the passage of state right-to-work (RTW) laws.[16] There is little doubt that the intent of RTW law proponents was to make unions less secure and to slow down or even halt their rate of growth.

Essentially, an RTW law prohibits negotiation by employers and unions of any formal agreement requiring union membership in a union as a condition for continued employment. As a result, union shops may be banned by state RTW laws, which then take precedence over federal law in this area. It is clear that states that enacted such legislation anticipated that they would make unions less secure and slow down or halt their rate of growth. To the extent that they were successful, firms may also view these laws as a reflection of what future wage levels are likely to be.

Historical Overview. As of 1970, a total of nineteen states had RTW laws. Table 4.3 lists these states, along with the corresponding date of adoption by either legislative enactment or constitutional amendment. Three of these states (Florida, Nebraska, and South Dakota) had constitutional amendments prohibiting union security agreements prior to the passage of the federal Taft-Hartley Act in 1947. But not until 1947 and the inclusion of the hotly contested section 14(b) of this act did the impetus for RTW laws gain momentum. It is this section of the federal legislation that allows individual states to ban union shops, and it is this component of the act that continues to be at the heart of the RTW controversy.

TABLE 4.3

STATE RIGHT-TO-WORK LAWS AND CONSTITUTIONAL
AMENDMENTS AS OF 1970
(year of adoption)

State	Constitutional Amendment	Statute
Alabama		1953
Arizona		1947
Arkansas		1947
Florida	1944	
Georgia		1947
Iowa		1947
Kansas	1958	
Mississippi	1960	1954
Nebraska	1946	1947
Nevada		1951
North Carolina		1947
North Dakota		1947
South Carolina		1954
South Dakota	1946	1947
Tennessee		1947
Texas		1947
Utah		1955
Virginia		1947
Wyoming		1963

Source: Right-to-Work: An Overview, Congressional Research Service, Library of Congress, April 1975.

Note: Louisiana has an agricultural RTW law enacted in 1956.

Political pressure to curb union strength had been building in several states for a number of years prior to 1947, and immediately following the federal legislation eleven states passed statutes that incorporated restrictions on union security provisions. States continued to pass RTW laws throughout the 1950s, with Wyoming rounding out the list in 1963.

However, examining only those states that currently have RTW laws belies the extent to which this issue dominated political debate at the state level in the 1940s and 1950s. The union security issue has arisen in several other states, and there has been both ebb and flow in the disposition of such legislation. Table 4.4 lists the states that have adopted and subsequently repealed various kinds of laws in this area. In addition to the nineteen states that currently have RTW laws, six other states (Delaware, Hawaii, Indiana, Louisiana, Maine, and New Hampshire) adopted and then repealed laws restricting union security agreements. Indiana was the last state to formally repeal such a law, in 1965. Table 4.5 lists those states in which some union security measure was submitted to the voters and defeated. By far the greatest amount of activity occurred during the 1950s, reaching a peak in 1958 when referendums were submitted to voters in California, Colorado, Kansas, Ohio, and Washington. These referendums were defeated in every state except Kansas. Since 1958 the union security measure has been formally put forth in only

TABLE 4.4

STATES IN WHICH RIGHT-TO-WORK OR OTHER LAWS RESTRICTING UNION
SECURITY AGREEMENTS HAVE BEEN REPEALED

State	Year Adopted	Year Repealed
Delaware	1947	1949
Hawaii	1945	1959
Indiana	1957	1965
Louisiana*	1954	1956
Maine	1947	1949
New Hampshire	1947	1949

Source: Right-to-Work: An Overview, Congressional Research Service, Library of Congress, April 1975.

*Louisiana's statute is now applicable only to agriculture.

TABLE 4.5

STATES IN WHICH RIGHT-TO-WORK MEASURES HAVE BEEN
DEFEATED BY REFERENDUM

State	Year Defeated
California	1944, 1958
Colorado	1958
Idaho	1958
Maine	1948
Massachusetts	1948
New Mexico	1948
Ohio	1958
Oklahoma	1964
Washington	1956, 1958

Source: Right-to-Work: An Overview, Congressional Research Service,
April 1975.

four states. Thus, it appears that most states destined to have RTW laws had them firmly on the books by 1958. Since 1958 the issue has assumed far less attention in state political arenas and, as a result, has probably created more certainty in the minds of businessmen about their continued existence within a state.

Review of Previous Work. Of particular interest in this study is the relationship between RTW laws and industrial location activity. On this point there exists little empirical analysis, and what evidence does exist is inconclusive. For example, Soffer and Korenich (1961) conclude that "right-to-work laws do not seem to have contributed, on balance, to the expansion of non-agricultural jobs and industries" (p. 54). Their study compared the industrialization experience of two groups (RTW and non-RTW) of the most agriculturally oriented states in the contiguous central and western regions. The maintained hypothesis was that there would be no clear-cut differences in basic economic measures between states that have and states that do not have RTW laws. The measures used to proxy economic activity were employment in nonagricultural industries, annual wages and salaries of production workers, union membership, number of business establishments, and per capita income in the period 1939 to 1947–49 compared with that of 1947–49 to 1956–58. Their analysis consisted of two-way comparisons of changes in these measures between RTW law states and non-RTW law states. The basic problem with such a simple descriptive two-way analysis is that it does not take into account the fact that the significance as well as the sign of the relationship between variables may be changed if the independent variable (RTW) is considered *simultaneously* with other independent variables that are also hypothesized to affect the dependent variable. That is, the effect on economic activity of RTW laws must be evaluated in a ceteris paribus framework. In addition, their results may be sensitive to the *timing* of their study. Recall that the debate and legislative activity reached a peak in 1958. Also, many other states seriously considered passing an RTW measure; some states actually enacted such legislation, only to repeal these restrictions at a later date. Given the chronology of legislative activity, it may be convenient to think of the late 1950s as the watershed for locational incentives provided by RTW laws. Thus, we would anticipate that the migration of industry between RTW law states and non-RTW law states would be observed subsequent to this period. Furthermore, even in the absence of uncertainty over which states would ultimately have an RTW law, the sluggish nature of industry migration implies that observed changes in the location pattern of industries would not begin to be observed by the analyst until the early 1960s. Soffer and Korenich examined changes in economic activity prior to this period.

Most of the economic literature has been devoted to the effects of RTW laws on union membership and bargaining power. The specific issue is the extent to which passage of an RTW law by a state inhibits or retards union growth and power within that state. Several observers have argued that this legislation has had only minimal direct impacts on union organization. Meyers (1955, 1959) argues that a right-to-work statute, in isolation from the whole body of state labor legislation, has had a minimal impact on union growth or power. The issue is merely a symbolic one. According to Marshall (1963), the main impact of an RTW law is to demonstrate the political power of unions.[17] This conclusion has not gone unchallenged. A number of observers, including Kuhn (1961) and Shister (1958), have argued that RTW laws have indeed proved to be an impediment to union growth and, furthermore, that union growth rates would have been significantly higher had there been no RTW laws. For example, Shister concludes that the impact on the growth of union membership has been substantially larger than its impact on the bargaining power of established unions. Barkin (1961) agrees with the first part of Shister's conclusion but disagrees with second part. He believes that RTW laws have tended to give legal confirmation to antiunion sentiment and that they therefore not only impede new organizational gains but also weaken union positions in presently organized plants.[18] The problem with all these studies is that they failed to provide any tangible evidence on a statistical plane that would merit acceptance of their conclusions. Their conclusions were based on deductive inferences from very sketchy summary statistical data.

In three recent empirical studies, by Lumsden and Peterson (1975), Moore and Newman (1975), and Moore (1980), the evidence suggests that RTW laws have only minimal direct impact on union membership and bargaining power. Moore found no empirical support for the hypothesis that the presence of RTW laws significantly lowers the wages of union members. In fact, RTW laws may have influenced trade union wage policy in the direction of increasing union relative wage rates. In their efforts to promote union membership, union leaders may be forced to push for higher wages and union benefits to a larger degree in RTW states than in non-RTW states. According to Moore's estimates, based on data from the Income Dynamics Panel collected by the Survey Research Center at the University of Michigan, union membership increases workers' wage rates by 25.69 percent in RTW states but only 12.8 percent in non-RTW states.

These recent empirical studies suggest that ex post the RTW issue may be more symbolic than real. Why unions and proponents of RTW laws were willing to spend millions of dollars fighting over a symbolic issue remains an unanswered question, however.

Theoretical Considerations. Why do states pass RTW laws?[19] The answer to this question is not obvious but is nevertheless essential to our understanding of the effects of an RTW law on industry location decisions. Does a state with an RTW law deliberately attempt to create a *legal* climate in which unions find it difficult to organize and flourish, or is an RTW law merely a legal reflection of a strong bias against unions on the part of that state's labor force? The stronger and more pervasive the antiunion sentiment existing in the labor force, the less effective the legal constraint; the law is primarily symbolic. Unions would find it difficult to grow and become effective even in the absence of such a statute. However, if the legal restraints created by RTW laws are not symbolic of worker preferences, then the issue is whether an RTW law significantly reduces union strength. Can states make their labor force more attractive to industry, at the margin, by passing an RTW law? If so, how does the legal restriction manifest itself in real economic benefits to firms?

The traditional explanation for the economic effects of RTW laws obviously centers on the effects created by the absence of a union security clause. Since a union shop is prohibited by this law, the impact is felt directly on a union's main resource—dues. Presumably, the constant threat of losing income diverts union activities away from the bargaining table, and the union therefore becomes less effective in pushing wage demands and other employment-related benefits. As pointed out by Gallaway (1966), however, this threat may cause a union to substitute wage demands for employment gains in the absence of a union shop. Hence, the end result may be higher union/nonunion wage ratios in RTW law states.[20] In other words, unions attempt to "sell" themselves to existing members by driving up union wage rates more than they would have in the absence of an RTW law. The reduction in their guaranteed endowment (union shop) causes them to substitute higher wage demands for employment gains.[21]

Whether RTW laws in fact have real or symbolic effects may be of secondary importance, however, as long as individual economic agents act *as if* they do indeed have real effects.[22] Given the millions of dollars spent by groups on both sides of the issue, it is difficult to imagine that they perceived, ex ante, no real effects. Thus, to the extent that firms attempt to economize on search costs by utilizing easily identifiable signals of business climate, and to the extent that passage of this legislation provided firms with more information concerning the business climate of a particular state, we are led to the following hypothesis:

HYPOTHESIS 3: *Passage of an RTW law makes a state's labor force more attractive, at the margin, to new industry (and investment) than the labor force of a state with no RTW legislation.*

Also, to the extent that firms treated the passage of RTW laws as a signal of what future wage levels were likely to be, assuming that they anticipated lower wage levels, we would expect these effects to be more pronounced for particular types of industries—those in which labor costs are important. We can translate this statement into the following hypothesis:

HYPOTHESIS 4: *Relatively labor-intensive industries are more sensitive to the passage of RTW laws than relatively capital-intensive industries.* [23]

Finally, since the passage of RTW laws represent a one-time change in location characteristics, the effects on industry redistribution between states with such legislation and states without such legislation should decay over time. Once industry location adjustments have been made, the existence of RTW laws will no longer act as an important location influence. Thus:

HYPOTHESIS 5: *The effects of the passage of RTW laws will decay over time as industries complete their adjustments to a one-time change in location characteristics.*

UNIONIZATION

One frequently mentioned reason for regional shifts in employment is the extent of unionization in one region relative to another. The general presumption is that in highly organized states, typically those in the North, unions have been successful in imposing higher-than-average wage costs on employers. Movement to the South is, therefore, seen as a flight from high-union states.

Historical Overview. In Table 4.6 the growth of union membership in the United States over the period 1930–78 is presented both in absolute numbers and as a percentage of employees in nonagricultural establishments. Betwen 1930 and 1978 trade union membership rose from 3.4 million to 20.2 million, a 497 percent growth rate. As a result, union membership was almost six times larger at the end of this forty-eight-year period. However, in terms of the proportion of total nonagricultural employees unionized, union membership in 1978 was no greater than it was in the late 1930s.

TABLE 4.6

TOTAL UNION MEMBERSHIP AS A PERCENT OF EMPLOYEES IN NONAGRICULTURAL
ESTABLISHMENTS 1930-78

Year	Number[a]	Percent	Year	Number	Percent
1930	3,401	11.6	1955	16,802	33.2
1931	3,310	12.4	1956	17,490	33.4
1932	3,050	12.9	1957	17,369	32.8
1933	2,689	11.3	1958	17,029	33.2
1934	3,088	11.9	1959	17,117	32.1
1935	3,584	13.2	1960	17,049	31.4
1936	3,989	13.7	1961	16,303	30.2
1937	7,001	22.6	1962	16,586	29.8
1938	8,034	27.5	1963	16,524	29.1
1939	8,763	28.6	1964	16,841	28.9
1940	8,717	26.9	1965	17,299	28.4
1941	10,201	27.9	1966	17,940	28.1
1942	10,380	25.9	1967	18,367	27.9
1943	13,213	31.1	1968	18,916	27.8
1944	14,146	33.8	1969	19,036	27.0
1945	14,322	35.5	1970	19,381	27.3
1946	14,395	34.5	1971	19,211	27.0
1947	14,787	33.7	1972	19,435	26.4
1948	14,319	31.9	1973	19,851	25.8
1949	14,282	32.6	1974	20,199	25.8
1950	14,267	31.5	1975	19,611	25.5
1951	15,946	33.3	1976	19,634	24.7
1952	15,892	32.5	1977	19,695	24.8
1953	16,948	33.7	1978	20,246	23.6
1954	17,022	34.7			

Source: U.S. Department of Labor, Bureau of Labor Statistics, Handbook
of Labor Statistics, Bulletin 2070 (1980), Table 165, p. 412.

[a]In thousands of employees.

This does not mean that union growth in relative terms remained static. As we can see, the real growth (percentage organized) in union membership increased steadily until 1954, when the fraction unionized reached its zenith at 34.7 percent. Unions experienced their largest short-term real growth in 1937, when the fraction unionized rose from 13.7 to 22.6 percent.

However, the period after 1954 can be characterized as a period of slow but steady decline in real union membership. One of the factors contributing to this decline has been the rapid growth of employment in sectors that are largely nonunion, that is, costly to organize. This includes government, finance, trade, and services.

This has occurred simultaneously with the relative decline in employment in some sectors that have historically been strongly organized (manufacturing, mining, and railroads). The decline in relative union membership has also been brought about by some important demographic changes in the labor force. Blue-collar workers have historically been unionized in higher proportions than white-collar workers. This may be due to any number of factors, including their view of the employee/management relationship as being adversarial. Even in the traditionally high-union industries such as manufacturing, however, the proportion of blue-collar to white-collar occupations has been falling. Finally, the dramatic increase in female labor force participation since the mid-1950s has probably contributed to at least part of the decline in real union membership. Females have in the past been difficult to organize (in part because of their low labor force attachment); hence, their increased representation in the labor market has not augured favorably for continued union growth.

Though there was a fairly steady increase in union membership until 1954 and a fairly steady decrease after 1954, there has been substantial year-to-year variation in this growth pattern. This variation can be seen in Figure 4.1, where we plot the annual percentage change in union membership over the period in question. Notice that some of the largest gains in union membership occurred during the Great Depression. This fact posed some problems for the business-cycle explanation for union growth. According to this argument, unions experience procyclical growth patterns; that is, favorable business conditions make union organizing activities easier and less costly. Ashenfelter and Pencavel (1969) provided a single behavioral relationship that allowed them to largely explain away this anomaly of the 1930s. Essentially, changes in union membership throughout this century can be explained by movements in the relative benefits and costs of union membership to individual workers over time. Thus, the 1933–37 spurt in union membership was in good part the result of labor's grievances (proxied by unemployment) and a favorable political climate (proxied by percentage of membership in the House of Representatives affiliated with the national democratic party). Consequently, as the authors point out, there is no need to resort to Bernstein's ad hoc "social unrest" explanation for the *countercyclical* growth patterns exhibited in the 1930s.[24]

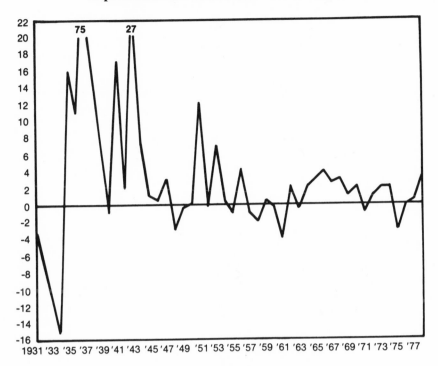

Figure 4.1
TRADE UNION GROWTH IN MEMBERSHIP
(annual percentage change)

The regional distribution of union membership is displayed in Table 4.7 for four selected years. There are a few interesting patterns that emerge from the data. First, as expected, the proportion of employees in nonagricultural unionized establishments has fallen in almost every state over this period. The only notable exception is New York, where real union membership rose from 34.4 to 39.2 percent. Second, the variation in the degree of unionization between states is substantial. For example, in 1978 the degree of unionization ranged from a low in North Carolina of 6.5 to 39.2 percent in New York. Finally, the degree of unionization in the South (SA, ESC, and WSC) is substantially lower than any other region of the United States.[25] This fact has long intrigued economic and labor historians. Most observers agree that the success of union operations depends critically upon the prevailing attitudes within society. For any given effort, union leaders will have greater success in recruiting new members if

TABLE 4.7

TOTAL UNION MEMBERSHIP AS A PERCENT OF
NONAGRICULTURAL EMPLOYMENT BY STATE, 1953, 1964, 1974, 1978

	1953	1964	1974	1978		1953	1964	1974	1978
New England (NE):					**South Atlantic (SA):**				
Maine	21.4	20.8	16.2	18.3	Delaware	18.4	24.0	20.1	21.1
New Hampshire	24.6	20.1	15.1	13.3	Maryland	25.2	22.9	21.6	21.0
Vermont	18.9	18.7	17.7	17.5	Dist. of Columbia	21.2	22.9	21.6	21.0
Massachusetts	30.1	28.0	24.4	24.4	Virginia	17.4	15.8	13.8	12.7
Rhode Island	27.4	28.3	27.3	27.1	West Virginia	44.1	44.7	38.2	36.8
Connecticut	26.5	27.0	25.1	21.9	North Carolina	8.3	7.4	6.9	6.5
					South Carolina	9.3	7.4	8.0	6.7
Middle Atlantic (MA):					Georgia	15.0	14.0	14.5	13.6
New York	34.4	38.5	38.0	39.2	Florida	16.2	14.0	12.5	11.7
New Jersey	35.2	32.3	28.2	23.0					
Pennsylvania	39.9	38.7	37.5	34.2	**East South Central (ESC):**				
					Kentucky	25.0	27.0	25.1	22.4
East North Central (ENC):					Tennessee	22.6	19.2	18.7	17.7
Ohio	38.0	36.7	33.2	29.5	Alabama	24.9	18.7	19.9	19.2
Indiana	40.0	36.4	33.2	29.3	Mississippi	14.7	13.5	12.0	12.7
Illinois	39.7	38.4	34.9	31.5					
Michigan	43.3	42.7	38.4	34.6	**West South Central (WSC):**				
Wisconsin	38.3	33.4	28.7	27.8	Arkansas	21.5	17.0	16.8	15.0
					Louisiana	19.5	18.7	16.3	16.0
West North Central (WNC):					Oklahoma	16.1	15.1	15.0	13.5
Minnesota	38.1	34.0	25.3	24.4	Texas	16.2	14.1	13.0	11.0
Iowa	25.0	22.6	21.2	19.2					
Missouri	39.7	37.9	32.3	30.0	**Mountain (MT):**				
North Dakota	15.6	14.8	15.1	14.7	New Mexico	14.2	14.5	14.1	12.1
South Dakota	14.4	10.0	11.0	10.3	Montana	47.0	35.2	25.7	24.1
Nebraska	19.7	19.2	15.1	15.3	Idaho	21.5	19.0	15.5	14.3
Kansas	23.9	18.6	14.1	12.8	Wyoming	28.6	19.4	18.2	14.9
					Colorado	27.8	22.3	18.9	15.2
Pacific (PAC):					Arizona	27.7	18.5	16.0	13.8
Washington	53.3	44.0	36.7	33.1	Utah	26.3	18.0	14.9	13.0
Oregon	43.1	34.2	26.5	23.1	Nevada	30.4	32.8	27.4	22.9
California	35.7	33.3	28.2	23.7	United States	36.6	28.9	25.8	23.6

Sources: 1953 from Troy (1957); All other years from U.S Bureau of Labor Statistics, Directory of National and
International Labor Unions in the United States, 1965 and Directory of National Unions and Employees

there is general sympathy for labor's goals. There appears to be a general consensus in the literature that public attitudes in the South regarding unions are significantly different from those in the non-South.

Marshall (1968) discusses a few real economic factors that can account for the lower degree of unionization in the South. First, there has been a tendency for new industries in the South to locate in non-metropolitan areas. This tendency lowers the level of union activity, since union organizational strengths are usually higher in urban areas. Second, the abundance of low-income agricultural workers in the South has been an important obstacle to union growth within this region. Third, there is a positive correlation between market concentration and union membership. The hypothesis is that large oligopolistic firms are more easily organized than scattered smaller firms. Because of the South's higher proportion employment in smaller competitive industries, union organizing success has been impeded. Finally, employment in government has increased significantly in the South, but most southern states discourage collective bargaining among their employees.[26]

However, Moore and Newman (1975) found that states in the South were less organized even after properly controlling for labor force composition and industrial structure. Thus, it appears that public attitudes in the South would result in lower unionization rates for this region even if its labor force composition and industrial structure were identical to the non-South's.

Review of Previous Work. In one of the most influential empirical studies on the regional location of manufacturing, Victor Fuchs (1962) examined the comparative growth rates for manufacturing industries among states for the period 1929–54. Using census data, several hypotheses concerning the determinants of location change were tested. Some of these include the effects of interstate differences in wage rates, climate, and population density (measure of available space for location). The results indicated that economic variables strongly influenced comparative rates of growth and implied that a firm's choice of location was significantly affected by location-specific market characteristics.

Of particular importance to this inquiry, however, is Fuch's empirical work relating to the importance of interstate differences in unionization. He found that the relative extent of unionization was significantly related to comparative growth in manufacturing employment among states. His results provide support for the hypothesis advanced by many students of location theory that the comparative absence of unions has been favorable to the growth of manufacturing employment in some states between the years 1929 and 1954. Unfortunately, his empirical work did not consider the influences of state corporate taxes and RTW laws.

Theoretical Considerations. It is widely accepted that unions have the power to raise wages in establishments where they have bargaining rights.[27] This power derives from their ability to impose costs on firms via strikes, slowdowns, and other tactics that are greater than the costs of the wage increases demanded. Other functions of unions include regulation of nonwage conditions of employment for their members—including the speed of production, grievance procedures, and seniority systems. Thus, a union attempts through collective bargaining to make the terms of employment of its members better than they would be in the absence of the union. Of course, any improvements in the terms of employment necessarily raise the costs of production to the firm. For example, to the extent that organized labor can successfully restrict or penalize hiring, firing, layoffs, and overtime, then *overhead costs* for a firm employing unionized labor are likely to be higher than those of an otherwise identical firm employing unorganized labor.

Thus, firms may wish to avoid states with highly organized unions when decisions are being made concerning alternative locations for expansion. For new industry expansion this may be especially important, because such enterprises have to face the inevitable costs associated with organizational strikes, jurisdictional disputes, and the resulting disruptions in production plans. These organizational costs may be minimized by locating in areas where the probability of their occurrence is minimized, that is, in "nonunion" states.

To some extent, the degree of unionization within a state may also reflect the prevailing government attitude toward business. States in which organized labor has grown politically "strong" may have enacted increasingly higher unemployment compensation and workmen's disability benefits and stricter regulations governing working conditions.

Unionization rates may be viewed by firms as an indication of labor costs, either directly in terms of higher wages, or indirectly through their impact on work rules (affecting overhead costs). Firms may also use the degree of unionization in a state as an estimate of the probability that they will face an organized work force. Consequently, we have the following hypothesis:

HYPOTHESIS 6: *Ceteris paribus, firms will find "nonunion" states more attractive for location or expansion than "union" states.*

Our final hypothesis is derived in the same manner as hypotheses 2 and 4. To the extent that organized labor increases the wage costs of a firm above what they would have been in the absence of the union, then:

HYPOTHESIS 7: *Relatively labor-intensive industries are more sensitive to changes in unionization rates than relatively capital-intensive industries.*

SUMMARY

This chapter has transformed three controversial explanations for the Sunbelt phenomenon into empirically testable hypotheses. These hypotheses were generated by relating state corporate income taxes, right-to-work laws, and unionization rates to their theoretically anticipated effects on costs of production. To the extent that these factors vary between states and regions, they will provide explanatory power only to the degree that the differentials *changed*. With this in mind, we provided a historical overview of each of these factors, focusing on the secular changes in South/non-South differentials. In addition, we reviewed the empirical results from previous work on industry location. Our conclusion from this review was that many of these earlier empirical studies suffered from either weak data, poor methodology, or inappropriate specification. More recent location studies were successful at resolving these problems, but their conclusions cannot be generalized beyond their limited sample of industries.

NOTES

1. It is interesting to note that we are ignoring one extremely popular explanation. It is frequently alleged that industries are moving to the South to take advantage of the warmer and more equable climate (a notion implicit in the origin of the term "Sunbelt"). While it may be that employers and employees both prefer warmer climates, it is hard to imagine why it has taken them so long to reveal this preference. Since climate differences are no greater now than in the past, it is unlikely that climate can account for much of the *acceleration* of industry migration to the Sunbelt.

2. The impact of local property taxes on industry location has been examined for interurban migration. There is some evidence to support the hypothesis that low property tax urban areas experience higher growth rates than high property tax urban areas. See Hodge (1979) and Carlton (1979).

3. The thirteen states having graduated income tax schedules were Arizona, Arkansas, Hawaii, Iowa, Kentucky, Louisiana, Maine, Mississippi, Nebraska, North Dakota, Ohio, Vermont, and Wisconsin.

4. Five states had no corporate income tax. These states were South Dakota, Texas, Wyoming, Nevada, and Washington. If we include these states, the minimum is obviously zero.

5. The relative tax is defined as a state's tax rate divided by the average rate for all states. As in most economic discussions, it is relative prices that matter.

6. A more thorough discussion of this criticism of survey questionnaire techniques can be found in Tiebout (1957).

7. For a complete review of the early empirical work in this area see Due (1961). Some of the studies reviewed include Bloom (1955), Campbell (1958), Floyd (1952), Larson (1957), and Garwood (1952).

8. It was on the basis of these results that Fuchs (1962) decided to completely ignore tax differentials in his important study on the changes in the location of manufacturing between 1929 and 1954.

9. The analysis was carried out using firm location data provided by DB for two time periods, 1967–71 and 1972–75.

10. Taxes are said to be economically efficient if they do not introduce distortions in the allocation of resources either within the firm or across firms in different locations. A more complete discussion of these taxing goals is provided in Brazer (1961).

11. These services include police and fire protection, water supply, sewage disposal, access streets, and the like. However, these services are usually supplied at the local level, not at the state level.

12. To the extent that taxes alter relative factor returns, they will also affect the optimal mix of resources within a firm. For example, if one tax lowers the return on capital (increases its user cost), there will exist an incentive for firms to substitute into more labor-intense production techniques. Whether there will be a net increase in the employment of labor will depend on whether the substitution effect dominates the scale effect.

13. This would mean that a firm's decision regarding its optimal capital/labor ratio would no longer be affected. It would not, however, eliminate the effects on spatial allocation, since firms would tend more to locate in "low" tax states than they would in the absence of the tax. Also, it would not eliminate the allocative effects between the corporate and noncorporate sectors within a state.

14. The seminal contribution on this issue is Harberger (1962). For an excellent theoretical application of Harberger's model to the issue of industry location see McLure, Jr. (1970).

15. One of the assumptions in the Harberger model is a closed economic system. Though not unduly restrictive at the federal level, it is clearly inappropriate when dealing with state

taxes, since labor, capital, and goods are vastly more mobile between states and regions than between nations. It should be pointed out that a firm cannot avoid this tax by chartering in a nontax state and doing business in the taxed state.

16. The Taft-Hartley Act, enacted in 1947, allows union shops. The union shop is a union security agreement between management and the union that specifies that workers employed by a firm must join the union within some specified period of time. However, the Taft-Hartley Act also includes the famous section 14(b), which permits an individual state to outlaw within that state the union shop provisions that the federal law allows.

17. For others who share this opinion see Kuhlman (1955), Nadworney (1966), Sultan (1958), and Witney (1958).

18. Others who have challenged the Meyer's thesis include Glasgow (1967) and Northrup and Bloom (1963).

19. Several studies have examined the determinants of the passage of RTW laws. In this regard see Moore, Newman, and Thomas (1974); Palomba and Palomba (1971); and Tollefson and Pichler (1974).

20. The evidence on union/nonunion wage ratios between RTW and non-RTW states provided by Moore (1980) is consistent with this hypothesis.

21. This results from the relative position of the union's wage preference paths under alternative union security clauses. Wage preference paths for both an open and a closed shop lie to left of the union shop path. Hence, the open shop leads to higher equilibrium wage rates and lower levels of employment than would exist under a union shop. These wage preference paths result from union preference functions that treat wage rates and employment as substitutes.

22. Otherwise, we must conclude that symbolic advantage commands a very high price in terms of both money and time.

23. See equation (4.3) above.

24. See Bernstein (1954).

25. West Virginia stands out as a dramatic exception within the South. This state's high degree of unionization (36.8 percent in 1978) can be attributed largely to its heavy concentration of mining, a traditionally well organized industry.

26. In a study by Moore and Newman (1975), a South dummy variable was found to negatively affect the probability of a state passing a public bargaining law. That is, southern states are less likely to pass public bargaining legislation requiring mandatory negotiations or at least permitting but not necessarily requiring collective bargaining for state and local government employees.

27. There is a substantial body of literature devoted to estimating the relative wage advantage of union members over labor in the nonunion sector. The seminal contribution in this area is Lewis (1963). He found that the aggregate proportionate union wage advantage was 15 percent in the 1955–58 period. A plethora of empirical studies followed the work by Lewis. Some of the important studies include Ashenfelter (1972), Boskin (1972), Johnson and Youmans (1971), Stafford (1968), Throop (1968), and Weiss (1966).

Chapter 5

Empirical Analysis
of Industry Migration

IN THIS CHAPTER the empirical measures of the influences outlined in the previous chapters are specified and tested. This inquiry into the effects of state corporate tax rates, degree of unionization, and RTW laws on industry migration between states and regions is confined to the manufacturing sector. We focus on the manufacturing sector because it has historically been the obvious target of state and local efforts designed to promote their economic development. The common presumption is that the creation of manufacturing jobs results in substantial multiplier effects leading to additional job opportunities in other types of industries. Manufacturing activities are usually considered as the primary source of exports from the area, which in turn enhances that area's ability to purchase products from outside areas. In addition, manufacturing firms seem to have more flexibility with respect to location than industries directly dependent on natural resources or proximity to individual consumers (e.g., mining or wholesale and retail trade). The emphasis is on the *redistribution* of industry between states, that is, the rate of growth of an industry within a state relative to the rate of growth of an industry across all states. The purpose of the analysis is to explain, not existing location of plants, but rather *comparative changes* in location as measured by changes in total employment. The data do not distinguish between the physical movement of plants across locations and differential growth rates of firms that remain in a given location. Thus, it is not clear whether an industry expands (contracts) in one state relative to another because of the physical movement of plants and facilities or as a result of the expansion (contraction) of existing facilities. However, while this is an interesting question, it is not a crucial distinction for the present analysis.

DATA AND VARIABLE DEFINITIONS

Industry Growth. The measure of growth and redistribution utilized here is a comparative change between states in total employment within an industry. Our point of reference is the change in employment for each industry that occurred at the national level. The objective is to distinguish between growth-induced change that occurs because of national trends and growth-induced change that occurs as a result of factors associated with a particular state. We start with the measure of relative gains and losses used in Chapter 2,

$$E_{si}^1 - E_{si}^0 \left(\overline{E}_i^1 / \overline{E}_i^0 \right)$$

where E_{si}^1 represents total employment in state s, industry i, in the terminal year, and E_{si}^0 denotes the same for the initial year. The corresponding employment levels for the United States are $\overline{E}_i^1$ and $\overline{E}_i^0$, respectively. Since states differ significantly in absolute size, however, it is useful to have a measure of relative gains and losses expressed in percentage terms. Although there are well-known problems associated with all percentage change measures (e.g., imparting exaggerated growth rates to states that have initially low employment levels), the virtue of the following specification is that it yields measures that are conceptually simple, easily interpreted, and readily compared with other studies.[1] Converting the above state differential into percentage terms yields

$$SD = \left(E_{si}^1 / E_{si}^0 \right) - \left(\overline{E}_i^1 / \overline{E}_i^0 \right) \tag{5.1}$$

It is intended to capture the importance of local factors in producing a divergence between actual state growth and that which might be expected on the basis of national trends. The prediction $\left(\overline{E}_i^1 / \overline{E}_i^0 \right)$ represents the growth a state would have experienced had no factors peculiar to that state intervened to affect the level of economic activity. A positive value of SD means that the state grew faster than the United States, and we say that the state "gained" employment; if SD is negative, the state grew less rapidly than the United States, and we say it "lost" employment.

Data on two-digit manufacturing employment for each state are taken from *Employment and Earnings*, published by the U.S. Bureau of Labor Statistics (BLS). Recall that the purpose of this analysis is to determine whether state corporate tax differentials, unionization rates, and RTW laws help explain the acceleration of industry movement to the south that began in the early 1960s. This movement was documented for the period 1957–79 in Chapter 2. However, it is felt that, in the analysis to follow, more information can be extracted by examining shorter intervals of time. Since the results from measuring relative gains and losses may be sensitive to the choice of an interval, care was taken in selecting intervals such that two conditions were satisfied. First, the interval had to be of sufficient length for the calculation of SD to be independent of cyclical movements within the interval. Second, changes were measured between similar phases of the business cycle. The resulting trend indicators would be consistent with any magnitude of cyclical amplitude. With these observations in mind, the relative change in employment is defined over three overlapping time periods: 1957–65, 1965–73, and 1973–79. These intervals are of sufficient length and are roughly in the same phase of the business cycle to imply long-term movements from the resulting calculation of SD.[2] Thus, for each state in which corresponding employment data are available, there are three observations per industry.[3]

Table 5.1 presents the U.S. growth rates $(\overline{E}_i^1/\overline{E}_i^0)$ and the mean SD for the South and the non-South in each time period. Notice that, with the exception of lumber and wood products, the state differentials in the South exceed the corresponding differentials in the non-South by a substantial margin. Also, it appears that the growth differentials in the South were fairly uniform across the three time periods, which suggests that this movement is continuing without any noticeable abatement.

Corporate Income Tax. The measure of corporate income tax employed in this study differs from measures used in previous studies. The important distinction is that we use a *change* in a state's *relative* tax position and not its absolute tax rate. Unless one has an explicit disequilibrium model in mind, induced movements of industry between states will depend upon *changes* in relative taxes and not upon their levels. For example, if all states increased their corporate tax rates in the same proportion, no redistribution of industry between states would follow. The change in a state's relative tax position is defined in the following manner:

TABLE 5.1

INDUSTRY GROWTH RATES FOR THE UNITED STATES AND MEAN SD BY REGION

Industry Group	(SIC)[a]	Growth United States 1957-65	1965-73	1973-79	Mean State Differential (SD) South 1957-65	1965-73	1973-79	Non-South 1957-65	1965-73	1973-79
Textile Mill Products	(22)	.9434	1.0909	.8765	.0587	.1864	.0041	.0140	-.1369	-.1289
Apparel & Other Textile Prods.	(23)	1.1191	1.0620	.9070	.3827	.2971	.0224	-.0717	-.0428	.0440
Lumber & Wood Products	(24)	.9518	1.1608	1.0101	-.0432	-.0957	-.1726	-.0020	-.0836	.1896
Furniture & Fixtures	(25)	1.1506	1.2355	.9822	.1946	.1011	-.1024	-.1193	-.0379	-.0953
Paper & Allied Products	(26)	1.1200	1.1025	1.0031	.1182	.2455	.0676	.0305	-.0023	-.0214
Printing & Publishing	(27)	1.1257	1.1341	1.1120	.1178	.1973	.0930	.0316	.0691	.0543
Chemicals & Allied Products	(28)	1.1207	1.1430	1.0691	.0713	.1058	.1069	-.0316	-.0260	.1418
Rubber & Misc. Plastics	(30)	1.2659	1.4703	1.1292	.0902	.3266	-.0932	-.0651	-.1638	-.0831
Leather & Leather Products	(31)	.9469	.8048	.8651	.2153	.3620	-.0060	-.0367	-.0023	-.0002
Stone, Glass & Clay Products	(32)	1.0553	1.1391	.9902	.2259	.1146	.0609	.0072	.0233	.1352
Primary Metals	(33)	.9649	1.0050	.9959	.2844	.3822	.1214	.0219	.1281	-.0052
Fabricated Metals	(34)	1.0830	1.2032	1.0403	.3878	.3700	.1559	.0573	.1287	.2141
Machinery, Ex. Electric	(35)	1.0942	1.2038	1.1895	.8026	.5712	.2064	.2575	.1176	.1876
Electric, Electronic Equip.	(36)	1.2180	1.2194	1.0748	.8793	.5613	.1616	.5103	-.1900	-.0417
Transportation Equipment	(37)	.9612	1.0303	1.0767	.3683	.6036	.0281	.0608	.2108	.1024

Source: Calculated from data in U.S. Department of Labor, Bureau of Labor Statistics, Employment and Earnings, States and Areas, 1938-78, 1979 and Supplement to Employment and Earnings, States and Areas, 1977-79.

[a]Standard Industrial Classification Manual (SIC), U.S. Office of Management and Budget, 1972.

Definitions: Growth $= \overline{E}_i^1 / \overline{E}_i^0$

$$SD = (E_{si}^1 / E_{si}^0) - (\overline{E}_i^1 . \overline{E}_i^0)$$

where $E_{si}^1 =$ Employment in state s, industry i in terminal year.

$E_{si}^0 =$ Employment in state s, industry i in initial year.

$\overline{E}_i^1 =$ Total U.S. employment, industry i, terminal year.

$\overline{E}_i^0 =$ Total U.S. employment, industry i, initial year.

$$\text{TAX} = \left(T_s^1/\overline{T}^1\right) - \left(T_s^0/\overline{T}^0\right) \qquad (5.2)$$

where T_s^0 and T_s^1 denote the corporate tax rate for state s in the initial and terminal year, respectively, and $\overline{T}^0$ and $\overline{T}^1$ represent the average tax rates for all states in each year.[4] The tax rate for each state is obtained from *Facts and Figures on Government Finance,* published by the Tax Foundation. Choice of the appropriate rate is complicated slightly by the fact that a few states have graduated tax schedules. For these states the tax rate used is the maximum nominal rate applied to net income.[5] In addition, some states allow for various deductions in arriving at taxable earnings within the state. Rather than attempting to adjust for these differences, the nominal quoted rate is used as an indicator of the tax burden on corporations.

Unionization. The extent of unionization within a state is defined as total union membership as a fraction of the nonagricultural labor force. Data on union membership by state prior to 1964 are taken from Troy (1957). He has membership data, by state, for only two years, 1939 and 1953. Starting in 1964, these data are collected and published by the BLS in its *Directory of National Unions.* Again, the appropriate measure of this effect is the change in the relative degree of unionization. This is defined as follows:

$$\text{UNION} = \left(U_s^1/\overline{U}^1\right) - \left(U_s^0/\overline{U}^0\right) \qquad (5.3)$$

where U denotes the fraction of the labor force unionized.[6] The subscripts and superscripts are as previously defined. This represents one measure of the change in the relative importance of organized labor within a state.[7]

Right-to-Work Laws. To capture the effects of a favorable business climate and an indirect measure of future labor costs, a dummy variable (RTW) is included that takes a value of unity for states that enacted a right-to-work law prior to 1963 and zero otherwise.[8] Since this is a once-and-for-all change, it is anticipated that the incentives created by the passage of an RTW law die out over time, much the same as do the effects of a one-time change in the money supply.

INDUSTRY REGRESSIONS

In this section, regression results are first reported at the industry level across states. Since there exists substantial variation in parameter estimates, the data are pooled in the next section to obtain estimates across industries. Imposing common slopes and intercepts, with appropriate interactions, enables one to systematically examine reasons for the observed variation. In the process, we can determine whether the effects of changes in state differentials in corporate taxes, unionization, and business climate have significantly affected the mass of industry location patterns.

Regression results for each of the fifteen industries in the sample are reported in Table 5.2. Before proceeding with a discussion of the results, it is necessary to fully specify the variable definitions. The TAX variable is a lagged, ten-year change. For relative industry growth between 1957 and 1965, the tax variable is defined as a change between 1948 and 1958. The corresponding changes for TAX in the second and third periods are 1956–66 and 1964–74, respectively.[9] Lack of historical data on union membership by state prior to 1964 constrains the choice of dates for lags; as a result, the relative changes in UNION are not identical to those in TAX. The UNION variable is defined as a change over the periods 1953–64, 1964–74, and 1968–78.

The reason for using lagged tax changes rather than contemporaneous changes is simply that lags in industry response to a given change in relative tax rates are anticipated.[10] Owing to the short-run fixity of capital and the lead time required for the expansion of plant and equipment prior to the actual employment of labor, observed changes in SD are likely to be a response to tax changes that occurred in previous periods. This lagged response by firms was predicted by our decision model developed in Chapter 3. Since no theoretical reasons exist for choosing the length of the lag, a ten-year lag is chosen and imposed on all industries in the sample.[11]

Overall, we notice that the variables included in the model have the anticipated signs, but the effects of the two labor cost variables and the tax rate effects vary across industries. The coefficient on the RTW variable is significantly positive in eleven of the fifteen industries, while the UNION coefficient is significantly negative in four of

TABLE 5.2

REGRESSION RESULTS: INDUSTRY GROUPS ACROSS STATES
(t-values in parentheses)

Industry Group	(SIC)	TAX	UNION	RTW	Constant	R^2	F	d.f.	Joint F
Textile Mill Products	(22)	-.151* (-2.10)	.155 (0.44)	.114 (1.58)	-.059 (-1.47)	.11	3.38	80	1.30
Apparel & Other Textile Mill Products	(23)	-.058 (-0.94)	-.362 (-1.13)	.273* (4.57)	.002 (0.04)	.22	9.48	100	12.04
Lumber & Wood Products	(24)	.077** (1.98)	-.138 (-0.72)	.047 (1.16)	.017 (0.77)	.05	1.58	93	.90
Furniture & Fixtures	(25)	-.058 (-1.11)	-.589* (-2.22)	.211* (4.24)	-.086 (-3.08)	.28	10.31	79	11.89
Paper & Allied Products	(26)	-.063 (-1.36)	-.071 (-0.29)	.116* (2.51)	.015 (0.57)	.10	3.32	93	3.24
Printing & Publishing	(27)	-.066* (-2.59)	-.326* (-2.56)	.123* (4.79)	.041 (2.67)	.27	15.71	126	15.37
Chemicals & Allied Products	(28)	-.081 (-1.34)	-.156 (-0.49)	.076 (1.32)	.029 (0.77)	.05	1.78	94	1.15

Industry						R^2	F	n	F-stat
Rubber & Misc. Plastics	(30)	-.071 (-0.83)	-.108 (-0.28)	.366* (3.78)	-.110 (-2.33)	.27	5.68	47	7.30
Leather & Leather Products	(31)	-.074 (-0.76)	-.482 (-0.95)	.166 (1.56)	.054 (0.86)	.13	2.39	48	2.10
Stone, Glass, & Clay Products	(32)	-.053 (-1.21)	-.345 (-1.55)	.161* (3.88)	.026 (1.01)	.17	7.11	105	8.90
Primary Metals	(33)	-.136* (-2.58)	-.133 (-0.53)	.322* (5.84)	.028 (0.91)	.31	15.81	107	17.42
Fabricated Metals	(34)	-.234* (-3.94)	-.408 (-1.36)	.270* (4.49)	.104 (2.93)	.33	16.15	99	12.03
Machinery, except Electric	(35)	-.390* (-3.07)	-1.70* (-2.62)	.439* (3.53)	.143 (1.90)	.29	13.44	99	11.61
Electric, Electronic Equipment	(36)	-.289* (-2.14)	-1.30* (-1.86)	.458* (3.40)	.162 (2.05)	.21	8.68	96	8.39
Transportation Equipment	(37)	-.306* (-2.75)	-.340 (-0.60)	.272* (2.64)	.101 (1.64)	.17	6.30	90	3.84

Note: F-statistic for the null hypothesis that the coefficients on UNION and RTW are jointly significant.

*Significant at .05 or higher.

**Significant at .10.

the industry regressions. To a large extent, both variables may be capturing similar effects, that is, they may be highly collinear, and hence the standard errors on the coefficients may be inflated. In this case, it may be difficult to disentangle their relative influences. However, it would be incorrect to drop either variable on the basis of the reported t-value. Since there are strong apriori reasons to believe that they have independent effects, the true situation may not be that one of the variables has no effect but simply that the sample data do not enable us to pick it up. These estimates are presented as the best that can be obtained from the data in their present form.[12] In the last column of Table 5.2 we report the F-statistic for the null hypothesis that the coefficients on UNION and RTW are jointly insignificant. With the exception of textiles, lumber, and chemicals, the null hypothesis can be rejected at the .05 level in every case. The most surprising of these three exceptions is textiles. It is well known that textiles were one of the first northeastern immigrants in the South.[13] This movement began decades prior to the time period covered in this study, although the regional shift continued through the 1960s and 1970s. One of the most popular explanations for this phenomenon alleges that the textile industry migrated to the South to escape the highly unionized, high-wage states of the Northeast. The data do not support this explanation for the time period covered in this study, however. Therefore, while textiles are still, on net, moving South, this phenomenon may be related to other locational advantages. In particular, tax rate differentials certainly appear as one important reason.[14]

The tax coefficient is significantly negative in seven industry regressions. It appears that the durable goods sector of manufacturing is more sensitive to changes in state differentials in the corporate income tax than the nondurable sector. Only one industry within the nondurable group, textiles, is significantly affected by tax rate differentials. There is an anomaly that is hard to explain. Notice that the tax coefficient for lumber is significant, but with the wrong sign. One possible explanation for this counterintuitive result is that the elasticity of substitution between capital and labor may be sufficiently high such that the scale effect is dominated by the substitution effect following increases in the corporate income tax. Recall that our measure of industry migration is denominated in labor units. In general, we assume that a regional shift in capital takes labor with it, that is, the scale effect dominates. But the ease of substitution can act to offset this effect, either making the net tax effect insignificant, or actually resulting in an increase in employment, if the substitution effect is high enough. However, whether this explanation accounts for the observed positive coefficient is a matter for future empirical work.

It is obvious that considerable variation in parameter estimates exist across industries. While we can conclude that changes in state differentials for the variables specified have contributed to the observed redistribution of industry between regions, there exist substantial differences in their individual effects. Formally, analysis of variance tests for the homogeneity of intercepts and slope coefficients reveal significant differences across industries. The F-statistics are 6.81 and 3.07, respectively. All null hypotheses of homogeneity are rejected. This poses an interesting question: Do these point estimates vary in a systematic manner?

POOLED REGRESSIONS

At this point, the data for all industries are pooled, and the same regression is estimated across states and industries. In the preceding section it was observed that the point estimates of the coefficients differed significantly between industries. As mentioned earlier, imposing common slopes and intercepts, with appropriate interactions, will enable us to determine whether there are any systematic components in this variation. In the process, we can determine whether state differences in corporate taxes, unionization, and RTW laws significantly affect the mass of industry location decisions.

Across States and Industries. Table 5.3 reports the regression results from pooling the industry data. The first row presents the fully constrained estimates (i.e., we are imposing common slopes and intercepts on all industries). Furthermore, the U.S. growth rate $\left(E^1/\overline{E}^0\right)$ is constrained to equal unity. This constraint is implicit in the definition of the dependent variable (SD). Recall that SD is a difference between the growth rate in a particular state and the growth rate for the United States, that is, for each industry we have $\left(E_s^1/E_s^0\right)$ $- \left(E^1/\overline{E}^0\right)$. The U.S. growth rate is used as a prediction of what the growth rate for each state would have been assuming that no factors

TABLE 5.3

POOLED REGRESSIONS: ACROSS STATES AND INDUSTRIES
(t-values in parentheses)

	Constant	TAX	UNION	RTW	$(\overset{1}{E}/\overset{0}{E})$	R^2	F	d.f.
1. Fully constrained	.038 (3.15)	-.125* (-6.00)	-.475* (-4.52)	.228* (11.02)	1.00	.14	78.35	1412
2. No constraint on U.S. growth rate	-.184 (-1.85)	-.123* (-5.90)	-.466* (-4.44)	.229* (11.09)	1.206* (13.27)	.23	105.10	1411
3. With time period dummies	.051 (2.75)	-.118* (-5.54)	-.460* (-4.37)	.229* (11.08)	1.00	.15	47.70	1410
4. With industry dummies	.003 (0.09)	-.128* (-6.34)	-.445* (-4.38)	.225* (11.22)	1.00	.21	21.82	1398
5. With time period & industry dummies	.019 (0.54)	-.120* (-5.81)	-.431* (-4.22)	.226* (11.30)	1.00	.21	19.77	1396

Note: Results for dummy variable regressions are fully reported in Appendix B.

*Significant at .01.

unique to that state intervened to affect the level of economic activity. This formulation, common in the regional science literature, assumes that whatever forces are causing an industry to grow at the national level (e.g., productivity gains, income elasticity of demand, or technological change) affect all regions and states equally. If this is the case, then national growth-inducing factors are regionally invariant, and hence this specification would imply a unit coefficient on $(\overline{E}\,^1/\overline{E}\,^0)$. This may or may not be a valid assumption, and it therefore merits closer inspection. In row 2 this constraint on U.S. growth is relaxed. The results are interesting. The coefficient on national growth is 1.206 and is significantly different from unity.[15] However, notice that the coefficients on the explanatory variables, TAX, UNION, and RTW, are unaffected. Thus, while we can conclude that the assumption of unity imbedded in SD is rejected by the data, the relaxation of this constraint does not alter the conclusions concerning the impact of our three independent variables. As a result, we will maintain our use of SD as the specification in all regressions to follow.

The important thing to note from Table 5.3 is that all variables enter with the expected sign and that the coefficients are stable under the alternative specifications. Hence, the hypothesized effects of tax differentials, unionization, and RTW laws on industry migration between states are supported by the data. One of the most interesting findings, which differs from results in previous studies, is the significant, independent role played by state corporate income tax differentials in explaining industry movement between states and localities. As mentioned earlier, previous studies attempted to explain changes in manufacturing employment between areas by absolute tax levels. Furthermore, past studies assumed that contemporaneous tax rates were crucial. In this study we consider changes in relative tax rates, and we allow industry time to adjust. The statistical results reported above lend considerable support to the argument by many observers that ''low'' taxes have the effect of attracting business into an area.

Also, the estimates indicate that passage of RTW laws in some states had the effect of redistributing industry employment toward those states, ceteris paribus. These results are contrary to those of Soffer and Korenich (1961). The difference in results may be largely attributable to the difference in time periods covered in the present study and theirs. To the extent that firms need time to adjust to changing locational characteristics, data on employment changes prior to the 1960s will not capture the effects of RTW laws. We have argued that the debate and legislative activity surrounding state right-to-work laws lasted throughout the 1950s and came to a head in 1958 when referendums were submitted to voters in six states. Since 1958 the measure has been put forth in only four states. Therefore, we can consider 1958 as a watershed in the activity spawned by the Taft-Hartley Act. Whatever location incentives were created by RTW laws would have begun to take hold at this time. One ancillary hypothesis concerning the persistence over time of this RTW effect will be examined in the next section.

Finally, the results support the earlier findings of Fuchs (1962) that changes in unionization have important influences on industry location decisions. As a state's degree of unionization rises, whether it results from a change in industry composition or results from increased union activity within the same industrial composition, future industry growth declines relative to the U.S. average. In the industry regressions this effect may have been camouflaged by the possible collinearity between UNION and RTW. One could argue that states with a right-to-work law are also likely to have a slower growth in the degree of unionization and that states with a highly organized labor force are less likely to pass RTW laws. This would have the effect of inflating the standard errors and, hence, reduce the associated t-values. To the extent that they are collinear, the results in Table 5.3 provide an even stronger test, because both coefficients are strongly significant and have the correct sign. Therefore, the results suggests that the effects of both variables are sufficiently strong for the estimated coefficients to be statistically different from zero in spite of the effect of collinearity in increasing the standard errors. This would, in turn, suggests that RTW laws and degree of unionization have independent effects.

Before examining additional hypotheses, we discuss the sensitivity of our conclusions to both alternative lags and variable definitions. Consider first the specification of a ten-year lag for the tax effect.[16] In Table 5.4, point estimates for six alternative lag structures (including the ten-year lag) are displayed. Holding everything else constant in the regression equation, we are asking the data to select the preferred lag. In addition, we want to determine whether the rejection of the null hypothesis that $\beta = 0$ is sensitive to our choice of lag structure.[17] Notice that the TAX coefficient is significant for all six lag structures and that the effects of UNION and RTW remain unaltered. However, the data appear to prefer the ten-year lag, which is the structure used throughout this study.[18]

This experiment also reveals an interesting pattern that merits further discussion. Notice that the significance level of the tax coefficient rises as the length of the lag structure increases. This is true up to the ten-year lag, beyond which the significance level diminishes. This clear pattern suggests that the sensitivity of industry migration following a change in tax differentials between states rises as we allow time for location adjustments to take place. Recall that we have no a priori theoretical basis for selecting a particular lag structure. Nevertheless, we can say beforehand that a firm's fixed investment will cause some inertia in its migration response. Obviously, we expect very little *immediate* firm migration within an industry in response to a change in the structure of interstate cost of production differentials. But, with time, the amount of migration observed should increase. In Chapter 3 we suggested that "older" plants will move before "newer" plants (especially if newer capital is more efficient than older capital). Thus, we anticipate a migration flow. What the results in Table 5.4 suggest is that this flow reaches its peak ten years subsequent to the initial migration stimulus.

Second, consider the asymmetry in definitions between the dependent variable, *SD,* and the independent variables, TAX and UNION. Would the conclusions be altered if both explanatory variables were defined in the same manner as *SD?* In order to check this possibility, it is necessary to estimate the regression on a restricted sample, since several states have zero tax rates in one or more periods. Defining TAX and UNION symmetrically with *SD* we have

$$\text{TAX} = \left(T_s^1/T_s^0\right) - \left(\overline{T}^1/\overline{T}^0\right)$$

and

$$\text{UNION} = \left(U_s^1/U_s^0\right) - \left(\overline{U}^1/\overline{U}^0\right)$$

But, for all states in which the tax rate is zero in period 0, we run into obvious division problems. Table 5.5 presents the point estimates for both symmetrical and asymmetrical definitions on a sample excluding all observations in which $T_s^0 = 0$. The qualitative results

TABLE 5.4

POOLED REGRESSIONS WITH ALTERNATIVE LAGS FOR
CORPORATE TAX RATES
(t-values in parentheses)

Variable	Length of Lag for TAX					
	2-Year	4-Year	6-Year	8-Year	10-Year	12-Year
TAX	-.100** (-2.07)	-.089* (-2.75)	-.102* (-3.72)	-.101* (-4.50)	-.125* (-6.00)	-.076* (-5.09)
UNION	-.574* (-5.48)	-.557* (-5.31)	-.514* (-4.85)	-.495* (-4.67)	-.475* (-4.52)	-.494* (-4.69)
RTW	.247* (11.94)	.244* (11.78)	.239* (11.50)	.232* (11.11)	.228* (11.01)	.232* (11.17)
Constant	.384 (3.08)	.042 (3.41)	.037 (3.01)	.043 (3.50)	.038 (3.15)	.033 (2.65)
R^2	.12	.13	.13	.13	.14	.14
F	66.31	67.54	69.92	72.38	78.35	74.49
d.f.	1412	1412	1412	1412	1412	1412

*Significant at .01.

**Significant at .05.

Definitions for TAX:

Years Lagged	Period for SD		
	1957-65	1965-73	1973-79
2	1956-58	1964-66	1972-74
4	1954-58	1962-66	1970-74
6	1951-58	1960-66	1968-74
8	1950-58	1958-66	1966-74
10	1948-58	1956-66	1964-74
12	1946-58	1954-66	1962-74

are the same under both definitions. For comparison, the last column reproduces the results for the unrestricted sample. The only change between the unrestricted and restricted regressions is a minor reduction in the t-values on TAX. This can be attributed largely to the composition of each sample. In the process of eliminating observations, we have disregarded a significant amount of information, specifically those states with no corporate income tax.[19] Nevertheless, it appears that our results are invariant with respect to variable definitions.

TABLE 5.5

POOLED REGRESSIONS: SYMMETRIC AND ASYMMETRIC DEFINITIONS
(t-values in parentheses)

Variable	Model I	Model II	Unrestricted
TAX	-.158* (-5.05)	-.100* (-3.82)	-.125* (-6.00)
UNION	-.566* (-4.55)	-.596* (-4.64)	-.475* (-4.52)
RTW	.204* (8.17)	.211* (8.37)	.228* (11.02)
Constant	.044 (2.60)	.065 (4.03)	.038 (3.15)
R^2	.13	.11	.14
F	47.82	41.01	78.35
d.f.	1028	1028	1412

*Significant at .01.

Definitions:

	Model I	Model II
SD	$(E^1_{si}/E^0_{si}) - (\bar{E}^1_i/\bar{E}^0_i)$	$(E^1_{si}/E^0_{si}) - (\bar{E}^1_i/\bar{E}^0_i)$
TAX	$(T^1_s/\bar{T}^1) - (T^0_s/\bar{T}^0)$	$(T^1_s/T^0_s) - (\bar{T}^1/\bar{T}^0)$
UNION	$(U^1_s/\bar{U}^1) - (U^0_s/\bar{U}^0)$	$(U^1_s/U^0_s) - (\bar{U}^1/\bar{U}^0)$

At this point, it is worth summarizing the empirical results obtained thus far. The regression estimates lend considerable support to the argument that corporate tax differentials between states as well as the extent of unionization and a favorable business climate (enactment of an RTW law) have been major factors influencing the redistribution of industry between regions. Of particular interest is the degree to which the present results stand in contrast to those in previous studies.

Time Interactive Model. We have argued that since the passage of RTW laws represents a one-time change in location characteristics, the effects on industry redistribution between states with, and states without, such legislation should decay over time. That is, once industry location adjustments have been made, the existence of an RTW law will no longer act as an important influence. Thus, if we were to examine the pattern in the RTW coefficients over time, both the size and the significance level should fall at some point. To check on the time path of the coefficients, a time interactive model is estimated. The model takes the following functional form:

$$SD = \beta_0 + \beta_1 X + \beta_2 (D_2 X) + \beta_3 (D_3 X) + \beta_4 D_2 + \beta_5 D_3 + e \ (5.4)$$

and

$$D_2 = \begin{cases} 1 \text{ if an observation falls in period 1965–73} \\ 0 \text{ otherwise} \end{cases}$$

and

$$D_3 = \begin{cases} 1 \text{ if an observation falls in period 1973–79} \\ 0 \text{ otherwise} \end{cases}$$

The dependent variable is relative growth defined by equation (5.1). The data matrix X consist of a column of ones and the observations on the explanatory variables TAX, UNION, and RTW. This allows both intercepts and slopes to vary from period to period. The dummy variables (D_i) have been used in an additive and multiplicative fashion—in the former case, to allow for differential intercepts; in the latter case, to allow for differential slopes. This technique is equivalent to running separate regressions for each of three periods. However, this formulation permits a more direct approach to determining whether the individual coefficients differ significantly between periods. Each period regression can be obtained from equation (5.4) in the following manner:

Period 1957–65: $\hat{SD} = \hat{\beta}_0 + \hat{\beta}_1 X$
Period 1965–73: $\hat{SD} = (\hat{\beta}_0 + \hat{\beta}_4) + (\hat{\beta}_1 + \hat{\beta}_2)X$
Period 1973–79: $\hat{SD} = (\hat{\beta}_0 + \hat{\beta}_5) + (\hat{\beta}_1 + \hat{\beta}_3)X$

Thus, the coefficient on X (β_1) is the regression slope in the period 1957–65, and the coefficient of $D_i X$ represents the *difference* between the slope in the ith period and that in the first period. Whether the differences are significant can be determined by simply examining their associated t-values.

Fitting equation (5.4) to the data yields

$$\hat{SD} = .029 - .139(\text{TAX})* - .374(\text{UNION})** + .278(\text{RTW})*$$
$$\quad (1.31) \quad\quad (-3.25) \quad\quad\quad (-1.89) \quad\quad\quad\quad (7.02)$$
$$\quad - .012(D_2 \cdot \text{TAX}) - .547(D_2 \cdot \text{UNION})*** + .097(D_2 \cdot \text{RTW})***$$
$$\quad\quad (-0.19) \quad\quad\quad\quad (-1.79) \quad\quad\quad\quad\quad\quad (1.84)$$
$$\quad + .036(D_3 \cdot \text{TAX}) - .049(D_3 \cdot \text{UNION}) - .232(D_3 \cdot \text{RTW})*$$
$$\quad\quad (0.70) \quad\quad\quad\quad (-0.19) \quad\quad\quad\quad (-4.37)$$
$$\quad - .031(D_2) + .042(D_3)$$
$$\quad\quad (-1.00) \quad\quad (1.35)$$

with $R^2 = .17$ and 1404 degrees of freedom. The figures in parentheses are t-values, and the asterisks indicate that a coefficient is significant ($* = .01$, $** = .05$ and $*** = .10$ levels). A few interesting patterns emerge. First, the coefficients on $(D_i\text{TAX})$ are not significantly different from zero, implying that the impact of state corporate tax differentials has not changed from the first period. Second, we observe that the UNION effect increased slightly in the second period but was not significantly different in the last period. Finally, our interest lies primarily with the time pattern of the RTW coefficient. Notice that RTW laws were a significant influence in the first period and that this effect increased slightly in the second period. In the 1970s, however, RTW laws no longer significantly accounted for any of the observed redistribution of industry across states and regions.[20] This pattern is consistent with our hypothesis concerning the impact of a one-time change in location characteristics. This would imply that by the mid-1970s industries had largely completed their adjustment to the relocation incentives created by the passage of RTW laws in the 1950s.

Systematic Coefficient Variation across Industries. We are now in a position to examine reasons for the significant differences in point estimates across industries. In this section, two different reasons for the variation are discussed and tested. First, to the extent that the corporate income tax represents a tax on returns to capital and RTW laws and unionization are labor cost proxies, coefficient estimates should vary across industries according to capital intensity. Second, to the extent that "newer" industries are in some sense "footloose," they should be in a position to respond more rapidly to changes in interregional cost structures than "older" established industries.[21]

For the capital-intensity hypothesis we first obtain estimates of the capital/labor ratio (K/L) for each of the fifteen industries in the sample. The capital/labor ratio is defined as gross book value of depreciable assets divided by total payroll. This ratio is derived for each industry at the national level. We know that capital intensity varies over states and regions within industries, but using K/L for each industry at the state level would create problems, since the capital/labor mix for any particular industry within a state is a function of relative prices of inputs within that state.

Cacculated capital/labor ratios for each industry are reported in Table 5.6. Data on total payroll and gross book value of depreciable assets by two-digit industry classification are taken from the U.S. Bureau of the Census *Annual Survey of Manufactures* for three years, 1957, 1964, and 1972. The K/L estimates in 1957 are used as a measure of the capital intensity of each industry at the beginning of the first migration period, 1957–65. Likewise, K/L in 1964 and 1972 are associated with the second and third migration periods, respectively. To test each capital-intensity hypothesis, a pooled regression is estimated with K/L interacted with each explanatory variable. The regression takes the following functional form:

$$SD = \beta_0 + \beta_1(\text{TAX}) + \beta_2(K/L)\,(\text{TAX}) + \beta_3\,(\text{UNION})$$
$$+ \beta_4(K/L)\,(\text{UNION}) + \beta_5\,(\text{RTW}) + \beta_6(K/L)\,(\text{RTW}) + e \quad (5.5)$$

The hypotheses to be tested by this procedure can be restated as follows:

(1) Relatively capital-intensive industries are more sensitive to changes in interstate tax differentials than relatively labor-intensive industries.
(2) Relatively capital-intensive industries are less sensitive to changes in interstate labor cost differentials than relatively labor-intensive industries.

Operationally, the interaction term should increase the effect of TAX, the larger the capital/labor ratio. Likewise, for both UNION and RTW, the interaction term should have the effect of moving the coefficients toward the origin. The interactive results are reported in Table 5.7. Block A contains the tax effect that includes the K/L interaction term. Blocks B and C report the same for RTW law and

TABLE 5.6

ESTIMATED CAPITAL/LABOR RATIOS BY INDUSTRY GROUP

Industry Group	(SIC)	1957	1964	1972
Textiles	(22)	1.57	1.69	1.96
Apparel	(23)	.27	.38	.46
Lumber	(24)	1.38	1.64	1.61
Furniture	(25)	.73	.75	.84
Paper	(26)	2.62	3.25	2.59
Printing	(27)	.86	1.02	1.12
Chemicals	(28)	3.20	3.95	4.45
Rubber	(30)	1.36	1.57	1.96
Leather	(31)	.40	.45	.50
Stone, Glass, & Clay	(32)	2.19	2.68	2.69
Primary Metals	(33)	2.47	3.21	3.67
Fabricated Metals	(34)	1.06	1.22	1.31
Machinery	(35)	1.04	1.11	1.23
Electrical Equip.	(36)	.80	.88	1.08
Transportation Equip.	(37)	.89	1.06	1.17

Source: U.S. Bureau of the Census, Annual Survey of Manufactures, 1957, 1964, and 1972.

Note: Capital/labor ratio defined as gross book value of depreciable assets divided by total payroll.

unionization effects. In the last two cases, the interaction term has the anticipated effect, which is consistent with the second hypothesis. However, our tax rate hypothesis is not supported by the data. In fact, the coefficient on $(K/L)(TAX)$ is the wrong sign. At first blush, this suggests that capital-intensive industries are less sensitive to interstate corporate tax differentials, a result that is at the very least counterintuitive. However, this result may be an artifact of specifying the migration of industry in terms of changes in employment. If the

TABLE 5.7

POOLED REGRESSION WITH CAPITAL/LABOR RATIO INTERACTION

Variable	Coefficient	t-value	Joint F [a]
TAX Effect			
A. TAX	-.167	(-4.35)	
(K/L)(TAX)	.026	(1.39)	18.26
UNION Effect			
B. UNION	-.702	(-3.65)	
(K/L)(UNION)	.140	(1.49)	10.90
RTW Effect			
C. RTW	.327	(9.87)	
(K/L)(RTW)	-.060	(-3.90)	67.61
D. Constant	.039	(3.19)	
R^2	.16		
F	43.38		
d.f.	1409		

[a]Joint F for null hypothesis that $\beta_i = \beta_{i+1} = 0$.

elasticity of substitution between capital and labor varies positively with K/L, an increase in tax rates on returns to capital might actually lead to an increase in employment as labor is substituted for capital. This remains a matter of speculation, however.

Finally, we have argued that expanding industries are more likely to be "footloose" and therefore that they should be more responsive to changes in interstate costs differentials. Rapidly growing industries will be opening new plants and thus have the opportunity to seek out the optimal location. Static or declining industries, on the other hand, are relatively immobile owing to the fixed costs in their present location. As Creamer (1943) has pointed out, "an industry in which new capacity is being constructed can be shifted more easily than one burdened with considerable unused capacity" (p. 88).

In order to test this hypothesis, it is necessary to obtain some estimate of the rate at which new plants (capacity) was being added within each industry.[22] To get some idea of the rate at which new capacity was being added within each industry, we calculate an expansion variable (EXP), which is defined as the ratio of the number of new establishments to the total number of establishments, that is, the ratio of new to total. For each industry the exact form of this expansion measure is

$$EXP = (EST^1 - EST^0)/EST^1 \qquad (5.6)$$

where EST^1 represents the number of establishments in the terminal year and EST^0 denotes the same for the initial year. What constitutes a new plant is dictated by available data. The *Census of Manufacturers,* published by the U.S. Bureau of the Census, provides data on the number of establishments for each of the two-digit industry groups. Considering the time periods for *SD,* we have five census years from which to work: 1954, 1958, 1963, 1967, and 1972. Thus, the number of *new* establishments is assumed to be the difference in the number of establishments between successive census years. The total number of operating establishments for each industry in each of the census years is reported in Table 5.8. The EXP variable used in the analysis below is also reported. For the first time period, the corresponding expansion measure is defined between 1954 and 1958. The corresponding measure in the second and third time periods are reported in columns 7 and 8. Note that for a few industries the associated expansion rate is negative. We may interpret this as representing a relatively stagnant growth, assuming the absence of widespread plant consolidations. According to our measure, rubber, electronic equipment, and transportation equipment were adding plant capacity at a fairly substantial rate throughout all three periods. For example, in the transportation industry roughly 29 percent of the total operating establishments in 1958 were added between 1954 and 1958.

To test the expansion hypothesis, a regression is estimated in

TABLE 5.8

NUMBER OF OPERATING ESTABLISHMENTS BY INDUSTRY IN THE U.S.
AND ASSOCIATED EXPANSION RATES

| | Number of Establishments | | | | | Expansion Rate (EXP)[a] | | |
	1954	1958	1963	1967	1972	1954-58	1958-63	1967-72
Textile Mill Products	8,070	7,675	7,104	7,056	7,201	-.052	-.080	.020
Apparel	31,372	29,358	28,457	26,385	24,438	-.069	-.032	-.080
Lumber & Wood Products	41,484	37,878	36,150	36,849	33,949	-.095	-.048	-.085
Furniture & Fixtures	10,273	10,179	10,478	10,010	9,233	-.009	.029	-.084
Paper & Allied Products	5,004	5,271	5,713	5,890	6,038	.051	.077	.025
Printing & Publishing	32,531	35,456	38,090	38,001	42,103	.082	.069	.097
Chemicals & Allied Prods.	11,075	11,309	11,996	11,799	11,425	.021	.057	-.033

Rubber & Misc. Plastics	3,845	4,462	5,728	6,458	9,237	.138	.221	.301
Leather & Leather Prods.	4,845	4,549	4,047	3,695	3,201	-.065	-.124	-.154
Stone, Glass, & Clay	11,162	15,055	15,838	15,602	16,015	.259	.049	.026
Primary Metals	6,174	6,446	6,513	6,821	6,792	.043	.045	-.004
Fabricated Metals	22,042	24,782	26,991	27,413	29,525	.111	.081	.072
Machinery, ex. Electric	25,601	29,867	33,703	37,743	40,792	.143	.114	.075
Electric, Electronic Equip.	5,758	8,091	9,948	10,753	12,270	.288	.187	.124
Transportation Equipment	5,348	6,625	7,179	7,439	8,802	.193	.079	.155

Source: U.S. Bureau of the Census, Census of Manufactures, 1954, 1958, 1963, 1967, and 1972.

aEXP = (EST^1 - EST^0)/EST^1.

which each of the explanatory variables is interacted with EXP. The form of the regression is

$$SD = \beta_0 + \beta_1 (\text{TAX}) + \beta_2(\text{EXP})(\text{TAX}) + \beta_3(\text{UNION})$$
$$+ \beta_4(\text{EXP}) (\text{UNION}) + \beta_5(\text{RTW}) + \beta_6(\text{EXP})(\text{RTW}) + e \quad (5.7)$$

The point estimates are reported in Table 5.9. As expected, the interaction term has the effect of driving the coefficients away from the origin; that is, rapidly expanding industries are more sensitive to changing location characteristics across states than slower-growing or declining industries.

In conclusion, we have estimates that suggests two possibilities for the observed variation in parameter estimates across industries. The results indicate that the effects of changing economic characteristics of particular states and regions do not affect all industries to the same degree, but particular effects depend upon the capital intensity of an industry and the rate of capacity expansion. The importance of both the capital-intensity and the expansion hypotheses as explanations for interindustry coefficient variation is twofold. First, they are consistent with microeconomic predictions concerning the effect of factor shares on a firm's response to changes in factor costs and the impact of fixed costs on the speed of adjustment in locations. Second, it allows us to suggest a reconciliation for the difference in results between this study and previous work. Recall that most studies have utilized limited industry samples. As suggested by the significant differences in coefficient estimates across industries, what may have been true for some industries does not apply to others. Clearly, then, the present results are not inconsistent with earlier studies but merely reflect a broader sample of industries.

Decomposition of Industry Migration to the South. Of the systematic variation in relative employment growth explained by the basic model in Table 5.3, we are now concerned with the relative influence of each of the independent variables, TAX, UNION, and RTW, in accounting for the movment of industry to the South. To get some rough approximation fo how much of the predicted growth differential in the South was attributable to changes in relative taxes, unionization, and RTW laws, we decompose the predicted value of *SD* across all industries in the following manner:

TABLE 5.9

POOLED REGRESSION WITH EXPANSION RATE INTERACTION

Variable	Coefficient	t-value	Joint F[a]
		TAX Effect	
A. TAX	-.093	(-4.25)	
(EXP)(TAX)	-.804	(-3.85)	26.53
		UNION Effect	
B. UNION	-.346	(-3.10)	
(EXP)(UNION)	-2.253	(-2.32)	12.39
		RTW Effect	
C. RTW	.173	(7.97)	
(EXP)(RTW)	1.107	(6.48)	84.27
D. Constant	.035	(3.03)	
R^2	.19		
F	56.01		
d.f.	1409		

[a] Joint F for null hypothesis that $\beta_i = \beta_{i+1} = 0$.

$$w \cdot \sum_s \left(\hat{SD}_s \cdot E_s \right) = \beta_0 + \sum_i \beta_i \left[w \cdot \sum_s X_{is} \cdot E_s \right] \tag{5.8}$$

where

$E_s = (E_s^1 + E_s^0)/2$ is the average employment in state s between the
initial and terminal dates $(0, 1)$

$w = 1/\Sigma E_s$ is the reciprocal of the sum of average employment across
states in the South

X_i = represents each of the explanatory variables in the regression
β_i = denotes the estimated coefficients for each X
β_0 = denotes the estimated intercept

In this procedure we are weighting each state's influence by its proportion of total employment in the South. On the basis of this decomposition, the model predicts an overall 24.1 percent relative growth advantage for the South, and of this advantage the amount attributable to each independent variable is given by

$$.241 = \text{Constant} + \text{Tax Effect} + \text{Union Effect} + \text{RTW Effect}$$
$$= .035 + .030 + .020 + .710 \qquad (5.9)$$

Utilizing the estimates from this equation, roughly 12 percent of the predicted advantage can be accounted for by the tax effect, 71 percent by the RTW law effect, and 2 percent by unionization; the remaining 15 percent can be attributed to the intercept.[23] It is obvious that RTW laws played a fairly substantial role in industrial migration to the South; and, given its relative importance, unraveling the interaction between the legal environment in which collective bargaining takes place and resulting effects on location decisions is a promising area for future research. In essence, the dummy variable (RTW) represents our ''specific ignorance,'' and it would be of some importance to decompose the effects that are being captured by this variable.

Although the tax effect has played a minor role when compared with the influence of RTW laws, it has nevertheless been a significant contributor to the overall migration of industry employment to the South. Finally, unionization influences appear to be the least important of the three hypothesized variables.

ALTERNATIVE EXPLANATIONS

Although the present results appear to strongly support the hypotheses that changes in interstate differences in corporate tax rates, degree of unionization, and the enactment of RTW laws (our proxy for business climate) have been important determinants of the movement of industry to the South, there are alternative interpretations of the growth process in the Sunbelt. The first alternative relates directly to our interpretation of the regression results. Suppose the migration of industry to the South had nothing to do with changes in these institutional characteristics. For example, one might argue that reductions in transportation and communication costs over time may have allowed firms to move farther away from the Northeast and hence that this movement would have proceeded *as if* firms were responding to differences between the South and the non-South in the aforementioned variables. As a result, in a regression attempting to account for this migration, anything strongly correlated with "South" would naturally appear to be an important influence. According to this interpretation, the results we have obtained are merely the artifact of a spurious correlation, and therefore we are erroneously attributing southern migration to these interstate differentials.

A second alternative stems from a difference in theoretical perspective rather than from a mere argument with the regression results. There are a number of regional growth theories that provide different viewpoints on the causes and processes of regional economic growth. While they are not necessarily mutually exclusive, each theory tends to emphasize different causal mechanisms in the growth process. In the following discussion, we will examine a few of the most popular regional growth theories.[24] Ultimately, our objective is to determine whether they individually or collectively rule out our conclusions based on the results presented above.

Export Base Models. The essential idea behind these models is that some activities in a region are particularly "basic" in the sense that their growth leads and determines the region's overall development. Other "nonbasic" activities are merely the outgrowth or by-product of the region's overall development. These theories identify basic activities as those which bring money into the region from other regions, by producing goods for export. Thus, export base theory states that a region's growth rate is a function of its export performance. In its extreme form, growth in a region can result only if its export base increases.[25]

The development of export base models and interpretation of regional economic growth within this context is usually associated with the names of North (1955), Perloff and Wingo (1961), and Thomas (1963). North, for example, proposed a five-stage regional export base model. After a region spends a brief period in a subsistence stage, the regional economy begins to grow with the development of exporting of staple commodities to more advanced regions. With the resultant inflow of capital and the provision of an export-oriented infrastructure, a further stage of export intensification and regional development begins. In time, this leads to the development of a residentiary industry that serves local markets. In the final stage, expansion of the residentiary industry may reach a point where it enters the export market, thereby extending the region's export base.

One illustration of the use of an export base model is the study by Bolton (1966). His purpose was to estimate the impact of defense spending on U.S. regions and individual states over the period 1947–62. The technique entailed the use of a simple model of regional growth, one in which the rate of growth in personal income is predicted by the rate of growth in exogenous income. "Exogenous" refers to income that comes from outside a region, especially the income derived from selling goods and services to other regions. All defense purchases (defense income) are classified as exogenous. Defense income as a percentage of total exogenous income is assumed to provide an index of the relative dependence of a state or region on defense activity. The impact of defense income on regional growth depends both upon the weight of defense income relative to total exogenous income and upon the rate of growth in defense purchases as well.

While Bolton found modest evidence to suggest that the growth of income in some states and regions was "greatly stimulated" by defense purchases, only one of these states, Mississippi, was located in the South. Only eight states in the South had their growth "moderately stimulated" by defense spending. The remaining six states in the South were "little affected." Finally, only four states in the United States had experienced "growth depression" as a result of reductions in defense spending within these states.

Bolton's study is germane to our discussion for two reasons: (1) it represents a rigorous application of the export base theory to regional economic growth within the United States; and (2) it provides a fairly direct test of one very popular explanation for the Sunbelt phenomenon. Based upon Bolton's estimates, it seems doubtful that the acceleration of economic growth in the South can be entirely (or even largely) attributable to national defense spending patterns. Nevertheless, the export base theory is a valuable contribution to our understanding of the regional growth process. This was amplified by Borts (1960) when he found strong support for a model of regional growth based on the demand for a region's exports.

Product Life-Cycle Models. Though Vernon (1966) developed the product life-cycle model as one possible explanation for changing industry location patterns between nations, it has been applied to similar changes between regions within a country.[26] The product life cycle envisages a product evolving through three distinct stages in its life cycle. First there is an *innovation stage* where a new product is introduced. At this point, producers are confronted with a number of critical but transitory conditions that have certain spatial dimensions. The product will be relatively unstandardized, which means that its input requirements, its processing, and its final specification are not established with any degree of certainty. Thus, during the initial innovation stage a new product is manufactured in the home region and is introduced in other regions by export. This implies that the innovation stage, requiring a high input of R&D, will be carried out in large urban industrial agglomerations (i.e., the Northeast).

Second, as the product matures, a certain degree of standardization takes place. In this stage the producer's need for flexibility declines; that is, a "set of product standards opens up technical possibilities for achieving economies of scale and encourages long-term commitments to some given production process and some fixed set of facilities" (p. 196). The reduction in uncertainty of operations and the uncertainty over input mixes means that concern about production costs replaces concern over product characteristics. Growth in demand for the product now makes it profitable to expand production to low-cost locations, specifically in other regions in the United States where labor costs are "cheap." Once firms begin locating in a new area and are successful, the uncertainty over the profitability of this new location may be reduced. Other firms may then use this as a signal and will, in turn, emulate the location decisions of firms having already undertaken the move.[27]

Finally, at an advanced stage in the standardization of some products, less developed regions may offer competitive advantages as a production location. "If we can assume that highly standardized products tend to have a well-articulated, easily accessible national market and to sell largely on the basis of price (non-price competition is reduced by standardization of the product), then such products will not pose the problem of market information as accutely for a movement into less-developed regions" (p. 202).

Rees (1979) postulates that the decentralization of manufacturing employment as a whole and the technological changes involved in these shifts to the Southwest can best be explained by a product life-cycle model. Within the United States, the manufacturing belt of the Northeast has traditionally served as the seedbed of the American manufacturing system where most innovations have been nurtured. But, according to Rees, the decentralization of standardized technology in the third stage of the product cycle may have provided a constant tendency toward the erosion of the manufacturing belt's function as the only major manufacturing seedbed in the nation.

Utilizing shift-share analysis similar to that employed in the present study, Rees finds some evidence in support of the product-cycle hypothesis but admits that a complementarity exists between the role of regional resource endowments, certain government policies (e.g., defense spending), and increasing internal demand in bringing about the wane of the manufacturing heartland and the concomitant growth of the South.

Unbalanced-Growth Theories. The basic characteristic of unbalanced-growth theories is that regional growth rates during a nation's early stages of development may manifest significant *divergence.* This conceptual framework, unlike neoclassical equalization theroies, envisages market forces tending to increase, rather than decrease, the inequalities between regions. However, following this period of regional divergence, market forces eventually cause a movement toward regional equality.

Probably the two most popular regional inequality theories are Myrdal's (1957) "cumulative causation" model and Hirschman's (1958) "growth poles" model. Myrdal's model is based on the assumption that particular changes in the national economy do not, as neoclassical growth models predict, call forth offsetting changes. Instead, market forces set in motion supporting changes that move the system in the same direction as the initial change, but much further. Thus, once particular regions have acquired an initial advantage based on location, transportation, or some other attribute, new increments of growth will tend to be concentrated in the already expanding regions. The result is that little investment or growth occurs in the remaining areas of the nation.

These forces are, in turn, reinforced by what Myrdal calls "backwash effects." The lagging regions, faced with the higher returns obtainable in the growth regions, tend to lose their skilled workers, entrepreneurs, and capital. At the same time, goods and services originating in the expanding regions flood the markets in the lagging areas, which inhibits the development of indigenous enterprise. Both cumulative causation and spread effects work toward producing an initial period of interregional divergence in growth.

There are market forces that tend to work toward regional convergence, however. Myrdal calls these forces centrifugal "spread effects." Economic growth and development in the expanding regions may stimulate demand for agricultural and mineral products in the stagnating regions. If these spread effects dominate the backwash effects, a new process of cumulative causation may begin, leading to sustained economic growth within the formally stagnant regions.

Hirschman's model is similar to Myrdal's, but the key role in differential growth between regions is attributed to "polarization" effects. According to Hirschman, national development occurs initially around one or more "growth poles." Interregional growth inequality is thus a natural consequence of national growth. However, if an imbalance between regions resulting from the dominance of polarization effects occurs during early stages of growth, counterbalancing forces will eventually be set in motion to induce growth in lagging regions. These forces are called "trickle down" effects.

Rigorous empirical applications of the unbalanced-growth theories to the recent regional growth patterns exhibited in the United States have not yet been formulated. However, in a recent study Weinstein and Firestine (1978) relate these stages of growth to regional development in the United States. The evidence presented in support of these theories is mostly impressionistic and of a very low order of rigor (i.e., no operational hypotheses were structured).[28] Nevertheless, their argument proceeds as follows: (1) prior to 1880, no particular region dominated growth; (2) between 1880 and 1910 the Northeast and the Midwest became the manufacturing belt; and (3) after this period spread effects began to take hold, and during World War II these spread effects became even more pronounced.

A Simple Test against the Alternatives. In the preceding discussion we have presented alternative explanations for the Sunbelt phenomenon. The first suggested an alternative interpretation of the regression results, while the second class of alternatives provided another conceptual framework for evaluating the regional growth process. Do these alternative explanations necessarily rule out our hypotheses for the migration of industry to the South?

One way to distinguish between our interpretation of the results and those suggested by the preceding discussion is to divide the sample into two groups, South and non-South, and to treat each as entirely separate worlds. To the extent that interstate differentials in taxes, business climate, and unionization matter, we should be able to explain *intra*regional movement as well.

With this in mind, separate regressions were estimated for each region, expressing all changes relative to each region's average. The results are reported in Table 5.10. With the exception of unionization in the South, all the variables appear with the expected sign and are highly significant. This would strongly suggest that our interpretation of the previous results has merit and that, whereas our test does not rule out the possibility of national structural trends in industry migration from the Northeast, it certainly indicates that a firm's choice of destination is influenced by the local economic considerations outlined above.

Another interesting result is that RTW is highly significant in both regressions. This is *inconsistent* with the view that holds RTW laws to be a uniquely southern phenomenon. Instead, the passage of RTW laws has not only resulted in the redistribution of industry across regions but has also led to the redistribution of industry employment *within* both the South and the non-South.[29] Thus, the RTW controversy should hardly be considered a South/non-South issue, especially if one considers that, of the nineteen states that currently have such legislation, 37 percent are outside the South. Furthermore, of the states that at one time or another had legal restrictions on union security agreements, 45 percent were non-South

TABLE 5.10

POOLED REGRESSIONS: SOUTH/NON-SOUTH
(t-values in parentheses)

	South	Non-South
TAX	-.080** (-1.84)	-.117* (-6.59)
UNION	-.120 (-0.73)	-.595* (-6.30)
RTW	.211* (6.07)	.273* (7.04)
Constant	.071 (2.52)	-.026 (-1.86)
R^2	.09	.13
F	18.15	42.56
d.f.	578	830

Note: All variables defined relative to region averages.

*Significant at .01.

**Significant at .10.

states. Therefore, these stylized facts and the empirical results in this study contradict the view that the RTW law epitomizes the institutional characteristics of the South.

SUMMARY

There have been many explanations advanced to account for the acceleration of industry migration to the South. Despite the rather impressive gains in employment in the South, there has been no attempt to empirically test, within one consistent model, three of the most controversial explanations. The primary purpose of this chapter was to fill this void by extending our empirically validated knowledge concerning the influence of interstate differentials in corporate tax rates, unionization rates, and business climate (enactment of RTW laws).

Contrary to conventional wisdom, the results of this study lend considerable support to the argument that corporate tax rate differentials between states as well as the extent of unionization and a favorable business climate have been major factors accounting for a portion of the redistribution of industry to the South. Evidence also reveals substantial variation in the coefficient estimates across industries, but that this variation is systematic and can be at least partially attributable to the capital intensity and the rate at which an industry is expanding or contracting capacity. These two findings provide at least a partial reconciliation for the ambiguous results from previous empirical studies, especially with respect to the conflicting evidence concerning the role of state taxes in this process. Expanding the sample to include other industries, as this study does, reveals that previous results based upon limited industry samples cannot be generalized.

More specific results are: (1) tax rate differentials and RTW laws have not only affected movement *to* the South but have also influenced the redistribution of industry employment *within* the South; (2) the time pattern of coefficients on RTW support the hypothesis that the incentives from a one-time change in location characteristics decay over time as firms complete their adjustments (thus, by the mid-1970s most industries had completed their locational adjustments to the passage of RTW laws in several states in the 1950s and (3) the RTW variable in both a South and a non-South regression "carries its own weight," and hence the widely held notion that RTW laws are a uniquely southern phenomenon cannot be supported by these data.

At the very least, the results from this study are certainly consistent with the notion that government policymakers at the state and local levels have played a more influential role in the Sunbelt phenomenon than most of them have been willing to admit. This is particularly relevant to the ongoing debate over the appropriate role for the federal government in ameliorating the effects of interstate tax and expenditure "competition." To the extent that state and local governments compete for industry employment with tax incentives or other forms of financial incentives, does this argue for the federal enactment of measures designed to restrict these kinds of activities?

In a series of reports, the Advisory Commission on Intergovernmental Relations (ACIR) explicitly addressed this question.[30] Without discussion of what these federal actions might entail, the commission stated that a serious problem would be created for our federal system (and, by implication, require federal action) if there existed clear evidence that two conditions brought about by interstate tax differentials were present: (1) that several states were losing jobs and capital investment to other states because their tax levels were too high; and (2) that states losing jobs will be unable to stop this outflow within a reasonable period of time. That is, states may not be able to halt this outflow because the requisite tax and spending cutbacks would cause severe public service hardships.

The commission's task then turned to an evaluation of the impact of state and local tax differentials on the movement of capital and jobs from the Frostbelt states to the Sunbelt states. The ACIR concluded that state and local tax differentials, as they influence interregional development, do not currently constitute a problem for the federal system. That is, these differentials have not significantly affected the redistribution of industry employment either within or between regions. The results in this study, along with the findings of Hodge (1979) and Romans and Subrahmanyam (1979), are clearly at odds with the commission's conclusions.

Assuming that the present results are correct, does this suggest that federal intervention in this area is warranted? Using the commission's first criterion, the answer would appear to be yes. However, one might argue, on substantially different grounds, that federal action to restrict tax ''competition'' between states would introduce additional inefficiencies in the spatial allocation of resources.[31] In short, it may not be a socially optimal policy for the federal government to insulate ''high'' tax states from the economic consequences of their own actions. To the extent that tax differentials may cause firms to ''vote with their feet,'' then the resulting vote would ultimately induce states to alter their behavior. At one point, one would expect an alteration of their tax and expenditure policies—certainly if the vote created a strong enough mandate.[32]

Considerably more work is needed before we understand the effects of a state's full menu of tax and expenditure policies. While the theoretical basis for studying the effect of taxes on location has been well understood for over a decade—at least since McLure's 1970 article—and buttressed by a substantial literature on tax capitalization and related general equilibrium phenomena, the empirical literature in this area demands additional work. By implication, the results of this study reveal potentially high returns to further investigation of the empirical implications embodied in the theoretical literature.

NOTES

1. Fuchs (1962) found that several alternative measures of relative gains and losses yielded the same general picture of locational change. Whether this specification of growth introduces a bias will be discussed below.

2. The census years 1960 and 1970 are not used for two reasons. First, they are manifestly on different phases of the business cycle. Second, choice of census years has no natural appeal aside from providing researchers with a rich source of data not available in other years. This study is not faced with a census year data constraint. The year 1979 is the latest year for which employment data are available at this writing.

3. Alaska and Hawaii are excluded from the sample. For the first time period, only those states for which employment data are published in 1957 are included. If states excluded in the first period have the corresponding employment figure for 1965, they are then included in the second period. The same exclusion principle is followed for the third period. Because of the paucity of employment data by state, two industries are excluded from the sample. These are petroleum and coal products and instruments and related products. In addition, food and kindred products and tobacco products are excluded because of their ties to specific areas. For example, Fuchs (1962) found that many food industries are primarily oriented to local markets; hence, their locational change is related to the redistribution of income and population, factors not covered in this study.

4. The reader will note the asymmetry in definitions between SD and TAX. The tax variable could just as easily be defined in the same manner as relative industry growth, that is,

$$\text{TAX} = \left(T_s^1/T_s^0\right) - \left(\bar{T}^1/\bar{T}^0\right)$$

But for several states the tax rate is zero, and in such cases obvious division problems are encountered. Whether the results below are sensitive to changes in the definition of TAX will be discussed in a later section.

5. The maximum marginal tax rate is usually encountered at a sufficiently low income level to mitigate against any potential problems arising from graduated tax schedules.

6. This measure is chosen so as to maintain symmetry with TAX. Both independent variables are expressed in the same units, thus easing interpretation. The impact on parameter estimates of changing this definition will be discussed below.

7. Strictly speaking, this measure assumes that all industries entering a given state draw from the same population with the probability of drawing a unionized labor force directly proportional to the measure U. Some industries are systematically more unionized than others, however, and it is doubtful that they draw from the same pool. This measure is chosen because

it is the only one available by state (i.e., unionization rates by industry and state are not published).

8. One can correctly argue that RTW and UNION are highly collinear. That is, a state with an RTW law is likely to have substantially lower unionization rates, and symmetrically, states with high unionization rates are less likely to enact RTW laws. If multicollinearity proves to be a serious problem in the sense that estimated coefficients have an unsatisfactorily low degree of precision (inflated standard errors), we are faced with a classic case of weak data. The remedy lies in the acquisition of new data. Whether this is truly a serious problem remains to be seen.

9. Lack of tax data for 1965 precludes defining TAX with a terminal date synonymous with the initial date for *SD*. All changes are therefore pushed forward one year.

10. The same reasoning applies to UNION effects. However, given the lack of historical union data, this is not possible.

11. Five alternative lags on TAX are included separately in the pooled regressions to follow. The effects on parameter estimates are discussed and evaluated below.

12. The results change dramatically once the data are pooled in the next section.

13. This movement is extensively documented in Fuchs (1962) and Perloff et al. (1960).

14. As will be seen later, textiles are relatively capital intensive, which may make them particularly sensitive to changes in corporate income taxes.

15. The *t*-value associated with the null hypothesis that $\beta = 1$ is 2.29, which is significant at the .05 level. Hence, the null hypothesis is rejected.

16. Remember that the lack of data prevent us from considering alternative lags for the unionization effect.

17. Since tax rate data for 1952 are not available, we have substituted 1951 tax rates in the six-year lag for the first period.

18. We say that the data prefer the ten-year lag in the sense that the regression F-statistic is maximized.

19. A total of 384 observations were "lost" in the restricted sample, or roughly 27 percent of the total sample.

20. Regression results for each period are reported in Appendix B. In the last period, the coefficient on RTW is significant at no higher than .10.

21. Firms within an established industry are burdened with existing capital facilities, and relocation can occur only after sufficient depreciation has occurred to warrant a move. This location constraint will be less binding the more mobile is their capital stock. On the other hand, a firm entering an industry can make its ex ante location decision unencumbered by previous investments in plant and equipment. See Chapter 3.

22. It is not necessarily the number of new firms that we are interested in for an industry can be expanding rapidly while at the same time it is losing firms, say, through mergers. In fact, the measure chosen here counts the number of operating "plants," whether each belongs to a single-plant firm or multiplant firm. Even so, we still may be getting bias measures to the extent that an industry is expanding through a large number of plant consolidations.

23. It is important to keep in mind that we are decomposing the *predicted* value of the dependent variable for the South, not the total variation in *SD*. Thus, the RTW effect accounts for roughly 71 percent of the predicted value of *SD*, not the total variation. The unexplained variation is about 86 percent.

24. A thorough critique of these theories with considerably more bibliographic detail can be found in the Keeble (1967) and Meyer (1963). In our discussion we do not concern ourselves with a critique of these theories as "theories," in the sense that they do or do not possess "internal logic." Our objective is merely to present these theories as alternative approaches to the study of regional economic development.

25. The implicit assumption in all export base models is that only an increase in demand for a region's exports leads to growth. But this fails to recognize that *internal* trade can also generate growth: Otherwise, how else can any closed economy (e.g., the world economy) grow?

26. However, as is the case with most stages-of-growth theories, it is difficult to structure operational hypotheses. This difficulty stems from a failure to formulate a demarcation rule for deciding whether a specific case lies within or without the acceptable bounds of the model. What is needed is a clear explanation of how and why a product (or region) moves from one stage to another at a particular time. See Yotopoulos and Nugent (1976) for a useful discussion on operationalizing stages-of-growth models.

27. See McCall and Pasal (1979) for a formal treatment of this effect.

28. In fairness to Weinstein and Firestine, it must be pointed out that testing these unbalanced-growth theories was not their objective.

29. In the pooled regression a dummy variable for the South was entered, and while it had the effect of reducing the significance of RTW, both variables were highly significant. This would suggest that both have independent influences.

30. See ACIR (1979 and 1978).

31. We abstract from constitutional questions arising from this form of federal intervention.

32. However, modification of behavior within Frostbelt states may involve actions other than lower taxes. One popular policy option considered by many of the high tax states is to enact laws that restrict business mobility. These are commonly referred to as *plant closure* laws. The purpose is to maintain present tax levels by preventing firms from voting with their feet. See McKenzie (1979) for an excellent and easily readable analysis of restrictions on plant mobility.

Part II
Interregional Wage Patterns, 1959–1978

Chapter 6

Why Regional Wage Differentials?

WHY WAGES DIFFER between regions at any point in time is a fairly straightforward question to answer. In a dynamic growing national economy we would expect to observe short-run interregional wage differentials because of incomplete adjustments to recent changes in the structural demand for labor across regions. Given that it takes time for workers to acquire information about changing labor market conditions and to obtain training that may be necessary to change jobs, we do not expect supply responses to be highly elastic in the short run.

However, why wages in one region of the United States are chronically lower than wages in other regions provides economists with a slightly more perplexing question. When viewed over a sufficiently long period of time, the "failure" of the market to equalize wage rates between different regions has led to continuing speculation about the factors with which these differentials are associated. Consequently, a rather substantial body of literature has been devoted to measuring and explaining this phenomenon by attempting to isolate those influences which could give rise to the observed differentials.

Of particular interest to most economists over the years has been the historical difference in wages (measured variously by per capita income, annual earnings, the wage bill, and weekly wages)[1] between the South and the non-South.[2] By whatever measure chosen, there is an overwhelming body of evidence that reveals that southern workers earn significantly less than their counterparts elsewhere. Furthermore, this differential has persisted over a long period of time.

Why do wages in the South tend to be chronically lower than wages in other regions? If one examines the literature in this area, it is readily apparent that there is no single, universally accepted explanation for this phenomenon. In fact, there are almost as many explanations as there are studies. A second and equally important question follows directly from the first one. What has been happening to these wage differentials over time? In earlier studies on this topic, the research focus was almost exclusively centered upon secular patterns in regional wage differentials. This research methodology evolved from a theoretical predisposition that viewed observed regional wage differentials as disequilibrium differentials. Hence, concern was focused upon their long-run movements. But, as we shall see, the research focus changed in the 1960s. More recent studies have tended to examine regional wage differentials at a single point in time. This change in research focus was due in part to an emergence of high-quality cross-section microdata files and also to a growing tendency to view the observed differentials as compensating (equilibrium) differentials. As a result, however, the movement in South/non-South wage differentials in the post-1960 period remains largely undocumented and is therefore open to speculation.

In light of the significant regional redistribution of economic activity that has occurred over the last two decades, these two questions, especially the latter, take on added importance. Our interest in accounting for the existence and movement in regional wage differentials is twofold. First, we are concerned with the determinants of regional income inequality. Since labor income represents a substantial portion of the average worker's wealth position, and since wage rates for labor services largely determine labor income, our concern with determining why wages differ between regions is obvious. Second, we have a slightly more academically motivated interest in regional wage differentials. The existence and movement in wage differentials in general, and regional wage differentials in particular, provide us with useful information concerning how well labor markets function to alocate labor among competing activities (including spatial reallocation). Indeed, the acid test of a model of labor markets is its ability to predict the magnitudes and movements in wage differentials observed in the labor market.

REGIONAL WAGE DIFFERENTIALS IN A REGIONAL GROWTH MODEL

Under a neoclassical model of regional labor markets, with its assumptions of perfect and costless information and mobility, long-run equilibrium is characterized by regional factor price equalization.[3] Any short run disparities in factor returns across regions will be eliminated by the movement of resources from low-return to high-return regions.

This section is devoted to a description of the essential elements of a widely used aggregate model of economic growth. This model is presented for two reasons: (1) because it has implicitly (and, in some cases, explicitly) provided the theoretical foundation for most of the previous empirical work on regional wage differentials and (2) because it serves to identify some of the crucial variables involved in the movement of regional earnings differentials over the long run.

In this model the observable patterns of wage growth are produced by initial disparities in resource endowments between regions. In other words, owing to a historical accident of southern economic development, the South is hypothesized to be operating at a different point on the same production function as the non-South. The production functions are assumed to be identical across regions and are subject to constant returns to scale.[4] Those regions with higher proportions of capital to labor will manifest higher wage rates and lower returns to capital. With the assumption of factor mobility, we would witness capital moving from high-wage regions (non-South) to low-wage regions (South). The resultant changes in the capital/labor ratios produced by these movements will raise the marginal product of labor in the latter and lower the marginal product of labor in the former (the opposite occurs for the marginal product of capital). The net effect is a convergence in regional wage differentials.

The model can be stated formally by specifying a regionally invariant linear homogeneous production function, $Y = f(K, L)$, where Y denotes output and K and L are capital and labor inputs, respectively. With linear homogeneity, the marginal physical product of labor, f_L, and the marginal physical product of capital, f_K, are functions of the capital/labor ratio, K/L. In addition, the wage rate and the return to capital will be equal to their respective marginal products:

$$f_L = g(K/L) = w; \qquad f_K = h(K/L) = r$$

Thus, if the wage rate is higher in one region than another, it implies that the capital/labor ratio is also higher in that region. The direction of resource movement and its impact on factor returns can be predicted by the following two relationships:

$$g'(K/L) > 0 \quad \text{and} \quad h'(K/L) < 0$$

Consequently, labor will flow from the low-wage region to the high-wage region, and capital will move in the opposite direction, since f_K is negatively, related to K/L.

This model presents a highly simplified description of reality. The real issue is not its simplicity but rather its predictive power, however. Borts (1960) found the predictive power of this model to be weak in the sense that it failed to explain the observed patterns of growth among regions between the intervals 1919 to 1929 and 1948 to 1953. On the other hand, Borts found that this highly aggregate theory of regional growth performed well in the period between 1929 and 1948.[5] Thus, he concluded that the data were inconsistent with the theory for the periods 1919–29 and 1948–53 but provided support for the theory during the 1929–48 period.[6]

The weakness of this theory is that it fails to recognize the diversity of economic activity carried on within and between regions. It abstracts from differences in demand, differences in production techniques that may result from the quality of labor, and differences in the composition of output. The traditional theory of interregional wage growth is therefore an oversimplification of the nature of the problem, because of its exclusive focus on differentials in K/L between regions. This focus on capital/labor ratios as the mechanism through which interregional wage differentials are eliminated has a second drawback. Contrary to conventional wisdom, not only had capital/labor ratios converged by 1958, but the southern ratios were actually higher than those in the North.[7] As a result, we are confronted with the task of explaining the absence of wage convergence in light of the convergence of capital/labor ratios.[8]

It appears that our observations on interregional wage differentials and capital/labor ratios do not square with our theoretical construct. Is it still possible to interpret regional wage data in terms of a long run equilibrium framework? One perspective would view the persistence of regional wage differentials as a disequilibrium phenomenon, in which the adjustment mechanism of labor mobility from labor-abundant to capital-abundant regions is seen as working only very slowly. But, as we argued, capital/labor ratios have already converged without a resultant elimination of interregional wage differentials.

A departure from the simple growth model perspective is to examine ways in which regional wage differentials may persist over an extended period. First, the observation of a significant and persistent wage differential across regions may be explained by institutional factors that act as barriers to the free flow of resources among regions. Such institutional factors as regional differences in the bargaining strength of unions[9] and labor market discrimination against nonwhites are sometimes offered as explanations for the incomplete and lengthy convergence process of regional wage differentials.

Second, the apparent contradiction between theory and fact can be rationalized by recognizing the heterogeneity of labor between regions. For example, the nonhomogeneity of the labor force between regions may be the result of a pattern of industrial specialization in the South that makes use of the relative abundance of unskilled workers, while northern industries make use of that region's relative abundance of skilled workers.[10] Thus, within each skill category we would anticipate economic forces to work toward the elimination of regional wage differentials. But the overall average wage across all skill categories would be higher in the North, reflecting that region's higher degree of human capital requirements. The simple growth model presented above assumes a homogeneous labor force and ignores differences between regions in industry mix.

If we modify our approach slightly by first recognizing the nonhomogeneity of labor between the the North and the South, how might a persistent *average* wage differential between the two regions exist in long run equilibrium? To the extent that at least part of the observed North/South wage differential is permanent, then we must account for the major factors leading to equilibrium differences in earnings across *individuals*.

OCCUPATIONAL WAGE DIFFERENTIALS

Competitive labor market theory predicts that in the long run there will be a tendency for labor of the same quality to obtain equality of "net advantage" irrespective of *place* of employment. The term "net advantage" is meant to include both the pecuniary and the nonpecuniary components of an occupation. Occupations are defined primarily by the kinds of tasks and skills required to perform the job. In addition, attached to any occupation are nonwage attributes such as riskiness, working conditions, variability of earnings, and prestige. Thus, almost by definition, we expect to observe wage differentials across workers in different occupations. Whether we assume that all individuals have identical taste or whether they differ in their assessment of the wage and nonwage components of a particular occupation, differential earnings will be needed to compensate individuals for: (1) acquiring the necessary skills (assuming that skills are required at a cost)[11] and (2) putting up with unfavorable employment conditions. Therefore, to the extent that occupations differ as to their "net advantages," wage differentials are not a reflection of a misallocation of labor but are instead compensating (equilibrium) differentials.

INTERINDUSTRY WAGE DIFFERENTIALS

In a competitive economy, with no impediments to factor mobility, long run equilibrium will yield equality of wages across industries for any given occupation. Therefore, in the long run, interindustry wage dispersion will reflect only interindustry differences in skill mixes. Therefore, in equilibrium, the competitive model implies, among other things, that there will be no association of industry wage levels either with the amount of labor employed or with the amount of capital employed. Furthermore, there will be no correlation between wage levels and capital/labor ratios.

However, we cannot ignore the possibility that nonwage aspects of a given occupation differ between industries. If these differences exist, they will generate interindustry wage differentials even within a specific occupation. Again, these nonwage attributes would include the pleasantness of work, risk to health, and the cyclical variability of employment. But, in the long run, wage differences among industries for any given occupation should be no greater than can be rationalized by differences in nonwage components.

REGIONAL WAGE DIFFERENTIALS

Recognizing the diversity of economic activity across regions, we must leave the simple, one-good world envisaged by the growth model outlined earlier. Nevertheless, economic theory allows us to make a general statement concerning interregional wage differentials: wages for the same type of labor should tend toward equality between regions over time.

We have claimed that occupational wage differences arise because the costs of acquiring the necessary skills to enter various occupations differ and because nonwage aspects of occupations vary considerably. In addition, these equilibrium wage differentials may be magnified if there exists a dispersion of individual tastes and preferences. By implication, occupational wage differentials are compensating differentials and hence are the only ones that persist in the long run. Abstracting from nonpecuniary differences in occupations across industries, industrial wages will differ only to the extent that industries differ in their occupational mixes. Consequently, we can conclude that regional wage differentials will persist in the long run only to the extent that industry mix differs across regions.

A number of empirical studies have attempted to control for differences between the South and the non-South in both industry mix and the quality of labor. Gallaway (1963) found that while the unadjusted wage differential between the South and the non-South[12] was approximately 20 percent in 1954, the adjusted wage differential (taking into account industry mix) was about 15 percent. Fuchs and Perlman (1960), performing the same sort of industry mix adjustment, found that wages in the South were between 15 and 21 percent lower than the national average in 1929, between 11 and 16 percent lower in 1947, and between 10 and 13 percent lower in 1954.[13] Thus, even after taking into account the differences in the industrial mix between regions, a sizable differential still remained to be explained.[14]

With the advent of more sophisticated econometric techniques and high-quality data files, more recent studies have been able to control for both industry and labor-quality variations across regions. Scully (1969) performed the most thorough and detailed examination of South/non-South wage differentials. He was able to standardize for industry, race, sex, and capital intensity. He was also able to control for educational levels of the work force by forming an index of the amount of educational expenditure for an average worker, by industry. As a proxy for unionization, Scully included a variable on the proportion of each industry's work force involved in strikes. He did not, however, control for occupational mix.

Based upon his regression results for average hourly wage rates paid to production workers in 1958, Scully arrived at the following conclusions. (1) The net effect of capital/labor ratios was to create a wage differential of about 8 percent in favor of the South. This was due to the fact that the South had a slightly higher mean capital/labor ratio than the North. Although wages were lower in the South even in the presence of a higher capital/labor ratio, this fact merely suggests that other factors have moved southern wages in the other direction.[15] (2) The net effect of human capital (education) created an approximate 10 percent differential in favor of the North. (3) Wage discrimination against nonwhites in the South resulted in about a 12 percent differential unfavorable to the South.[16] (4) Trade union activity, while unfavorable to the North, produced only about a 3 percent differential in wage rates. (5) Finally, the industrial structure differences between the North and the South produced a 20 percent differential unfavorable to the South.

According to Scully, these findings would indicate that the pursuit of regional wage convergence depends upon the elimination of human capital differences and discrimination. But, aside from the discrimination argument, most of the difference in wage rates between the South and the non-South can be accounted for by regional differences in the quality of the labor force and by the industry mix. As we have pointed out, these differentials are compensating differentials and are entirely consistent with competitive labor markets.

In recent years, another hypothesis has emerged in the empirical literature. Some observers, including Coelho and Ghali (1971) and Bellante (1979), argue that, once industry mix and labor heterogeneity have been accounted for, the remaining regional wage differential can be attributed to regional differences in the cost of living. They conclude that a comparison of *money* wages between regions is invalid so long as prices differ. Their results suggest that regional price variations exactly offset regional money wage differentials, leaving real wages equal across regions. But this conclusion fails to recognize that the lower cost of living may be a *result* of low wages, since many items in the consumption bundle are produced in cooperation with local labor. Thus, a wage differential of, say, 10 percent between regions cannot produce a 10 percent differential in the cost of living. First, many of the items consumed within a region are produced outside that region; hence, the price of those items is likely to be influenced by the wage level in other regions. Second, many items produced within the low-wage region are produced in cooperation with capital. Unless capital earns a lower rate of return in this region, the relative cost of living will not be as low as the relative wage.[17]

Along the same lines, Rosen (1979) assumes that differences in wages between regions represent compensating differentials that reflect differing area-specific (immobile) amenities. Assuming *universal* preferences for amenities among members of the population, an equalizing set of money wages and cost-of-living differences will be observed among regions. Those areas that have predominantly negatively valued amenities will be required to offer higher wages and lower prices in order to attract workers from more favorable areas. Thus, according to Rosen, we fully expect to observe equilibrium wage differentials that persist over time and that merely reflect the fact that amenities are not transferable between regions.

Several issues remain unsettled in this analysis, however. First, it is not clear which price captures the value of an area's favorable amenities. One possibility is to have these amenity values totally reflected in the price of land, with money wages being equal between regions. Second, if wages differ between regions, for whatever reason, capital will tend to flow in the direction of cheap labor, since there is no requirement that owners of capital live in the same area. Third, it is not clear what constitutes a favorable amenity. If there exists heterogeneity of tastes among members of the population, geographic sorting may tend to eliminate prevailing wage differentials. Finally, the amenity-related wage differential theory requires a dynamic mechanism to explain any secular change in the pattern of regional wage differentials.

Up to this point, we have referred only to long-run equilibrium outcomes; that is, economic theory predicts that in the long run each industry's wage level (and hence each region's wage level) will, ceteris paribus, vary in the same direction as its skill mix. However, occupations and industries also differ with respect to recent changes in the demand for labor. While long-run wage differentials will not be related to changes in the quantities of labor and capital employed (or to their ratios), this is not the case for short-run observations. With short-run inelasticities of labor supply, the competitive hypothesis implies that, for any given year, part of the interindustry and interregional wage dispersion is due to disequilibrium of industries expanding and contracting employment more than average. Though this sort of dispersion is reduced over time by the operation of the price system, the interpretation of cross-section observations on regional wage data must therefore be tempered with some degree of caution.

Fortunately, economic theory has more to say about movements of regional wage differentials than it does about cross-section magnitudes. Thus, our purpose in the remaining chapters is to document and analyze long-term changes in the pattern of regional wage differentials. Our primary task is to examine these patterns during the period of the Sunbelt phenomenon. In the next chapter, however, we set the stage for this analysis by documenting the historical pattern in South/non-South wage differentials.

NOTES

1. Early studies tended to use per capita income, annual earnings, or the wage bill because of severe data constraints. With the advent of more comprehensive data, current studies are able to take advantage of information that comes closer to the theorectically preferred measure.

2. Though the terms "South" and "non-South" have had various definitions over the years, it is doubtful that these various definitions alter the basic conclusion. In one exchange, however, the exact definition of "South" was fundamental to differences in results. See Coelho and Ghali (1971, 1973) and Ladenson (1973).

3. Perfect and costless information precludes long-run regional wage dispersion because of workers' lack of knowledge concerning changing labor market conditions and because of employers utilizing different production technologies. Mobility assumptions usually mean that

all resources, including labor, capital, and commodities, move freely across regions in response to any short-run disparity in returns.

4. One explanation for the persistence of interregional wage differentials is that the production functions of the two regions differ in such a way as to produce different value marginal product schedules for labor in the two regions. Gallaway (1963) found little support for this argument.

5. Borts contended that the role of demand for a region's output had a stronger influence than wage levels on the relative movements of capital and on the increase in wages in the different states. He suggested that this was probably the chief reason why regional wage convergence failed to appear in two out of the three periods.

6. Although this is probably the best theoretical/empirical work in the area of regional wage differentials, his data were rather crude, and the analysis was not carried out in a multiple regression framework, this meant that he could not hold "other things equal."

7. See Moroney and Walker (1966) and Scully (1969, 1971).

8. This does not mean that wage growth is unaffected by the migration of capital and labor but may simply imply that other factors, not incorporated in the model, have interacted to prevent wage convergence.

9. Segal (1961) has suggested that interregional variations in the policies of unions and management resulted in the establishment and perpetuation of regional wage differentials. "The basic explanation appears to lie in the failure of American unionism to organize more completely, and more uniformly in terms of geographic locations, the work force of many industries" (p. 154).

10. What caused the initial disparity in skill mix between the North and the South is a matter of speculation. We will have more to say about the possibilities in the next chapter.

11. Some occupations require longer periods of schooling and training. Because training is expensive, it follows that earnings subsequent to the completion of a period of training must be higher to compensate individuals for having taken on the extra expense. For a careful discussion of factors generating long-run occupational wage differentials see Reder (1955, 1962).

12. The South was defined separately as the East South Central and South Atlantic divisions, while the non-South included only states in the Middle Atlantic division.

13. Their definition of the South was the same as Gallaway's, but their basis of comparison was the national average.

14. Although industry mix adjustments by Gallaway and by Fuchs and Perlman failed to account for the entire unadjusted wage differential, it is clear that industrial structure adds to differences in earnings between regions. One might argue strongly that these adjustments were far from being complete. For example, no adjustments were made for differences in sex or racial composition of employment, size of cities, worker skills, and occupational mix.

15. It should be pointed out that there is a theoretical objection to the inclusion of capital/labor ratios in such a model estimated by Scully. The effect on wages of differences in capital/labor ratios across regions is exclusively a disequilibrium effect. In the long-run equilibrium, there will be no association between wage levels and capital/labor ratios. Since a cross-section regression implicitly assumes equilibrium, and since Scully's objective was to account for differences in wage *levels* across regions, it is not clear what his results really mean.

16. As Scully admits, the interpretation of the results as evidence of wage discrimination as opposed to evidence consistent with white/nonwhite productivity differentials is a matter of speculation. That is, there was no way for the data to distinguish between these two competing hypotheses.

17. See Borts and Stein (1964).

Chapter 7

Historical Overview of South/Non-South Earnings Differentials

ALTHOUGH THE FOCUS of this study is on changes in regional wage patterns that have occurred over the last two decades, we set the stage for the analysis by placing the current South/non-South wage differentials in historical perspective. Unfortunately, no systematic time series data on annual earnings or wage rates exist that span the entire period since the Civil War. Therefore, in order to obtain some overall picture of the historical pattern in earnings differentials between the South and other regions, it is necessary to bring together the results of several independent estimates of earnings levels by region. The objective of this exercise is twofold: (1) to document the extent of these earnings differentials at various periods of time and (2) to examine the secular trend in regional earnings differentials. We proceed in two stages. First, we examine the magnitude and movement of South/non-South earnings differentials in the postbellum period of the 1800s. While no formal analysis is undertaken to explain the origins of lower earnings in the South, some tentative hypotheses are offered. But it remains for future research to determine whether they have empirical validity. Second, we continue our examination of the dynamic pattern in South/non-South earnings differentials through the first half of the twentieth century.

Based upon the cumulative weight of evidence from several studies, it appears that relative earnings for most workers in the South were lower at the turn of the century than they were prior to the Civil War. In the vast majority of cases, however, most of this widening occurred in the 1860s; thereafter, the South's relative position tended to improve slightly. The patterns in the 1800s stand in sharp contrast to the patterns after 1900. Since the turn of the century, these wage differentials have appeared to narrow considerably, punctuated by a few short periods of relative stability.

THE 1800s

Lebergott (1964) provides estimates of average daily earnings and average annual earnings for various categories of workers between the years 1850 and 1899. Long (1960) also provides estimates of average daily wage rates for workers during this same period, but for considerably more detailed industry and occupational groupings. Both authors provide these estimates by cities, states, and regional divisions. With a minimum of effort we can make interregional comparisons by first expressing averages within a particular division as a fraction of the associated average for the nation as a whole. The resulting index (South/non-South) can then be plotted against time to visually capture possible secular trends.

We start by examining average earnings for common laborers, farm laborers, and workers in three industry groupings (woolen manufacturing, cotton manufacturing, and steel manufacturing) estimated by Lebergott. He goes into considerable detail explaining the techniques used to estimate these earnings levels and the qualifications needed to interpret them.[1] For our purposes, the averages for each census division are expressed as a ratio of the U.S. average. Table 7.1 presents the resulting index of average daily earnings for common laborers for the nine geographic divisions. Note that estimates of average daily earnings in the first two rows include board, a common method of wage payment during this period. Unlike the trend in other occupations and industries, relative earnings of common laborers in the South showed a modest improvement between 1850 and 1890. The index in the South Atlantic (SA) division rose from .78 to .82 during this period. This pattern was also evident in the East South Central (ESC) division, where relative earnings rose from .78 to .90. However, relative earnings in the West South Central (WSC) division fell from 1.09 to .99. The most dramatic reduction in relative earnings occurred in the Pacific (PAC) division, where average wages were almost six times the national average in 1850, but by 1890 they were only 34 percent above the national average.

Interregional Wage Patterns, 1959–1978

TABLE 7.1

INDEX OF AVERAGE DAILY EARNINGS FOR COMMON LABORERS
BY GEOGRAPHIC DIVISIONS: 1832-90
(U.S. = 1.00)

Year	NE	MA	ENC	WNC	SA	ESC	WSC	MT	PAC
1832*	1.10	1.15	.77	.84	.73	.79	--	--	--
1850*	1.26	.98	.95	.92	.79	.80	1.15	--	6.55
1850	1.16	1.03	1.00	.89	.78	.78	1.09	--	5.74
1860	.97	1.00	.95	.92	.79	.87	1.20	1.89	2.50
1869	1.01	1.02	1.02	1.00	.68	.83	1.04	1.75	1.48
1880	1.04	1.03	1.06	1.16	.78	.89	--	--	--
1890	1.02	.99	1.03	1.01	.82	.90	.99	--	1.34

Source: Calculated from data in Lebergott (1964), Table A-25, p. 541.

*Daily wages include board.

Indexes of average monthly earnings with board for farm laborers by geographic division are reported in Table 7.2. In this case, we have estimates as far back as 1818. Farm workers in the South experienced a definite secular decline in monthly earnings relative to their counterparts in other regions. In all three southern divisions (SA, ESC, and WSC), the index fell rather dramatically between 1818 and 1899. For example, in the ESC division, earnings were initially 10 percent *above* the national average. By 1899 this index had fallen to .74. Conversely, the index rose in the Northeast (NE and MA) and north central (ENC and WNC) divisions.

Tables 7.3–7.5 present the index of average annual earnings for full-time equivalent workers in woolen manufacturing, cotton manufacturing, and steel manufacturing, respectively. Concentrating on the only two southern divisions (SA and ESC) for which data are available over the entire period, we notice a fairly clear downward trend in the index for each industry. One interesting pattern emerges in cotton manufacturing, however. In the decade prior to the Civil War, the index rose dramatically and then fell substantially thereafter. We

TABLE 7.2

INDEX OF AVERAGE MONTHLY EARNINGS WITH BOARD FOR FARM LABORERS BY
GEOGRAPHIC DIVISIONS: 1818-99
(U.S. = 1.00)

Year	NE	MA	ENC	WNC	SA	ESC	WSC	MT	PAC
1818	1.26	1.04	.94	1.07	.85	1.10	--	--	--
1826	1.32	.95	.99	1.15	.81	1.06	--	--	--
1830	1.31	.96	.99	1.15	.81	1.06	--	--	--
1850	1.20	1.03	1.05	1.11	.76	.88	1.04	--	6.27
1860	1.08	.93	1.01	1.01	.81	1.03	1.14	--	2.50
1870	1.20	1.08	1.02	1.03	.60	.77	.85	--	1.76
1880	1.19	1.17	1.32	1.27	.75	.87	1.10	2.11	2.12
1890	1.28	1.13	1.14	1.14	.68	.76	.92	1.56	1.63
1899	1.25	1.10	1.16	1.24	.64	.74	.81	1.81	1.72

Source: Calculated from data in Lebergott (1964), Table A-23, p. 539.

TABLE 7.3

INDEX OF AVERAGE ANNUAL EARNINGS FOR WOOLEN MANUFACTURING,
FULL-TIME EQUIVALENT, BY GEOGRAPHIC DIVISIONS: 1849-99
(U.S. = 1.00)

Year	NE	MA	ENC	WNC	SA	ESC
1849	1.05	.92	1.02	1.09	.93	.86
1859	1.00	1.01	1.13	.98	.89	.80
1869	1.07	.99	.85	.70	.66	.60
1879	1.04	1.01	.80	.64	.66	.65
1889	1.02	1.01	.84	.82	.71	.84
1899	1.07	1.00	.84	.76	.65	.70

Source: Calculated from data in Lebergott (1964), Table A-28, p. 544.

TABLE 7.4

INDEX OF AVERAGE ANNUAL EARNINGS FOR COTTON MANUFACTURING,
FULL-TIME EQUIVALENT, BY GEOGRAPHIC DIVISIONS: 1849-99
(U.S. = 1.00)

Year	NE	MA	SA	ESC
1849	1.10	.91	.68	.64
1859	1.02	.92	.84	.78
1869	1.02	.94	.67	.70
1879	1.05	1.00	.73	.70
1889	1.08	1.10	.67	.69
1899	1.19	1.19	.63	.65

Source: Calculated from data in Lebergott (1964), Table A-27, p. 543.

will provide some possible explanations for this empirical observation at the end of this section. Also, notice that most of the reduction in relative earnings for southern workers occurred in the 1860s, with some modest rebound in the 1870s and 1880s. Despite these gains, relative southern earnings in 1899 were below their prewar levels.

TABLE 7.5

INDEX OF AVERAGE ANNUAL EARNINGS FOR IRON AND STEEL MANUFACTURING,
FULL-TIME EQUIVALENT, BY GEOGRAPHIC DIVISIONS: 1859-99
(U.S. = 1.00)

Year	NE	MA	ENC	WNC	SA	ESC	WSC	CALIF
1859	1.06	.99	1.01	1.26	.87	.88	1.31	.31
1869	1.13	1.01	.97	1.37	.70	.76	1.22	1.14
1879	--	1.06	1.06	--	.80	.74	--	1.41
1889	--	1.02	1.07	--	.78	.79	--	1.19
1899	--	1.02	1.07	--	.82	.66	--	1.09

Source: Calculated from data in Lebergott (1964), Table A-29, p. 545.

We can obtain considerably more control for industry and oc-cupational classifications by examining regional earnings differentials using data provided by Long. Table 7.6 provides indexes of daily wage rates in three manufacturing industries represented in three re-gions: eastern, southern, and western states. These industries are ci-gars and tobacco, paper manufactures, and saw and planing mills. In all three industries, wages were consistently lower in the South. Fur-thermore, relative wages in the South were lower in 1880 than in 1860, but most of this widening occurred between 1860 and 1865; thereafter, the South/non-South differential remained roughly con-stant. These data have the advantage of enabling us to compare wages for the same firms, occupations, and industries over time.[2] As Long points out, however, these estimates should be interpreted with cau-tion, since data are restricted to a very small number of establish-ments. For example, the number of establishments in the South are: one for cigars, one for paper, and two for saw and planing mills. The smallness of this sample of establishments has several pitfalls. First, wages vary considerably among establishments *within* the same in-dustry. Second, these manufacturing classifications are broad; a man-ufacturer of tobacco products in one region may produce plug to-bacco; in another, mainly fine-cut. Finally, wage data for occupations may vary from one establishment to another as a result of errors in recordkeeping. A larger sample of establishments for each region would have caused these errors to cancel out in the process of aver-aging.

From the *Census of Manufactures,* 1860–1890, Long was able to construct estimates of average earnings for seventeen separate in-dustries in five different regions. These data cover hundreds of estab-lishments and more than 100,000 workers. Hence, estimates are less subject to the pitfalls outlined above. From Long's estimates, we can calculate an index by expressing each industry's average within a region as a ratio of the corresponding U.S. average. These indexes of average annual earnings are reported in Table 7.7. The only qual-ification of importance concerns the inclusion of certain southern states in non-South regions. Delaware, Maryland, and West Virginia are included in the Middle Atlantic, and Kentucky is included in Central states. It is not clear what biases are introduced, but this change in regional composition should nevertheless be pointed out, since these states are normally classified as southern states.

TABLE 7.6

INDEX OF DAILY WAGE RATES IN THREE MANUFACTURING INDUSTRIES BY GEOGRAPHIC DIVISIONS: 1860-80
(U.S. = 1.00)

	Cigars and Tobacco			Paper Manufactures			Saw and Planing Mills		
	Eastern States	Southern States	Western States	Eastern States	Southern States	Western States	Eastern States	Southern States	Western States
1860	1.02	0.63	1.21	1.01	0.72	0.88	1.06	0.69	0.89
1865	0.92	0.53	1.83	1.01	0.39	0.99	0.80	0.69	1.16
1870	1.03	0.53	2.05	1.01	0.53	0.59	0.83	0.65	1.10
1875	1.14	0.56	1.90	1.01	0.58	0.60	0.75	0.63	1.14
1880	1.04	0.56	1.93	1.01	0.57	0.74	0.73	0.62	1.15

Source: Calculated from data in Long (1960), Table A-3, p. 129.

Note: Number of establishments in sample: Cigars and Tobacco, 4; Paper Manufactures, 7; and Saw and Planing Mills, 7.

TABLE 7.7

INDEX OF AVERAGE ANNUAL EARNINGS OF MANUFACTURING WAGE EARNERS IN SEVENTEEN INDUSTRIES BY GEOGRAPHIC DIVISIONS: 1860-90
(U.S. = 100)

Industry	New England				Middle Atlantic				South[a]				Central[b]				Pacific			
	1860	1870	1880	1890	1860	1870	1880	1890	1860	1870	1880	1890	1860	1870	1880	1890	1860	1870	1880	1890
Foundry and Machine Shop Production	1.00	.99	1.03	1.02	.93	1.00	.99	1.02	1.04	1.05	.79	.90	.96	.92	.98	.95	4.25	2.07	1.43	1.44
Carriages and Wagons	1.08	1.26	1.17	1.19	.96	1.03	1.02	1.03	.93	.78	.74	.84	.94	.91	.96	.94	2.55	1.76	1.54	1.42
Liquors, Malt	1.14	.97	1.02	1.09	.92	1.15	1.03	1.10	1.09	.85	.87	.85	.94	.89	.97	.90	2.39	1.05	1.01	1.24
Agricultural Implements	.99	.95	1.06	1.05	.94	1.01	.96	1.02	.95	.68	.69	.81	1.06	1.01	1.14	.99	2.46	1.28	1.31	1.62
Iron and Steel, Rolling Mills	1.18	.93	.90	.90	.98	.98	1.01	1.00	.82	1.02	.79	.75	1.15	1.06	1.05	1.04	--	--	--	--
Liquors, Distilled	1.43	1.25	1.03	1.10	1.35	.92	1.02	1.21	.72	.48	.59	.51	.99	1.10	1.03	1.02	2.57	1.05	1.19	.66
Glass	.96	.86	1.03	.87	1.01	1.00	1.02	1.00	.93	.30	.80	.83	.93	1.25	.92	.98	--	--	--	--
Cigars and Cigarettes	1.05	1.20	1.18	1.16	.98	.97	1.06	.96	1.08	1.40	.72	1.14	.91	.95	1.01	.97	2.93	.82	.78	.98
Flour and Grist Mills	.91	.96	1.14	1.14	.98	1.00	1.02	1.07	.76	.49	.55	.53	1.07	1.29	1.19	1.11	2.75	2.20	1.82	1.62
Leather	1.14	1.24	1.06	1.05	.97	1.05	.98	.97	.81	.39	.59	.61	.98	.85	1.06	1.04	2.09	.98	1.37	1.28
Lumber, Sawed	.97	.99	.86	.99	.90	.99	.89	.92	.81	.83	.80	.93	.93	1.00	1.12	.98	2.34	1.62	1.59	1.58
Iron and Steel, Blast Furnaces	1.06	1.58	1.11	1.12	1.00	1.03	1.13	.99	.74	.78	.76	.92	1.12	1.01	.94	1.10	--	--	--	--
Paper	1.00	1.04	1.01	1.04	.94	.98	.95	1.00	1.37	.98	.74	.96	1.06	.96	1.05	.94	1.41	1.63	1.53	1.45
Woolen Goods	1.03	1.07	1.05	.98	1.01	.99	.99	.99	.77	.56	.56	.71	1.09	.81	.77	.81	2.39	1.21	1.31	.72
Cotton Goods	1.05	1.05	1.04	1.08	.96	.96	.95	1.06	.91	.66	.69	.80	1.29	.95	.95	.91	2.83	1.42	1.61	.81
Brick and Tile	.75	1.05	.95	.99	1.06	.96	1.14	1.10	.75	.65	.81	.68	.99	.91	1.09	.87	--	--	--	--
Chewing and Smoking Tobacco	--	--	--	--	1.26	1.17	1.52	1.45	.94	.61	.65	.73	1.12	1.37	1.30	1.32	--	--	--	--

Source: Calculated from data in Long (1960), Table A-9, p. 150.

[a] Delaware, Maryland and West Virginia are included in the Middle Atlantic.

[b] Kentucky is included in Central States.

Concerning relative earnings in the South, several interesting patterns emerge. Note that in 1860 four industries located in the South had average annual earnings above the U.S. average. By 1890, however, only one of these industries, cigars and cigarettes, had an index exceeding unity. This appears to contrast sharply with the index for cigars and tobacco in Table 7.6, where the index was substantially below unity and remained there throughout the period between 1860 and 1880. This difference may be partly attributable to differences in industry classification, or it may simply reflect the pitfall of small sample biases.[3] Fifteen of the seventeen industries had a lower index in 1890 than in 1860. This decline in relative earnings was especially noticeable for paper products, where the index fell from 1.37 in 1860 to .74 in 1890. Overall, these estimates suggest that relative earnings for workers in the South were lower in 1890 than they were in 1860. Notice, however, that there was substantial decennial-to-decennial variation in these indexes. This was especially true in the 1860s when twelve of the seventeen industries experienced precipitous reductions in relative earnings. Of the other five industries, four incurred losses in the 1870s. Finally, while most of these industries rebounded somewhat during the 1880s, they did not fully recoup their initial relative positions.

As we have seen, South/non-South earnings differentials by industry tended to widen in the post-bellum period. However, it is conceivable that the same industry may employ different combinations of occupations across regions. Considering this possibility, we now compare regional earnings ratios for the same occupations. Indexes of daily wage rates for various occupations are presented in Table 7.8. Long obtains estimates of daily wage rates from the U.S. Department of Labor (DOL). The DOL gathered daily wages for ten occupations in manufacturing industries and for four occupations more or less identifiable with the building trades. All except laborers were skilled, and all were from large cities; two in the South, and five each in the East and the West. As Long speculates, however, the number of reporting establishments was probably small.

For manufacturing occupations, daily wages tended to be higher in southern cities than in eastern or western cities. For example, boilermakers in southern cities had wages 44 percent above the U.S. average in 1870. By 1890 their wages were only 5 percent above the U.S. average. With three exceptions, relative daily wage rates in the

TABLE 7.8

INDEX OF DAILY WAGE RATES FOR VARIOUS OCCUPATIONS IN MANUFACTURING AND BUILDING TRADES BY GEOGRAPHIC DIVISIONS: 1870-90
(U.S. = 100)

	Western Cities					Eastern Cities					Southern Cities				
	1870	1875	1880	1885	1890	1870	1875	1880	1885	1890	1870	1875	1880	1885	1890
MANUFACTURING OCCUPATIONS:															
Blacksmiths	1.04	1.08	1.04	1.03	1.03	.97	.96	.97	.98	.98	1.01	.91	.97	.95	.94
Boilermakers	1.15	1.18	1.16	1.13	1.06	.90	.91	.92	.94	.96	1.44	1.47	1.47	1.07	1.05
Compositers	1.05	1.10	1.07	1.02	1.03	.98	.95	.96	.99	.98	1.07	1.06	.99	.97	.98
Cabinetmakers	1.01	.98	1.05	.90	.94	.99	1.00	.97	1.05	1.03	1.42	1.52	1.33	1.34	1.21
Iron Molders	1.06	1.08	1.06	1.05	1.04	.97	.96	.96	.97	.97	1.12	1.26	1.14	1.11	1.13
Laborers	1.00	1.02	1.09	1.02	1.01	1.01	.98	.93	.99	.99	.86	1.05	1.05	.96	.96
Machinists	1.11	1.09	1.07	1.06	1.06	.97	.97	.97	.98	.98	.89	1.00	.97	.84	.83
Stonecutters	.91	.97	1.02	.98	1.06	1.08	1.03	.98	1.02	.96	1.08	1.01	1.11	.92	.82
Patternmakers, Ironworks	1.00	.98	.99	.99	.94	1.00	1.00	1.00	1.01	1.03	1.38	1.31	1.08	1.06	.96
Teamsters	1.01	.99	1.01	.99	1.00	1.01	1.00	1.00	1.01	1.00	.87	.93	.88	.88	.87
BUILDING OCCUPATIONS:															
Bricklayers and Masons	.97	.95	1.16	1.12	1.08	1.01	1.04	.91	.94	.96	.88	.87	1.00	.88	.83
Carpenters and Joiners	.96	.99	.96	.94	.91	1.03	1.01	1.06	1.06	1.08	.90	.97	.88	.85	.88
Painters, House	.92	.91	.90	.91	.88	1.05	1.06	1.07	1.06	1.10	.84	.73	.80	.86	.69
Plumbers	1.06	1.07	1.06	1.02	1.03	.99	.98	.99	1.00	.99	.88	.94	.84	.71	.69

Source: Calculated from data in Long (1960), Table A-4, p. 135.

Note: Based on data for twelve large U.S. cities comprising: eastern cities, Baltimore, Boston, New York, Philadelphia, Pittsburgh; western cities, Chicago, Cincinnati, St. Louis, St. Paul, San Francisco; southern cities, Richmond, New Orleans.

South were lower in 1890 than in 1870. On average, relative daily wage rates in southern cities fell by about 11 percent between 1870 and 1890.

In building trades occupations, relative earnings in southern cities were lower than the U.S. average through the period in question.[4] Also, the southern indexes were lower in 1890 than in 1870, but the deterioration was not as pronounced in building trades as in manufacturing.

The secular patterns of the various indexes reported above are presented in Figures 7.1–7.5. Several features of the South/non-South wage ratio dynamics are readily apparent. First, there existed substantial period-to-period variation in these ratios, with a fairly uniform tendency for the South's relative earnings position to fall sharply in the 1860s. Second, although there was a tendency for the South's relative position to improve after the 1860s, most earnings ratios failed

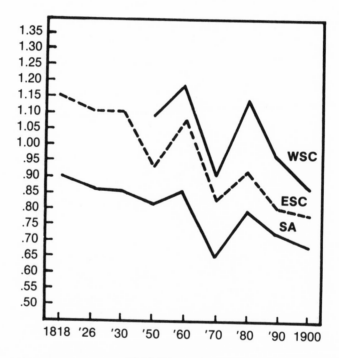

FIGURE 7.1
INDEX OF AVERAGE DAILY EARNINGS FOR FARM LABORERS
IN THREE SOUTHERN DIVISIONS

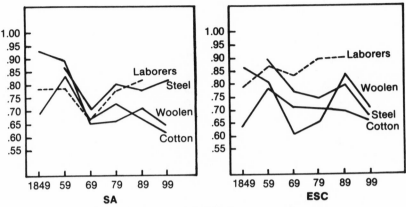

FIGURE 7.2
INDEX OF AVERAGE ANNUAL EARNINGS FOR FOUR INDUSTRIES

to regain their initial antebellum levels. As a result, relative earnings for workers in the South were lower in the 1890s than they were at the beginning of the war. Finally, there is some evidence to suggest that average earnings for several skilled occupations were actually

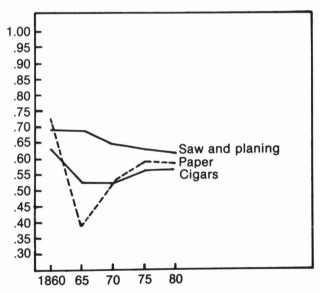

FIGURE 7.3
INDEX OF DAILY WAGE RATES FOR THREE MANUFACTURING
INDUSTRIES IN SOUTHERN STATES

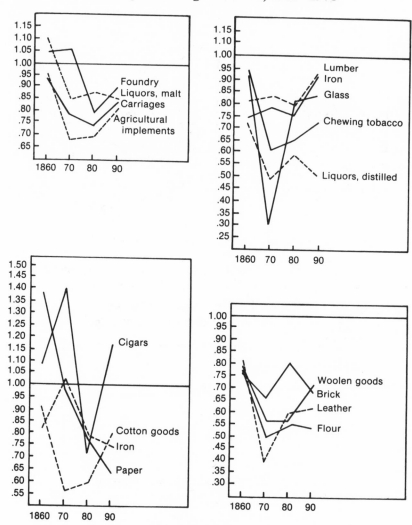

FIGURE 7.4
INDEX OF AVERAGE ANNUAL EARNINGS FOR
SEVENTEEN INDUSTRIES IN THE SOUTH

higher in the South than in other regions for a period after the war (Figure 7.5). But, without exception, the South's relative position in occupations declined throughout the period. Of the seven occupations with an index exceeding unity in 1870, only three of these occupations remained above unity in 1890.

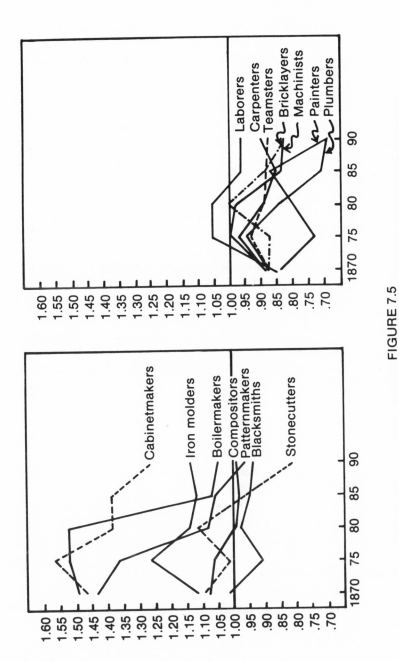

FIGURE 7.5
INDEX OF DAILY WAGE RATES FOR FOURTEEN OCCUPATIONS IN
SOUTHERN CITIES

What caused the South's deteriorating economic position, relative to other regions, after the Civil War? While no definitive (empirically validated) answer can be given, there are a few possible explanations that have been advanced in the literature. The remainder of this section is devoted to a brief survey of competing explanations.[5]

One of the most popular and widely accepted explanations for the deterioration in the South's economy considers the capital destruction brought about by the Civil War as the primary source. Since most of the war was fought in the South, war-related destruction of productive capital seems to be an obvious answer. However, Ransom and Sutch (1977) are skeptical of this explanation. As they point out, rapid recovery after massive wartime destruction appears to be the rule rather than the exception in modern history. They offer some causal evidence to suggest that capital destruction cannot have been the major cause. First, damage to rail lines and rolling stock was quickly repaired, and southern transportation was virtually restored to prewar capacity by 1870.[6] Second, manufacturing establishments in towns and cities of the cotton-producing states were producing 5 percent more output, with 5 percent more invested capital, in 1870 than they had in 1860. Finally, Ransom and Sutch find indirect evidence suggesting that there was no shortage of capital in agriculture either. They hypothesize that if loss of work animals (a one-third decline between 1860 and 1870) was a serious constraint on output, one would anticipate a substantial increase in the price of the remaining stock. Nevertheless, despite the considerable loss of work animals during the 1860s, the inflation-adjusted price of mules was lower in 1870 than it had been at any time during the 1850s.

Conrad and Meyer (1967) propose a completely different explanation. They suggest that during the war the South lost its export monopoly position in the world cotton market. With the disruption of cotton production caused by war, European factories replaced lost American supplies with Indian, Brazilian, and Egyptian cotton. Once growers in these countries made the change to cotton production, they were reluctant to switch back to other crops. Conrad and Meyer's argument assumes a good deal of producer inertia. Could this inertia have prevented the South from regaining its prewar export dominance? If we assume that the South attained its initial monopoly position because it had a comparative advantage in cotton production, then the end of the war would have allowed the South the same opportunity. That is, if Indian, Brazilian, and Egyptian producers found it unprofitable to compete with the South prior to the war, they would have arrived at the same conclusion after the war. This is because competition and profit-maximizing behavior would have dictated that European factories purchase their supplies from the cheapest source, with the world price of cotton being determined by the South's comparative advantage. Nevertheless, the South's prewar share of the cotton market was not recovered until the late 1870s.

Aldrich (1973) provides a more appealing explanation for the South's loss in the world market. Following the war, a combination of federal policies acted to bring about a reduction in prices. These deflationary policies resulted in a rapid postwar dollar appreciation, which had the effect of reducing foreign demand for U.S. cotton. It wasn't until 1879 that the federal government once again fixed the dollar exchange rates in the world money market.

Finally, in a slightly different vein, Wright (1974) attributes the South's slow recovery in cotton competition to the reduced rate of growth in the foreign demand for raw cotton because the world market for inexpensive cotton clothing was finally saturated. The fact that war briefly interrupted cotton production in the South and caused some market displacement was only tangentially related to the South's real problem. The fundamental problem was the South's heavy dependence on world demand for cotton. Wright claims that it would have been impossible for the South to continue along the growth path that existed prior to the war.

Whether the South's postwar decline resulted directly from the war or can be attributed to factors other than the war itself is an unsettled question. As is evident from this survey, there exist many possible explanations.

THE 1900s

Considerably more work has been undertaken to document and explain the dynamic patterns in regional wage differentials in the twentieth century, which is no doubt due to the existence of substantially better data, especially after the 1920s. Some of the more important studies include Borts (1960), Borts and Stein (1964), Hanna (1959), and Segal (1961). All revealed a noticeable, albeit slow, convergence in earnings between regions in the 1929–54 period. For example, Hanna's data show that the coefficient of variation for wage and salary income per capita between states declined between 1929 and 1948, then remained relatively constant up to 1951. Borts found the same general pattern of convergence and stability for roughly the same intervals. However, Segal's data on manufacturing wages suggest some convergence in the 1947–54 period. Unfortunately, very little is known about the dynamic patterns in wage differentials after this period, since more recent work has shifted the focus away from movements in regional wage differentials to the more narrow focus of attempting to account for these differences at a point in time.[7]

Perhaps this shift in research focus occurred as a result of a feeling that regional wage differences reflect some *permanent* underlying feature of the U.S. economy. That, coupled with the long historical persistence of these differentials, may have provided the impetus for the recent emphasis placed on "compensating wage differential" theories.[8] Whatever the cause of this shift in research focus, the current emphasis on wage-level comparisons leaves us with little reliable information concerning changes in the pattern of regional wage differentials over the past three decades. Furthermore, differences between studies in data sources, degree of aggregation, standardization procedures, and variable definitions make intertemporal comparisons difficult and confusing.

Therefore, in order to provide some insight into the dynamic patterns during the twentieth century we will limit the discussion to the period between 1919 and 1954. The next chapter provides a consistent and comprehensive analysis of South/non-South wage differentials subsequent to this period. Our description of the period between 1919 and 1954 will rely on the estimates of per capita personal income by state provided by Hanna (1959). It may be worthwhile to briefly summarize his major findings.

First, although estimates of per capita personal income in the United States varied considerably across states, the state ranks for 1919 tended to be the same ranks in 1929, 1939, 1949, and 1954. Second, Hanna found a pronounced narrowing of relative interstate differentials, as measured by the coefficient of variation.[9] Beginning at a level of 37 to 41 percent in 1929–32, the coefficient of variation decreased steadily through 1945 and varied within a narrow range of

21 to 24 percent after 1945. Finally, expressing state per capita incomes relative to the national per capita income, there was a tendency for the relatives of the lower-income states to follow the cyclical patern of income changes, whereas the relatives of upper-income states followed a countercyclical course.

This last finding has special implications for long-run movements in regional earnings differentials. The fact that the coefficients of variation move countercyclically leads to the expectation of some regression of the state per capita incomes toward their mean as income increases. Also, economic theory predicts movement of resources between regions such that initial differentials are eliminated.[10] To examine this issue, we have taken Hanna's data on state relatives of U.S. per capita personal income at the beginning of the period and the end of the period. The objective is to see if there was indeed some regression toward the mean, that is, some reduction in relative dispersion across states. Table 7.9 presents three-year averages of state relative per capita income centered on a cyclical peak. The 1919–21 and 1952–54 periods are taken as occupying roughly comparable positions on the business cycle. Since the state differentials are constantly shifting, the use of any single year as representative of a state's income level would have introduced a random element into the comparisons of initial and terminal years. Averaging over three years is designed to control for purely transitory components.

Between each of the two periods, the change was calculated and is presented in columns 3 and 6 of the table. The hypothesis is that for all states above the U.S. average (relative = 1.00) there will be a tendency for the state relative to fall. Conversely, for all states below the U.S. average, there will be a tendency for the state relative to rise. Table 7.10 documents the sign pattern for state relatives above and below unity. For the twenty states with relatives exceeding unity in 1919–21, fifteen states had lower relatives in 1952–54. On the other hand, of the twenty-nine states with relatives below unity in the initial period, twenty-three experienced a gain by the terminal period. It certainly appears that the hypothesis is supported. In order to judge the validity of this claim, however, the probability of obtaining these results merely by chance must be calculated. Assume that there was no systematic relationship between a state's initial position, with respect to the average, and the change in national economy that acted to eliminate these differentials, then the relative for each state would

TABLE 7.9

STATE RELATIVES OF UNITED STATES PER CAPITA PERSONAL INCOME,
1919-21 and 1952-54

State	1919-21	Average 1952-54	Δ	State	1919-21	Average 1952-54	Δ
New England:				East South Central:			
Maine	93.6	84.8	- 8.8	Kentucky	61.2	69.0	+ 7.8
New Hampshire	100.6	88.9	-11.7	Tennessee	55.3	67.5	+12.2
Vermont	89.4	78.9	-10.5	Alabama	47.8	62.2	+14.4
Massachusetts	137.1	108.6	-28.5	Mississippi	43.1	49.1	+ 6.0
Rhode Island	128.8	103.6	-25.2	West South Central:			
Connecticut	118.7	134.5	+15.8	Arkansas	50.2	55.0	+ 4.8
Middle Atlantic:				Louisiana	64.9	72.8	+ 7.9
New York	155.4	120.9	-34.5	Oklahoma	76.2	80.7	+ 4.5
New Jersey	122.4	124.3	+ 1.9	Texas	81.5	88.0	+ 6.5
Pennsylvania	112.8	104.3	- 8.5				

East North Central:			
Ohio	106.4	112.8	+ 6.4
Indiana	88.4	104.8	+16.4
Illinois	125.6	121.2	- 4.4
Michigan	107.7	115.1	+ 7.4
Wisconsin	92.2	98.3	+ 6.1
West North Central:			
Minnesota	87.0	91.3	+ 4.3
Iowa	85.9	90.9	+ 5.0
Missouri	89.1	97.5	+ 8.4
North Dakota	69.6	67.4	- 2.2
South Dakota	81.6	73.1	- 8.5
Nebraska	84.6	91.1	+ 6.5
Kansas	89.5	95.9	+ 6.4
South Atlantic:			
Delaware	107.7	135.8	+28.1
Maryland	110.0	109.9	- 0.1
D.C.	177.9	128.8	-48.1
Virginia	63.9	83.3	+19.4
West Virginia	77.7	71.8	- 5.9
North Carolina	53.9	66.5	+12.6
South Carolina	51.0	62.4	+11.4
Georgia	52.8	70.3	+17.5
Florida	66.1	88.2	+22.1

Mountain:			
Montana	94.0	99.6	+ 5.6
Idaho	90.0	84.4	- 9.6
Wyoming	135.7	103.2	-32.5
Colorado	110.2	99.3	-10.9
New Mexico	73.1	77.9	+ 4.8
Arizona	104.4	91.2	-13.2
Utah	84.3	84.7	+ 0.7
Nevada	143.6	135.3	- 8.3
Pacific:			
Washington	116.9	110.0	- 6.9
Oregon	112.6	101.6	-11.0
California	149.7	122.9	-26.8

Source: Calculated from data in Hanna (1959), Table 4, p. 38.

TABLE 7.10

SIGN PATTERN, FOR CHANGES IN STATE RELATIVES,
1919-21 TO 1952-54

	Sign of Change	
Value of Relative	+	-
Less than unity	23	6
Greater than unity	5	15

Source: Calculated from data in Table 7.9.

have an equal probability of increasing or decreasing between the initial and terminal years. Given this assumption, the probability of obtaining the observed results purely by chance can be calculated by using the binomial distribution. For states with relatives initially below unity, the probably of the observed sign configuration occurring by chance is

$$\text{Prob } (X \geq 23) = \sum_{i=23}^{29} \binom{29}{i} .5^i \approx 0$$

As is obvious, the probability of this sign pattern resulting by mere chance is virtually zero. Likewise, the same probability measure for states with an initial relative above unity is

$$\text{Prob } (X \geq 15) = \sum_{i=15}^{20} \binom{20}{i} .5^i \approx .021$$

Hence, the results under both sets of comparisons are consistent with the hypothesis of convergence. Thus, it appears that the pattern for regional wage differentials during the first half of the 1900s was toward uniformity.

SUMMARY

South/non-South earnings differentials tended to widen in the post-bellum period. However, most of this widening can be accounted for by the precipitous decline in relative earnings for southern workers during the 1860s. Although there was some tendency for the South's relative position to improve after the 1860s, most earnings ratios failed to regain their initial antebellum levels. As a result, relative earnings for southern workers were lower in the 1890s than they were at the start of the Civil War. Also, there is some evidence that average earnings for several skilled occupations were actually higher in the South than in other regions for a brief period after the war. But, without exception, the South's relative position in these occupations declined throughout the last half of the 1800s. Of the seven skilled occupations with an index exceeding unity in 1870, only three of these remained above unity in 1890.

After the turn of the century, the South's relative position continued to improve. Several empirical studies conclude that between 1920 and 1950 regional wage differentials tended to converge with far less relative dispersion at the end of this period than at its beginning. Unfortunately, very little information concerning the dynamic patterns in regional wage differentials exists after this period because the research focus in this area shifted to cross-section analysis. Owing to the many differences between studies in data sources, standardization procedures, and variable definitions, it is difficult to make intertemporal comparisons.

NOTES

1. The interested reader should consult Lebergott's discussion of methods and sources (chap. 6).

2. These estimates are derived from longitudinal establishment data provided by the Weeks report (1880).

3. Recall that estimates in Table 7.3 were based on data from only one establishment in the South. Also, we are comparing estimates of daily wages in Table 7.3 with annual earnings in Table 7.4. These indexes will not be inconsistent as long as days worked per week and weeks worked per year did not vary significantly by region.

4. The only exception was bricklayers and masons in 1880.

5. The remainder of this section is adapted from an excellent survey by Lee and Passell (1979); see especially chap. 12.

6. This is consistent with the observed precipitous decline in South/non-South wage differentials during the 1860s and the modest recovery in subsequent decades.

7. For examples of recent cross-section studies see Bellante (1979), Fuchs (1967), Gallaway (1963), Goldfarb and Yezer (1976), Hanushek (1973, 1978), and Scully (1969).

8. Earlier studies assumed that regional wage differentials represented a disequilibrium phenomenon. For example, Borts (1960) and Gallaway (1963) characterize each region as possessing identical linear homogeneous production functions, with observed wage differentials between regions being produced by initial disparities in resource endowments. Owing to some historical shuffling of resources, each region is seen as operating at a different point on the same production function. Those regions with higher proportions of capital to labor will manifest higher wages and a lower marginal product of capital. With no impediments to factor mobility, we would witness capital moving from high-wage regions (non-South) to low-wage regions (South). The net result is a tendency toward equality-of-factor returns. Empirical testing has yielded rather disappointing support for this model, however. Consequently, in the 1970s observers began to accept regional wage differentials as an equilibrium phenomenon. See Bradfield (1976), Batra and Scully (1972), Coelho and Ghali (1971), and Rosen (1979).

9. The coefficient of variation is the standard deviation expressed as a percentage of the mean, that is, σ/μ, a fairly common measure of relative dispersion about the mean.

10. See note 8 above.

Chapter 8

Regional Wage Differentials in the Post-1960 Period

IN THE LAST chapter we argued that the 1960s ushered in a change in research focus concerning regional wage differentials. Earlier studies tended to focus exclusively on long-term movements in regional wage differentials under the theoretical presumption that the economic system was in a state of disequilibrium. Since equilibrium can be characterized by regional wage equality, the observed wage differentials necessarily implied a reallocation of resources. Given the nature of the regional wage differentials, this meant that we would witness labor moving from low-wage regions (South) to high-wage regions (non-South) and capital moving in the opposite direction. However, the persistence of the North/South wage differential over an extended period of time led many observers to conclude that the system was *not* in disequilibrium but rather that interregional wage differentials were compensating (equilibrium) differentials.[1] One claim is that labor quality varies systematically between regions, with lower quality in the South. Thus, the implication is that earlier studies failed to accurately account for differences between regions in labor quality that, inter alia, produced the illusion of wage differentials. As a result, more recent studies have concentrated on cross-section analysis, attempting to account for differences in labor force composition and human capital endowments between regions.[2]

Because of this change in research focus, we currently possess little comprehensive and systematic data on the dynamic pattern of regional wage differentials in the post-1960 period. This is particularly unfortunate in light of the significant redistribution of economic activity that has occurred during the last two decades.

The objective of the present chapter is to fill this void by documenting changes in regional wage differentials during the 1960s and

1970s. To take into account the possibility of differences between regions in labor force composition and labor quality, we will examine wage differentials for various demographic groups. This will allow us to control for compositional differences in sex, race, age (experience), and educational levels. Also, we will control for industrial composition.

Because of data limitations, the two-decade period is divided into two overlapping intervals, 1959 to 1969 and 1969 to 1978. This division is necessary, since earnings data had to be taken from two different sources. Nevertheless, care is taken to maintain as much comparability as is possible.

SOUTH/NON-SOUTH WAGE RATIOS

Table 8.1 presents evidence that reveals the degree to which earnings of male workers in the South changed relative to their counterparts in other areas of the United States between 1959 and 1969. Table 8.2 reports the same information for the period 1969–1978. Numbers reported are ratios of average weekly wages for males and income in each year.[3] Comparisons are made for both white and nonwhite males. Columns 3 and 6 in each table give the associated gain or loss in the South/non-South wage ratio between the initial and terminal years for each of five age groups.

In both periods we observe an overall pattern of convergence in regional wage differentials. These data suggest that the relative earnings position of male workers in the South improved dramatically between 1959 and 1978.[4] A closer examination of the data, however, reveals several interesting patterns across both age and racial groups.

First, for white male workers, the change in the relative earnings position of southern workers between 1959 and 1969 varied somewhat from the pattern exhibited in the latter period. For instance, in the first decade, the South's relative position with respect to the Northeast remained largely unchanged, but in the 1970s southern workers increased their relative position by about 6 percent. The most dramatic interyear change occurred in the last period. Between 1959 and 1969 southern workers gained about 4 percent over their counterparts in the West. However, in the 1970s their relative position deteriorated by about 9 percent, on average. On the other hand, the

TABLE 8.1

RATIOS OF SOUTH/NON-SOUTH WEEKLY WAGES FOR MALE WORKERS
BY AGE FOR 1959 AND 1969

	White Males			Nonwhite Males		
Age	1969	1959	1969-59	1969	1959	1969-59
			South/Northeast			
20-24	.884	.871	.013	.765	.685	.080
25-34	.967	.869	-.002	.766	.694	.072
35-44	.859	.872	-.013	.717	.672	.045
45-54	.872	.861	.011	.693	.672	.021
55-64	.857	.882	-.025	.668	.680	-.012
			South/North Central			
20-24	.856	.824	.032	.690	.654	.036
25-34	.865	.851	.014	.695	.632	.063
35-44	.870	.856	.014	.675	.622	.053
45-54	.880	.843	.037	.637	.604	.033
55-64	.861	.868	-.007	.601	.629	-.028
			South/West			
20-24	.898	.786	.112	.769	.657	.112
25-34	.863	.805	.058	.660	.592	.068
35-44	.844	.817	.027	.634	.582	.052
45-54	.841	.822	.019	.564	.611	-.047
55-64	.827	.868	-.041	.631	.629	.002

Source: U.S. Census of Population, Public Use Sample, 1960 and 1970.

pattern for nonwhites reveals a steady relative improvement for southern workers when compared with each of the other three regions. In the 1960s nonwhites in the South gained a little over 3 percent on their counterparts elsewhere. In the 1970s their relative position improved by approximately 10 percent.

Second, even though the relative improvement in the South/non-South earnings ratio was larger for nonwhites, the absolute level of this ratio was substantially lower than for whites. In both periods, the average difference between races in the South/non-South wage ratio

Interregional Wage Patterns, 1959–1978

TABLE 8.2

RATIOS OF SOUTH/NON-SOUTH WEEKLY WAGES FOR MALE WORKERS
BY AGE FOR 1969 AND 1978

	White Males			Nonwhite Males		
Age	1978	1969	1978-69	1978	1969	1978-69
			South/Northeast			
20-24	1.108	.956	.152	1.071	.719	.352
25-34	.947	.929	.018	.786	.750	.036
35-44	.931	.953	-.022	.825	.643	.182
45-54	.989	.935	.054	.747	.635	.112
55-64	.996	.908	.088	.637	.817	-.180
			South/North Central			
20-24	.907	.891	.016	.748	.601	.147
25-34	.900	.907	-.007	.723	.672	.051
35-44	.920	.916	.004	.921	.605	.316
45-54	.929	.896	.033	.725	.621	.104
55-64	.931	.894	.037	.751	.686	.065
			South/West			
20-24	.834	.895	-.061	.728	.710*	.018
25-34	.859	.882	-.023	.736	.682	.054
35-44	.888	.883	.005	.638	.468	.170
45-54	.882	.874	.008	.651	.682	-.031
55-64	.839	.844	-.005	.738	.667	.071

Source: U.S. Bureau of the Census, Current Population Survey, 1969 and 1978.

*Average wage in West calculated from less than ten observations.

was about 20 percent. Thus, we can conclude that there is substantially less regional wage dispersion for whites.

Third, it is interesting to note again the significant contrast in the degree to which these regional gains for workers in the South are distributed between races. On average, nonwhites in the South gained more relative to their counterparts elsewhere than southern whites gained relative to their counterparts. One possible explanation that can be advanced to reconcile this difference relies on an assumption about the degree of racial discrimination existing within each region. It is commonly assumed that racial wage and occupational discrimination has been greater in the South than in other areas of the United States. With the passage of antidiscrimination laws, the potential impact on nonwhite wages would, therefore, be more pronounced in the South. However, for the 1960s there is some doubt about how much pressure affirmative action programs could have exerted, given the timing of this legislation, subsequent judicial interpretations, and the point at which earnings were observed in the terminal year of the sample. Affirmative action programs did not come into their own until somewhat late in the 1960s, and it is unlikely that enough time had elapsed prior to 1969 for government enforcement policies and the resultant private sector reactions to have had any appreciable impact on nonwhite wages.

Clearly, to the extent that federal affirmative action programs had a differential impact on nonwhite wages between the South and the non-South, these effects would have manifested themselves in the 1970s. As we have already mentioned, the average gain in nonwhite South/non-South wage ratios was substantially larger in the 1970s (3 percent in the 1960s as opposed to 10 percent in the 1970s). However, to what extent affirmative action programs can account for the approximate 10 percent relative gain for southern nonwhites is a matter of speculation. But, even if we assume that the differential impact argument has empirical validity, it is hard to imagine that it could fully account for the entire 10 percent relative gain. Therefore, it may be reasonable to assume that, whatever caused southern nonwhite relative earnings to rise in the 1960s, its effect carried over into the decade of the 1970s.

Another explanation for the differential regional gains between races exhibited in Tables 8.1 and 8.2 has to do with differences across whites and nonwhites in year effects (e.g., changes in the demand for labor) and cohort effects (comparing individuals of different vintage). Year effects refer to any change in economic activity that occurs between years that may in turn affect wage rates; this would include business-cycle activity and secular growth in earnings. The hypothesis is that year effects vary across regions and hence would impact on the South/non-South earnings ratios. Vintage effects refer to all differences in experiences associated with persons of different age (different cohorts) that are not solely a function of the aging process. For example, an individual who is 25 was obviously born a decade after an individual who is 35. What makes vintage effects important is the fact that these two individuals experienced qualitatively different environmental influences, especially schooling, and these differences will be reflected in earnings potential over the life cycle.

By comparing the same age group across years we are not following a single cohort through time; instead, we are holding age constant and allowing cohorts to vary. Thus, within an age cell, part of the observed change in wage rates between years may embody vintage effects. Do these vintage effects vary across regions? There is some evidence to suggest that, at least with respect to the quality of schooling, the South has been improving relative to the non-South. This improvement may be even more pronounced for blacks.[5] This improvement would obviously be reflected in regional wage differentials.[6]

Tables 8.3 and 8.4 rearrange the data to facilitate within-cohort comparisons. This is accomplished by pushing the second column for each race down by one row. For example, the first entry in Table 8.3, .859, is the South/non-South wage ratio for white males age 25–34 in 1959. In 1969 these individuals were between the ages of 35 and 44.[7] This is not strictly true for the second period, however, since the data do not span an entire decade. Hence, individuals age 25 in 1969 have not passed into the 35–44 age group by 1978. It is not clear what sort of bias may be introduced by this incomplete cohort phasing, but it is most likely of secondary magnitude.

Reading across a row, we observe year effects, holding cohort constant.[8] In the 1960s notice that the year effects for nonwhites are clearly smaller than the intercohort effects (reading across rows in Table 8.1). With the possible exception of the 35–44 age group, the pattern among nonwhites suggests that wage rates for older cohorts have not risen faster in the South. Rather, the gains displayed in Table 8.1 may simply reflect quality changes between cohorts that have been more pronounced in the South.[9] This intercohort improvement has meant that younger cohorts have experienced a secular increase in their earnings profiles, but within cohorts the South/non-South wage differential remained largely unchanged between 1960 and 1970.

TABLE 8.3

RATIOS OF SOUTH/NON-SOUTH WEEKLY WAGES FOR
COHORTS IN 1959 AND 1969

Age in 1969	White Males			Nonwhite Males		
	1969	1959	1969-59	1969	1959	1969-59
South/Northeast						
35-44	.859	.869	-.010	.717	.694	.023
45-54	.872	.872	.000	.693	.672	.021
55-64	.857	.861	-.004	.668	.672	-.004
South/North Central						
35-44	.870	.851	.019	.675	.632	.043
45-54	.880	.856	.024	.637	.622	.015
55-64	.861	.843	.018	.601	.604	-.003
South/West						
35-44	.844	.805	.039	.634	.592	.042
45-54	.841	.817	.024	.564	.582	-.018
55-64	.827	.822	.005	.631	.611	.020

Source: U.S. Census of Population, Public Use Sample, 1960 and 1970.

To the extent that nonwhite wages rose faster in the South during the 1960s, these gains may have been limited to the younger cohorts. We have only a hint of this possibility. The youngest cohort in Table 8.3 is the 35–44 age group. For this cohort, the year effects are more decided (but clearly smaller than the intercohort effects). Assuming that this pattern holds up for younger age groups, it may indicate that year effects favored more recent entrants in the labor market.

On the other hand, whites exhibited relatively larger year effects and smaller cohort effects during the 1960s. It would appear that intercohort differences for whites, unlike the pattern observed for nonwhites, have been fairly uniform across regions. Thus, we can conclude that during the decade of the 1960s relative wage rates rose

Interregional Wage Patterns, 1959–1978

TABLE 8.4

RATIOS OF SOUTH/NON-SOUTH WEEKLY WAGES FOR
COHORTS IN 1969 AND 1978

Age in 1978[a]	White Males			Nonwhite Males		
	1978	1969	1978-69	1978	1969	1978-69
			South/Northeast			
35-44	.931	.929	.002	.825	.750	.075
45-54	.989	.953	.036	.747	.643	.104
55-64	.996	.935	.061	.637	.635	.002
			South/North Central			
35-44	.920	.907	.013	.921	.672	.249
45-54	.929	.916	.013	.725	.605	.120
55-64	.931	.896	.035	.751	.621	.130
			South/West			
35-44	.888	.882	.006	.638	.682	-.044
45-54	.882	.883	-.001	.651	.468	.183
55-64	.839	.874	-.035	.738	.682	.056

Source: U.S. Bureau of the Census, Current Population Survey, 1969 and 1978.

[a]These data do not span an entire ten-year period. Thus, not every age within each group has passed into the next highest group. For example, individuals age 25 in 1969 are 34 in 1978. However, since the CPS data in 1979 do not contain comparable weekly wage information, we report 1978 data.

in the South but that these regional gains were largely restricted to whites. To the extent that rapid industry growth within the South increased the demand for labor, this would imply that whites were the primary beneficiaries. Nonwhites may have just been getting "better" in the South relative to their counterparts outside the South.

In the 1970s the pattern changes somewhat. For nonwhites the year effects are clearly more pronounced than they were in the 1960s. In fact, the year effects are as strong as the intercohort effects. Unlike the experience of the 1960s, the South/non-South wage ratios for nonwhites rose substantially even *within* cohorts. For example, southern nonwhites between the ages of 35 and 44 in 1969 gained roughly 10 percent relative to their non-South contemporaries by 1978. Recall that in the 1960s the improvement for southern nonwhites occurred primarily because of vintage effects that were stronger in the South, but within cohorts relative wages in the South remained largely unchanged.

Again, for whites the year effects dominate the intercohort effects. For example, when compared with workers in the Northeast, southern workers of the same vintage experienced an average 10 percent gain in relative wages, but the intercohort improvement was only about 4 percent. Therefore, there were no differential vintage effects between regions for white males in the 1970s.

SOUTH/NON-SOUTH WAGE RATIOS BY INDUSTRY

How sensitive are the previous results to differences between regions in industrial composition? That is, have the gains in relative wages for southern workers been the result of wage growth within a few select industries, or has the convergence been widely distributed across sectors? To take into account differences in industrial mix and the possibility that these may affect the interregional wage comparisons made earlier, we now examine the South/non-South wage differential for each of seven industries: mining; construction; manufacturing durables; manufacturing nondurables; transportation, communications, and utilities; wholesale and retail trade; and services. Unfortunately, owing to the limited number of observations for nonwhite males in many industry breakdowns, especially in the 1970s, wage comparisons cannot be made by race.

Tables 8.5–8.11 present the resulting South/non-South wage ratios for male workers (white and nonwhite) by age within each of the seven industry groups. Although we introduce a considerable amount of noise in several age cells in the 1970s, the overall pattern is clear: in almost every industry there is a preponderance of gains over losses. Nevertheless, there exists some variation in the magnitude of gains across industries that merits brief mention. The most impressive gains for southern workers occurred in mining and services. This was especially true for the decade of the 1970s. Fairly significant gains were also evident in construction and in wholesale and retail trade. Less regional wage convergence occurred in transportation, communications, and utilities. Within manufacturing (both durables and nondurables), we observe some variation across age cells in gains and losses. Nevertheless, most of the movement in regional wage ratios in manufacturing was toward equality.

Despite the variation in gains and losses between industries and between age cells within industries, however, the evidence strongly suggests that the regional wage convergence that occurred during the Sunbelt period has not been restricted to a few select industries. Instead, these gains have been fairly well distributed across age groups and industries.

SUMMARY

During the last two decades we have witnessed an overall pattern of regional wage convergence. Though this pattern varied somewhat between whites and nonwhites, the data reveal that the relative earnings position of male workers in the South improved dramatically between 1959 and 1978. In almost every age group the relative improvement in South/non-South wage ratios was larger for nonwhites; that is, on average, nonwhites in the South gained more relative to their counterparts elsewhere than southern whites gained relative to their counterparts. The differential gains between whites and nonwhites were related to the possible differences in the regional impact of affirmative action programs and to differential vintage effects.

During the decade of the 1960s, relative wage rates rose in the South, but these regional gains were largely restricted to whites. The gains for nonwhites were largely the result of intercohort improvement (vintage effects), which was larger in the South. It appears that nonwhites may have been getting "better" in the South relative to their counterparts outside the South.

In the 1970s this pattern changed. Both whites and nonwhites in the South experienced an improvement in their relative earnings position. Unlike the experience of the 1960s, the South/non-South wage ratios for nonwhites rose substantially even within cohorts.

TABLE 8.5

RATIOS OF SOUTH/NON-SOUTH WEEKLY WAGES FOR MALE WORKERS
BY INDUSTRY GROUP, 1959-69 AND 1969-78

<u>Mining</u>

Age	1969	1959	ΔR	1978	1969	ΔR
			South/Northeast			
20-24	.999	.992	.007	1.132	.847	.285
25-34	.950	1.111	-.160	1.083	.833	.250
35-44	.906	.993	-.087	.976	.834	.142
45-54	1.076	.986	.090	1.122	.841	.281
55-64	1.015	.898	.117	.944	.841	.103
			South/North Central			
20-24	1.116	.827	.289	1.149	.789	.360
25-34	.975	.940	.036	1.053	.846	.207
35-44	1.040	.958	.082	1.039	.787	.252
45-54	1.003	.931	.072	1.039	.794	.245
55-64	1.136	.907	.229	.924	.859	.065
			South/West			
20-24	1.045	.809	.236	.903	.835	.068
25-34	.932	.896	.035	.846	.787	.059
35-44	.917	.862	.055	.993	.751	.242
45-54	.944	.832	.112	.901	.753	.148
55-64	.929	.743	.186	.817	.698	.119

Sources: U.S. Census of Population, <u>Public Use Sample</u>, 1960 and 1970, and U.S. Bureau of the Census, <u>Current Population Survey</u>, 1969 and 1978.

Interregional Wage Patterns, 1959–1978

TABLE 8.6

RATIOS OF SOUTH/NON-SOUTH WEEKLY WAGES FOR MALE WORKERS
BY INDUSTRY GROUP, 1959-69 AND 1969-78

Construction

Age	1969	1959	Δ R	1978	1969	Δ R
			South/Northeast			
20-24	.805	.784	.020	1.029	.726	.303
25-34	.768	.725	.043	.959	.758	.201
35-44	.776	.767	.009	.904	.600	.304
45-54	.772	.745	.027	.932	1.000	-.068
55-64	.746	.705	.041	.869	.640	.229
			South/North Central			
20-24	.762	.725	.036	.881	.554	.327
25-34	.746	.705	.041	.762	.798	-.036
35-44	.731	.732	-.001	.859	.695	.164
45-54	.754	.750	.004	.783	.867	-.084
55-64	.746	.737	.008	.867	.825	.042
			South/West			
20-24	.769	.672	.096	.715	.467	.248
25-34	.736	.675	.060	.776	.512	.264
35-44	.753	.685	.068	.733	.573	.160
45-54	.732	.678	.054	.728	.624	.104
55-64	.688	.659	.029	.747	.494	.253

Sources: U.S. Census of Population, Public Use Sample, 1960 and 1970, and U.S. Bureau of the Census, Current Population Survey, 1969 and 1978.

TABLE 8.7

RATIOS OF SOUTH/NON-SOUTH WEEKLY WAGES FOR MALE WORKERS
BY INDUSTRY GROUP, 1959-69 AND 1969-78

Manufacturing Durables

Age	1969	1959	Δ R	1978	1969	Δ R
			South/Northeast			
20-24	.816	.790	.025	1.016	.918	.098
25-34	.845	.796	.049	.878	.872	.006
35-44	.810	.815	-.004	.916	.877	.039
45-54	.831	.788	.042	.875	.909	-.034
55-64	.868	.846	.002	.892	.912	-.020
			South/North Central			
20-24	.772	.752	.020	.805	.831	-.026
25-34	.825	.789	.035	.818	.845	-.027
35-44	.819	.800	.018	.883	.872	.011
45-54	.809	.765	.043	.815	.872	-.057
55-64	.818	.815	.003	.846	.869	-.023
			South/West			
20-24	.807	.709	.097	.796	.860	-.064
25-34	.800	.730	.070	.825	.813	.012
35-44	.747	.735	.012	.874	.817	.057
45-54	.743	.749	-.006	.744	.855	-.111
55-64	.748	.843	-.095	.748	.872	-.125

Sources: U.S. Census of Population, Public Use Sample, 1960 and 1970,
and U.S. Bureau of the Census, Current Population Survey, 1969
and 1978.

Interregional Wage Patterns, 1959–1978

TABLE 8.8

RATIOS OF SOUTH/NON-SOUTH WEEKLY WAGES FOR MALE WORKERS
BY INDUSTRY GROUP, 1959-69 AND 1969-78

Manufacturing, NonDurables

Age	1969	1959	ΔR	1978	1969	ΔR
			South/Northeast			
20-24	.882	.883	-.001	1.085	.925	.160
25-34	.840	.851	-.011	.894	.929	-.035
35-44	.788	.797	-.008	.852	1.010	-.158
45-54	.784	.849	-.065	.955	.925	.030
55-64	.752	.858	-.106	.930	.952	-.022
			South/North Central			
20-24	.850	.809	.041	.876	.855	.021
25-34	.801	.819	-.017	.880	.895	-.015
35-44	.806	.797	.008	.857	.945	-.088
45-54	.833	.803	.029	.919	.877	.042
55-64	.754	.784	-.029	.872	.940	-.068
			South/West			
20-24	.867	.768	.099	.829	.855	-.026
25-34	.834	.798	.036	.925	.874	.051
35-44	.788	.791	-.003	.802	.894	-.092
45-54	.795	.793	.002	.924	.874	.050
55-64	.750	.821	.071	.765	.837	.072

Sources: U.S. Census of Population, Public Use Sample, 1960 and 1970,
and U.S. Bureau of the Census, Current Population Survey, 1969
and 1978.

TABLE 8.9

RATIOS OF SOUTH/NON-SOUTH WEEKLY WAGES FOR MALE WORKERS
BY INDUSTRY GROUP, 1959-69 AND 1969-78

Transportation, Communications, and Utilities

Age	1969	1959	ΔR	1978	1969	ΔR
			South/Northeast			
20-24	.878	.861	.017	1.112	.872	.240
25-34	.862	.888	-.026	.852	.927	-.075
35-44	.852	.904	-.052	.907	.926	-.019
45-54	.847	.882	-.035	.964	.883	.081
55-64	.884	.930	-.045	.987	.813	.174
			South/North Central			
20-24	.854	.791	.062	.848	.845	.003
25-34	.874	.872	.002	.836	.865	-.029
35-44	.872	.867	.005	.875	.846	.029
45-54	.879	.854	.024	.909	.870	.039
55-64	.899	.938	-.038	.885	.816	.069
			South/West			
20-24	.853	.847	.005	.886	.849	.037
25-34	.844	.836	.007	.822	.898	-.076
35-44	.819	.833	-.013	.814	.814	.000
45-54	.791	.846	-.055	.845	.809	.036
55-64	.820	.882	-.062	.884	.805	.079

Sources: U.S. Census of Population, Public Use Sample, 1960 and 1970,
and U.S. Bureau of the Census, Current Population Survey, 1969
and 1978.

Interregional Wage Patterns, 1959–1978

TABLE 8.10

RATIOS OF SOUTH/NON-SOUTH WEEKLY WAGES FOR MALE WORKERS
BY INDUSTRY GROUP, 1959-69 AND 1969-78

Wholesale and Retail Trade

Age	1969	1959	ΔR	1978	1969	ΔR
			South/Northeast			
20-24	.867	.829	.038	1.089	1.183	-.094
25-34	.856	.823	.032	.960	.982	-.022
35-44	.866	.849	.017	.872	1.007	-.135
45-54	.858	.809	.049	.948	.910	.038
55-64	.806	.823	-.017	.973	.772	.201
			South/North Central			
20-24	.864	.825	.038	.896	1.016	-.120
25-34	.844	.801	.043	.865	.957	-.092
35-44	.838	.826	.011	.907	.912	-.005
45-54	.856	.814	.041	.933	.865	.068
55-64	.845	.858	-.012	.930	.801	.129
			South/West			
20-24	.881	.757	.123	.857	1.325	-.468
25-34	.869	.749	.120	.845	.932	-.087
35-44	.884	.798	.086	.900	.863	.037
45-54	.824	.770	.054	.892	.918	-.026
55-64	.815	.795	.020	.791	.813	-.022

Sources: U.S. Census of Population, Public Use Sample, 1960 and 1970,
and U.S. Bureau of the Census, Current Population Survey, 1969
and 1978.

TABLE 8.11

RATIOS OF SOUTH/NON-SOUTH WEEKLY WAGES FOR MALE WORKERS
BY INDUSTRY GROUP, 1959-69 AND 1969-78

Services

Age	1969	1959	ΔR	1978	1969	ΔR
			South/Northeast			
20-24	.900	.732	.167	1.014	.372	.642
25-34	.869	.783	.085	1.030	.878	.152
35-44	.771	.657	.114	.994	.404	.590
45-54	.750	.644	.112	1.010	.666	.344
55-64	.749	.688	.061	1.002	.631	.371
			South/North Central			
20-24	.964	.737	.227	.734	.201	.533
25-34	.897	.768	.129	1.277	.891	.386
35-44	.825	.713	.112	1.064	.476	.588
45-54	.769	.675	.094	.903	.633	.270
55-64	.780	.726	.054	.951	.538	.413
			South/West			
20-24	.984	.715	.269	.806	.131	.675
25-34	.886	.696	.190	1.052	1.049	.003
35-44	.776	.623	.152	1.148	.541	.607
45-54	.810	.657	.153	1.012	--	--
55-64	.769	.743	.035	.772	--	--

Sources: U.S. Census of Population, Public Use Sample, 1960 and 1970,
          and U.S. Bureau of the Census, Current Population Survey, 1969
          and 1978.

NOTES

1. As mentioned earlier, it also led some observers to assume that there existed impediments to resource mobility. They maintained the disequilibrium assumption but concluded that the persistence of interregional wage differentials resulted from the inability of capital and labor to move in sufficient quantities to bring about regional wage equality.

2. Another claim is that higher wage rates in the non-South are necessary to compensate individuals for the higher cost of living. Therefore, while nominal wages may differ between regions, real wages are equal. See Coelho and Ghali (1971).

3. For the first period data are taken from the 1 in 100 *Public Use Samples* (PUS) of the 1960 and 1970 Census of Population. Only males with positive weeks worked and positive earnings are included in the sample. In addition, individuals who are self-employed or who work in agriculture are excluded. Weekly wages are earnings last year divided by weeks worked last year. Hourly wage is not used because the hours per week variable in the microdata files refers to hours in the survey week, not to hours worked in the year in which income is reported. The resulting sample size from which averages were calculated is 275,076 in 1960 and 293,180 in 1970.

Since the 1980 PUS sample was not available at this writing, data for the second period are taken from the May 1969 and 1978 *Current Population Survey* (CPS). The same sample restrictions are used to extract earnings information for individuals. Although the May 1979 CPS was available, it did not contain weekly wage data consistent with the 1969 file, which affects only the composition analysis in the next chapter. The resulting sample size from which averages were calculated is 17,459 in 1969 and 18,653 in 1978.

4. A note of caution: ratios in 1969 cannot be compared across tables. They represent averages from two different samples. Nevertheless, it appears that the same pattern is revealed in both periods (samples).

5. Although measuring the quality of schooling is at best tricky, two crude measures have been used in the past. One is the ratio of expenditures on instruction to the number of students, and the other is the student/teacher ratio. The implicit assumption is that the amount of resources devoted to the education of each pupil reflects the resulting quality. For both measures, the South has historically ranked below the non-South, but the South has made dramatic improvements since 1920. For instance, in 1920 the South spent approximately $15 per pupil on instruction, which was only 39 percent of the corresponding allocation in the non-South. By the 1960s, however, this figure had risen to about 73 percent. The number of students per teacher is now roughly equal in the two regions, whereas in the late 1930s the student/teacher ratio was roughly 18 to 20 percent lower in the non-South. These indices suggest that the relative quality of education in the South has been rising over time, and this, in turn, may have resulted in differential vintage effects that favored male workers in the South. This trend in quality indices, along with the integration of blacks into formerly all-white schools, may have made the differential vintage effects even larger for nonwhites.

6. Welch (1966) has shown that differences in school systems can affect the productivity (transmission into earnings) of schooling.

7. Only three within-cohort comparisons are possible.

8. It should be pointed out that with interregional migration, we may still not be comparing the same individuals within a region.

9. Whether the intercohort difference is a result of a change in the educational composition of younger cohorts is the subject of analysis in the next chapter.

Chapter 9

Accounting for Regional Wage Convergence

IN ANY DISCUSSION of regional wage differentials, one inevitably faces a multitude of competing hypotheses that can be advanced to explain observed patterns in the data. In principle, these hypotheses can be subsumed within two broad categories based upon their avenues of influence. The first category includes influences that operate through a change in the composition of a region's labor force (e.g., selective migration). The second category focuses upon factors operating on the price (wage) of labor. This would include changes in the demand for labor. The objective of this chapter is to structure the data so as to determine how much of the change in the South/non-South wage ratios, both within and between cohorts, has been due to wage and composition effects.

THE EFFECTS OF LABOR FORCE COMPOSITION

Suppose both regions had the same labor force composition and differed only by the wages paid to each of the various kinds of labor. What would the South/non-South wage differential be under these conditions? In order to answer this question, recall that the wage ratio comparisons in the last chapter were made for separate age groups by race. For each age cohort, the average was simply a weighted average of the wages paid for the various kinds of labor within that group. Obviously, the resulting average wage will be sensitive both to wage differences within the group and to the distribution of workers across the various labor categories.

In this study each age cohort is composed of workers with different amounts of schooling.[1] Categorizing labor into groups based upon sex, age, education, and race follows the tradition established in the human capital literature. In the typical human capital model, earnings is treated as a function of years of formal schooling, age, race, and sex. Jointly, they serve as proxies for skills acquired in education, experience, and on-the-job training. While there are no theoretical reasons for the inclusion of race and sex in the human capital earnings equation, as a practical matter this distinction is based upon a belief that the effects of discrimination influence the determination of wages, given a certain level of skill and experience.[2] Thus, these observable attributes (age, schooling, and race) will serve to operationally categorize individuals into relatively homogeneous groups.

With this in mind, the South/non-South wage rates for each age group can be expressed as

$$R = \left(\Sigma w_i^s N_i^s / N^s \right) / \left(\Sigma w_i^n N_i^n / N^n \right) = \overline{w}^s / \overline{w}^n \tag{9.1}$$

where the subscripts run across schooling classes and the superscripts (s, n) indicate South and non-South, respectively. To see what would happen to R if both regions had the same labor force composition, we start by defining a hypothetical average wage for the non-South. This wage is determined by holding w_i^n constant and assigning to the non-South the labor force composition (schooling distribution) of the South. Thus, for each age cohort we have

$$\hat{w}^n = \Sigma w_i^n N_i^s / N^s \tag{9.2}$$

where i indicates schooling class. Assuming no change in w_i^n, this would be the resulting non-South wage if this region had the same schooling distribution as the South.

Utilizing equation (9.2), we can now define a hypothetical South/non-South wage ratio that reflects what the relative wage in the South would be if both regions had the same labor force composition but different wage rates. This is accomplished by constructing a Paasche-type wage index as follows:[3]

$$P_w = \left(\Sigma w_i^s N_i^s \right) / \left(\Sigma w_i^n N_i^s \right) = \overline{w}^s / \hat{w}^n \tag{9.3}$$

In this formulation, the non-South can be considered the base, with the South's distribution of labor being valued at non-South wages.

Table 9.1 reports the results of our hypothetical wage ratios for both decades. In the 1960s data are taken from PUS samples for the

1960 and 1970 Census of Population. In the 1970s data are taken from the CPS tapes in 1969 and 1978. With few exceptions, the hypothetical wage ratios in both decades are somewhat larger than the actual wage ratios reported in Tables 8.1 and 8.2. This is not surprising, since w_i^n tends to be larger than w_i^s. The important thing to note from this exercise is that the observed South/non-South wage differentials cannot be entirely attributable to differences between the

TABLE 9.1

HYPOTHETICAL SOUTH/NON-SOUTH WAGE RATIOS ASSUMING SAME LABOR FORCE COMPOSITION AND DIFFERENT WAGE RATES

| | White Males | | | | Nonwhite Males | | | |
| | PUS | | CPS | | PUS | | CPS | |
Age	1959	1969	1969	1978	1959	1969	1969	1978
				South/Northeast				
20-24	.883	.895	.955	1.137	.690	.783	.750	1.046
25-34	.892	.891	.944	.964	.718	.787	.759	.848
35-44	.903	.888	.966	.965	.700	.752	.665	.842
45-54	.877	.901	.943	.985	.679	.724	.618	.778
55-64	.890	.874	.903	1.004	.694	.681	.845	.700
				South/North Central				
20-24	.830	.864	.891	.914	.658	.701	.631	.803
25-34	.862	.874	.911	.908	.646	.713	.715	.755
35-44	.874	.875	.919	.928	.634	.687	.615	.940
45-54	.856	.891	.902	.934	.608	.641	.627	.748
55-64	.860	.868	.898	.936	.635	.609	.692	.798
				South/West				
20-24	.802	.904	.915	.837	.674	.816	.769	.773
25-34	.829	.888	.891	.875	.621	.753	1.104	.781
35-44	.860	.882	.904	.918	.642	.697	.528	.909
45-54	.862	.894	.896	.889	.639	.607	.754	.694
55-64	.891	.869	.864	.865	.646	.676	.791	.709

Sources: U.S. Census of Population, Public Use Sample, 1960 and 1970, and U.S. Bureau of the Census, Current Population Survey, 1969 and 1978.

Note: ratios defined as $\left(\Sigma w_i^s N_i^s\right)\Big/\left(\Sigma w_i^n N_i^s\right)$.

two regions in the composition of their work force. Even after forcing the same labor force composition upon both regions, a sizable differential remains to be explained. This suggests that pure wage effects are fairly significant.

THE EFFECT OF WAGE RATES

Suppose, on the other hand, that both regions had identical wage rates but differed in their labor force composition. Under these conditions, what would the resulting wage ratios be? To get some notion of the compositional effects, we define a Laspeyres-type quantity index in the following manner: [4]

$$L_Q = \left(\Sigma w_i^n N_i^s / N^s\right) / \left(\Sigma w_i^n N_i^n / N^n\right) = \hat{w}^n / \overline{w}^n \qquad (9.4)$$

This is the ratio that would exist if wages were held constant (in this case, at non-South levels) and labor force composition was allowed to vary.

Table 9.2 presents the resulting hypothetical South/non-South wage ratios. In this case, the effect of assigning non-South wage rates to the South's labor force ($\hat{w}^n$) is to almost entirely eliminate the South/non-South wage differential within each age group. Thus, if we could hold labor force composition constant in the South, and then provide this region with the non-South's wage structure, the observed interregional wage differentials could be reduced substantially (if not entirely eliminated).

WAGE AND COMPOSITION EFFECTS OVER TIME

At this point, we turn our attention to the dynamic patterns in the South/non-South wage differential. From the data presented in Tables 8.1–8.4 we observed a general pattern of regional wage convergence; that is, relative wages for southern workers improved substantially during the last two decades. The purpose of this section is to determine how much of this improvement can be accounted for by actual changes in southern wages (w_i^s) and by changes in the composition of the South's labor force (N_i^s). We will call the first change a *wage effect* and the second change a *composition effect*.

TABLE 9.2

HYPOTHETICAL SOUTH/NON-SOUTH WAGE RATIOS ASSUMING SAME WAGE RATES
AND DIFFERENT LABOR FORCE COMPOSITION

| | White Males | | | | Nonwhite Males | | | |
| | PUS | | CPS | | PUS | | CPS | |
Age	1959	1969	1969	1978	1959	1969	1969	1978
				South/Northeast				
20-24	.987	.988	1.000	.975	.992	.977	.959	1.023
25-34	.974	.973	.984	.982	.967	.973	.988	.926
35-44	.966	.966	.987	.964	.959	.953	.966	.980
45-54	.981	.968	.992	1.004	.990	.957	1.028	.959
55-64	.992	.980	1.006	.992	.980	.980	.968	.910
				South/North Central				
20-24	.994	.991	.999	.993	.993	.985	.953	.931
25-34	.986	.990	.996	.991	.979	.975	.940	.957
35-44	.979	.994	.996	.992	.980	.983	.984	.980
45-54	.985	.987	.993	.996	.996	.995	.991	.969
55-64	1.008	.993	.996	.995	.991	.987	.991	.942
				South/West				
20-24	.981	.992	.979	.998	.974	.943	.922	.942
25-34	.970	.972	.990	.982	.952	.877	.618	.943
35-44	.950	.957	.977	.967	.906	.909	.885	.702
45-54	.955	.941	.975	.992	.955	.928	.905	.938
55-64	.975	.952	.976	.969	.974	.933	.843	1.042

Sources: U.S. Census of Population, Public Use Sample, 1960 and 1970,
and U.S. Bureau of the Census, Current Population Survey, 1969
and 1978.

Note: ratios defined as $\left(\Sigma w_i^n N_i^s / N^s\right) / \left(\Sigma w_i^n N_i^n / N^n\right)$.

From equations (9.3) and (9.4), the South/non-South wage ratio
(R) can now be expressed alternatively as [5]

$$R = \left(\overline{w}^s / \hat{w}^n\right) \cdot \left(\hat{w}^n / \overline{w}^n\right) = P_W \cdot L_Q \qquad (9.5)$$

Using equation (9.5), we are now in a position to provide a method
for decomposing the change in the observed wage ratio (R) between

initial and terminal years into the wage effects and composition effects. Let the change in the ratio be expressed as

$$\Delta R = \left(P_w^1 \cdot L_Q^1\right) - \left(P_w^0 \cdot L_Q^0\right) \tag{9.6}$$

where the superscripts are: $1 =$ terminal year and $0 =$ initial year. Upon manipulation we have

$$\Delta R = L_Q^0\left(P_w^1 - P_w^0\right) + P_w^1\left(L_Q^1 - L_Q^0\right) \tag{9.7}$$

The first term on the right-hand side of this expression measures the amount of the change in R directly attributable to wage changes (wage effects), holding composition constant; the second term measures the amount due to the change in the distribution of labor within each age group (composition effect), holding wage rates constant.

The decomposition results for between-cohort changes are displayed in Tables 9.3 and 9.4. The analysis was carried out for white and nonwhite males separately. Column 1 for each race reproduces the gains (or losses) from Tables 8.1 and 8.2. Columns 2 and 3 contain the estimated wage and composition effects. Note that for both races, in the 1960s as well as the 1970s, the movement in the South/non-South wage ratios has been primarily due to wage effects.[6] That is, overall we observe no significant changes in the schooling composition of the southern labor force that could have accounted for the intercohort convergence in average wages. Thus, these data suggest that, whatever is causing convergence, it is having its impact directly on the schooling-constant price of labor.[7]

The within-cohort decomposition is presented in Tables 9.5 and 9.6. Within-cohort changes, in general, follow essentially the same pattern; wage effects tend to account for most of the relative gains. This pattern is particularly decided for white males and less so for nonwhites in the 1960s. In the 1970s almost all the changes in wage ratios for both races are driven by wage effects. Thus, even for within-cohort changes, schooling-constant wage effects account for most of the improvement in relative wages for southern males workers. To the extent that selective migration has altered the composition of any specific cohort in the South relative to the non-South, it has contributed less to the overall improvement in the earnings position of southern male workers than wage effects.

What do these results tell us about the reasons for the recent convergence in South/non-South wage differentials? At least for white

TABLE 9.3

DECOMPOSITION OF CHANGES IN SOUTH/NON-SOUTH WEEKLY WAGE RATIOS
1959-69

Age	ΔR	White Males Wage Effect	Composition Effect	ΔR	Nonwhite Males Wage Effect	Composition Effect
			South/Northeast			
20-24	.013	.012*	.001	.080	.090*	-.010
25-34	-.002	-.002*	.000	.072	.067*	.005
35-44	-.013	-.013*	.000	.045	.049*	-.004
45-54	.011	.024*	-.013	.021	.044*	-.023
55-64	-.025	-.016*	-.009	-.012	-.012*	.000
			South/North Central			
20-24	.032	.035*	-.003	.036	.042*	-.006
25-34	.014	.012*	.002	.063	.065*	-.002
35-44	.014	.001	.013*	.053	.053*	.000
45-54	.037	.035*	.002	.033	.033*	.000
55-64	-.007	.007	-.014*	-.028	-.026*	-.002
			South/West			
20-24	.112	.102*	.010	.112	.138*	-.026
25-34	.058	.059*	-.001	.068	.124*	-.056
35-44	.027	.022*	.005	.052	.050*	.002
45-54	.019	.031*	-.012	-.047	-.031*	-.016
55-64	-.041	-.022*	-.019	.022	.029*	-.027

Source: Calculated from data in U.S. Census of Population, Public Use Sample, 1960 and 1970.

*Dominant effect.

Definitions: Wage effect = $L_Q^0 (P_w^1 - P_w^0)$.

Composition effect = $P_w^1 (L_Q^1 - L_Q^0)$.

males, these results are consistent with a short-run employment growth hypothesis. This hypothesis implies a positive association between increases in wage rates and increases in the quantity of labor demand in the short run. The greater the increase in employment over the

TABLE 9.4

DECOMPOSITION OF CHANGES IN SOUTH/NON-SOUTH WEEKLY WAGE RATIOS
1969-78

Age	White Males			Nonwhite Males		
	ΔR	Wage Effect	Composition Effect	ΔR	Wage Effect	Composition Effect
South/Northeast						
20-24	.152	.181*	-.029	.352	.284*	.068
25-34	.018	.020*	-.002	.036	.088*	-.052
35-44	-.022	-.001	-.020*	.182	.176*	.006
45-54	.054	.042*	.012	.112	.166*	-.054
55-64	.088	.098*	-.010	-.180	-.139*	-.041
South/North Central						
20-24	.016	.023*	-.007	.147	.164*	-.017
25-34	-.007	-.003	-.004	.051	.038*	.013
35-44	.004	.009*	-.005	.316	.320*	-.004
45-54	.033	.031*	.002	.104	.120*	-.016
55-64	.037	.037*	.000	.065	.105*	-.040
South/West						
20-24	-.061	-.076*	.015	.018	.004	.014*
25-34	-.023	-.016*	-.007	.054	-.200	.254*
35-44	.005	.014*	-.009	.170	.337*	-.167
45-54	.008	-.007	.015*	-.031	-.054*	.023
55-64	-.005	.001	-.006*	.071	-.069	.140*

Source: Calculated from data in U.S. Bureau of the Census, Current
Population Survey, 1969 and 1978.

*Dominant effect.

Definitions: Wage effect = $L_Q^0 \left(P_w^1 - P_w^0 \right)$.

Composition effect = $P_w^1 \left(L_Q^1 - L_Q^0 \right)$.

TABLE 9.5

DECOMPOSITION OF CHANGES IN SOUTH/NON-SOUTH WEEKLY WAGE RATIOS
WITHIN COHORTS 1959-69

Age in 1969	ΔR	White Males Wage Effect	Composition Effect	ΔR	Nonwhite Males Wage Effect	Composition Effect
			South/Northeast			
35-44	-.010	-.004	-.006*	.023	.033*	-.010
45-54	.000	-.002	.002	.021	.022*	-.001
55-64	-.004	-.003*	-.001	-.004	.002	-.006*
			South/North Central			
35-44	.019	.012*	.007	.043	.041*	.002
45-54	.024	.017*	.007	.015	.006	.009*
55-64	.018	.012*	.006	-.003	.001	-.004*
			South/West			
35-44	.039	.051*	-.012	.042	.071*	-.029
45-54	.024	.032*	-.008	-.018	-.031*	.013
55-64	.005	.005*	.000	.020	.035*	-.015

Source: Calculated from data in U.S. Census of Population, Public Use Sample, 1960 and 1970.

*Dominant effect.

Definitions: Wage effect = $L_Q^0 \left(P_w^1 - P_w^0 \right)$.

Composition effect = $P_w^1 \left(L_Q^1 - L_Q^0 \right)$.

recent past, the more likely is an industry to encounter rising wages
as a result of inelasticities of labor supply. As we clearly documented
in Chapter 2, employment growth rates in the South have exceeded
those in the non-South by a substantial margin for at least the last
two decades. Further, in Chapter 5 we estimated a regression model
in which the state employment differential, expressed in percentage
terms, was regressed on changes in state corporate tax rates, unioni-

TABLE 9.6

DECOMPOSITION OF CHANGES IN SOUTH/NON-SOUTH WEEKLY WAGE RATIOS
WITHIN-COHORTS 1969-78

Age in 1978	White Males			Nonwhite Males		
	ΔR	Wage Effect	Composition Effect	ΔR	Wage Effect	Composition Effect
			South/Northeast			
35-44	.002	.020*	-.018	.075	.082*	-.007
45-54	.036	.019	.017	.104	.110*	-.006
55-64	.061	.057*	.004	.002	.084*	-.082
			South/North Central			
35-44	.013	.017*	-.004	.249	.212*	.037
45-54	.013	.013*	.000	.120	.131*	-.011
55-64	.035	.061*	-.026	.130	.169*	-.039
			South/West			
35-44	.006	.026	-.020	-.044	-.121*	.077
45-54	-.001	-.015	.014	.183	.147*	.036
55-64	-.035	-.030*	-.005	.056	-.040	.096*

Source: Calculated from data in U.S. Bureau of the Census, Current
Population Survey, 1969 and 1978.

*Dominant effect.

Definitions: Wage effect = $L_Q^0 \left(P_w^1 - P_w^0 \right)$.

Composition effect = $P_w^1 \left(L_Q^1 - L_Q^0 \right)$.

zation rates, and a business climate proxy (RTW). Obviously, business relocation decisions are a function of a host of other location-
specific characteristics, but our objective was not to provide a test of
a comprehensive list of location characteristics. Instead, we were interested in extending our empirically validated knowledge concerning
three controversial and empirically neglected issues. Nevertheless, in

the model estimated, we took the view that changes in employment within a state or region represented primarily demand shifts. Changes in relative cost of production between states (TAX, UNION, and RTW) induce industry migration, which in turn shifts the demand-for-labor curve. This implies a change in relative wage rates, ceteris paribus.

In order to make this connection between employment growth and wage growth, however, we are implicity assuming that changes in employment represent primarily shifts in the demand for labor. But the observed level of employment at any given point in time is an equilibrium position, and changes in employment can result from movements in either supply or demand. For example, it could be argued that the relative growth of employment in the South has been a result of outward shifts in the supply-of-labor curve. If it were the case that observed movements in employment were caused by shifts in the supply-of-labor function, increases in employment would have been accompanied by declining wages as the supply curve shifted relative to demand. In the present context, decreases in the relative growth of employment in the non-South and increases in the relative growth of employment within the South would have been followed by an *increase* in the South/non-South wage differential. If, on the other hand, employment changes were generated by shifts in the demand for labor, wages would move in the same direction. The recent convergence in South/non-South wage differentials is inconsistent with the labor supply explanation but provides support for the second explanation, which gives primary importance to demand-side factors.

SUMMARY

In chapter 8 we documented the recent convergence in regional wage differentials. Specifically, we observed an overall improvement in the relative wage position of male workers in the South. Our purpose in this chapter was to structure the data so that we could explore various hypotheses that can be advanced to explain the observed patterns in the data. The central question addressed was: To what extent has the convergence in South/non-South wage differentials been attributable to changes in the composition of the South's labor force versus a change in the actual wages paid to the same units of labor?

We found that very little of the South/non-South wage differential was eliminated by forcing the non-South to have the same labor force composition as the South. However, if we allowed both regions to retain their respective labor force composition, but paid southern workers the northern wage rate, almost all the differential could be accounted for.

To explain the dynamic patterns in the South/non-South wage differentials, we developed a technique for decomposing the change in wage ratios into a wage effect and a composition effect. The results indicated that overall the movement in South/non-South wage ratios has been primarily due to wage effects. That is, we observed no significant alteration in the composition (schooling distribution within age groups) of the southern labor force that could have accounted for the observed convergence in regional wage differentials, either between or within cohorts.

There is some evidence to suggest that wage convergence between the South and the non-South over the last two decades was due to the acceleration of industry growth in several southern states. The hypothesis is that these increases in demand for labor in the South exerted upward pressure on wages because of short-run inelasticities of labor supply.

One interesting implication that follows these conclusions is that the observed relative improvement in southern wages may be a temporary phenomenon. To the extent that the reduction in interregional wage dispersion can be attributed to industries expanding rapidly in the South, with short-run inelasticities in labor supply, subsequent supply-side reactions in the future may act to erode these gains. For example, if there is some permanent component underlying regional wage differentials (e.g., locational amenities),[8] and if the recent convergence has moved wages in the South above their long-run equilibrium relative value, then some supply-side response via selective migration of labor is anticipated. Conversely, if the rise in relative wages in the South can be attributed to changes in labor quality (a hypothesis we cannot rule out a priori), then increased wages will be permanent, since no rents are involved. However, further research is needed before this point can be resolved.

NOTES

1. Within each age group, individuals in the sample are classified into one of five schooling levels: 0–8 years, 9–11 years, 12 years, 13–15 years, and 16 or more years. We refer here to years of schooling completed.

2. There is, however, a statistically based reason for the inclusion of race and sex dummies in a multiple regression equation on earnings. We desire unbiased coefficient estimates on age and schooling. Omitting these dummies would, therefore, lead to specification bias.

3. A Paasche price index measures the cost of purchasing the given-year quantities at given-year prices relative to their cost of base-year prices. In this case, the non-South is treated as equivalent to the base year in a typical price index. The distribution of labor among schooling classes represents the consumption bundle.

4. The Laspeyres quantity index provides an estimate as to whether quantities have increased on the average between the base year and the given year. To make this quantity comparison, the same weights (w_i^n) are used in calculating the average. Again, recall that the non-South is considered equivalent to the base year.

5. Bellante (1979) uses a similar technique to decompose observed regional wage differentials for a single year, 1970.

6. The choice of the base in constructing this type of decomposition is rather arbitrary. One could just as easily have constructed a Paasche-type quantity index (P_Q) and a Laspeyres-type wage index (L_w) by defining a hypothetical South wage rate in the following manner:

$$\hat{w}^s = \Sigma w_i^s N_i^n / N^n$$

In this case, the decomposition would be $\Delta R = P_Q^0(L_w^1 - L_w^0) + L_w^1(P_Q^1 - P_Q^0)$. To test whether the results reported above were sensitive to the choice of an index, both techniques were developed. This alternative procedure can be found in Appendix C.

7. Holding constant differences between regions in industrial composition yields the same general results. The decomposition was performed separately for seven major industry groups: manufacturing nondurables; manufacturing durables; mining; services; wholesale and retail trade; construction; and transportation, communications, and utilities. Though some noise was introduced at both ends of the schooling distribution within several age groups, the results are consistent with those reported above and support the hypothesis that convergence in South/non-South wages has been primarily a schooling-constant wage effect. Unfortunately, this industry-constant decomposition could be performed only for the 1960s because sample sizes from the CPS tapes were insufficient to withstand this much stratification. These results are reported in Appendix D.

8. See Rosen (1979) for an analysis of wage differentials and location amenities. According to Rosen, differences in wages between regions represent compensating differentials that reflect area-specific (immobile) amenities. Assuming *universal* preferences for amenities among members of the population, an equalizing set of money wages and cost-of-living differences will be observed among areas. Those areas that have predominantly negatively valued amenities will be required to offer higher wages and lower prices of housing services in order to attract workers from more favorable areas. Thus, we fully expect to observe equilibrium wage differentials that persist over time and merely reflect the fact that amenities are not transferable between regions.

Chapter 10

Summary and Conclusions

BY CONVENTIONAL DATING, we are well into the third decade of what has become known as the Sunbelt phenomenon. Within the last few decades the historical pattern of uneven growth among U.S. regions has reversed itself. Older manufacturing areas, particularly those cities and states in the Northeast, have experienced a substantial reduction in their rates of growth, while at the same time "backward" areas in the South have been experiencing impressive gains in both per capita income and employment.

The primary purpose of this study was to extend our empirically validated knowledge concerning the importance of certain economic influences on the changing interregional employment and wage patterns during the 1960s and 1970s. In particular, attention was focused on the recent acceleration of industry migration to the South and the dynamic patterns in South and non-South wage differentials.

SUMMARY

Interregional Employment Patterns. At some point during the late 1950s or early 1960s, industry migration to the South began to accelerate, and by the end of the 1970s a considerable amount of industry redistribution (or relocation) had occurred. Overall, the South had become the primary growth center in the United States. In the manufacturing sector, the South experienced a relative gain of approximately 1,709,000 employees between 1957 and 1979. In the nonmanufacturing sector (excluding agriculture), the South's relative gain amounted to 3,482,000 employees. These relative gains had the effect of dramatically increasing the South's share of total manufacturing and nonmanufacturing employment.

Though numerous explanations have been advanced to account

for this movement to the South, few have been as controversial and unsubstantiated as arguments attributing southern growth to lower state and local taxes, a more favorable business climate, and lower levels of union activity. Unfortunately, notwithstanding the popularity of these arguments, there exists a paucity of work that attempts to statistically isolate these effects within a single empirical model. Thus, one of the major objectives of this study was to determine whether these explanations have empirical validity. The results can be summarized as follows:

(1) Empirical results lend considerable support to the argument that corporate tax rate differentials between states as well as the extent of unionization and a favorable business climate (proxied by the existence of a state RTW law) have been major factors influencing the redistribution of industry employment across regions. Of particular interest was the finding that corporate tax rate differentials and RTW laws have each played a significant independent role in the observed patterns of industry migration. This finding suggests that government policymakers at the state and local levels have played a more influential role in the Sunbelt phenomenon than most of them have been willing to admit.

(2) Also, evidence reveals considerable variation in the coefficient estimates across industries. That is, some industries were found to be more sensitive to changes in tax rate differentials, unionization rates, and RTW laws than other industries. However, this variation was found to be systmatically related to industry capital/labor ratios and to the rate of capacity expansion. These two findings, in turn, suggest a partial reconciliation for the ambiguous results from previous empirical studies, especially with respect to the conflicting evidence concerning the role of state taxes in stimulating industry relocation. Expanding the sample to include many industries, as this study does, revealed that previous results, based upon limited industry samples, cannot be generalized.

(3) The influence on industry migration of RTW laws has tended to decay over time. Following the peak in legislative activity during the late 1950s, industry employment was redistributed toward states that had enacted such laws, ceteris paribus. However, by the mid-1970s most industries had completed their locational adjustments stimulated by the passage of RTW laws in several state. This finding supports the hypothesis that the incentives from a one-time change in

location characteristics decay over time as firms complete their initial adjustments.

(4) Tax rate differentials and RTW laws have not only affected movement to the South (i.e., movement across regions); they have also influenced the redistribution of industry employment *within* the South. This merely reflects the fact that the South is far from being a homogeneous region. In addition, these results are inconsistent with the view that holds RTW laws to be a uniquely southern phenomenon. Therefore, the RTW law controversy should not be considered as a South/non-South issue, especially if one considers that, of the nineteen states that currently have such legislation, 37 percent are outside the South. Furthermore, of the states that at one time or another had legal restrictions on union security agreements, 45 percent were non-South states. Hence, these stylized facts, along with the present empirical results, contradict the view that RTW laws merely epitomize the social, political, and institutional characteristics of the South.

Interregional Wage Patterns. Alongside this substantial regional redistribution of industry employment we have witnessed a considerable convergence in South/non-South wage differentials. Our findings can be summarized as follows:

(1) During the last two decades we witnessed an overall pattern of regional wage convergence. Though this pattern varied somewhat between whites and nonwhites, the data revealed that the relative earnings position of male workers in the South improved dramatically between 1959 and 1978. On average, nonwhites in the South gained more relative to their counterparts elsewhere than southern whites gained relative to their counterparts. These differential gains between whites and nonwhites may possibly be related to the differences in the regional impact of affirmative action programs and to differential vintage effects.

(2) We found that very little of the observed South/non-South wage differential was eliminated by forcing both regions to have the same labor force composition. However, if we allow both regions to retain their respective labor force composition, but assign the northern wage rate to southern workers, almost all the observed wage differential could be accounted for.

(3) To what extent has the convergence in South/non-South wage

differentials been attributable to changes in the composition of the South's labor force (e.g., through selective migration) versus a change in the actual wage rates paid to a given composition of labor? To explain the dynamic patterns in the South/non-South wage differentials, we developed a technique for decomposing the change in wage ratios into a "wage effect," holding composition constant, and a "composition effect," holding wages constant. The results indicated that the movement of South/non-South wage ratios has been due primarily to wage effects. That is, we observed no significant alteration in the composition (schooling distribution within age cohorts) of the southern labor force that could have accounted for the observed convergence in regional wage differentials, either between or within cohorts.

(4) Finally, there is some evidence to suggests that wage convergence between the South and the non-South over the last two decades was due in large part to the acceleration of industry growth in several southern states. The hypothesis is that this increased demand for labor exerted upward pressure on wage rates because of short-run inelasticities of labor supply.

CONCLUDING REMARKS

The primary objective of this study has been to provide some additional insights into the nature of interregional growth patterns in general and the causes and consequences of growth in the South specifically. Unfortunately, owing to both exogenous and endogenous constraints imposed upon empirical studies of economic events, decisions invariably have to be made regarding the scope of analysis. This study is no exception. Consequently, we have not exhausted fruitful areas of research into the phenomenon in question.

With respect to industry migration, many variables that affect firm location decisions have not been examined in this study. We concentrated on three of the most controversial issues in the ongoing debate over why industry has been moving to the South. Several other economic as well as "environmental" influences have undoubtedly been at work to account for part of the observed differences in regional growth patterns. For example, unlike interurban location studies, we were unable to examine the effects of *local* tax differentials such as the influence of the property tax. In addition, since it certainly appears that the South has attained some of its own internal growth momentum, it would be interesting to determine to what extent agglomeration economies have begun to reinforce existing migration patterns. As the present results suggest, however, future empirical work should take into account industry-specific characteristics that cause differential migration responses between industries to a given migration stimulus.

One curious result begs additional work. Contrary to our prior expectations, RTW laws accounted for a very substantial portion of the explained variation in comparative employment growth across states. Determining exactly what effects are being captured by this variable would greatly expand our knowledge concerning the pattern of industry relocation. As it stands now, using a dummy variable to represent (proxy) business climate merely reduces our level of general ignorance, leaving a number of specific questions unanswered.

With regard to our analysis of changing patterns in regional wage differentials, one interesting implication remains unanswered; that is, the improvement in southern wages for male workers may be a temporary phenomenon. To the extent that the reduction in South/non-South wage differentials can be attributed to industries expanding rapidly in the South, with short-run inelasticities in labor supply, subsequent supply-side reactions may act to erode these gains. For example, if there is some permanent component underlying regional wage differentials (e.g., locational amenities), and if the recent convergence has moved wages in the South above their long-run equilibrium relative value, then some supply-side response via selective migration of labor is anticipated. Conversely, if the rise in relative wages in the South can be attributed to changes in labor quality, increased wages will be permanent, since no rents are involved. Further research is needed before this question can be resolved, however.

Thus, although this study has expanded our knowledge of the dynamic patterns of industry movement and the institutional influences impinging on industry migration, there are still many opportunities for further research. This is true as well for movements in South/non-South wage differentials.

Appendixes

Data for Industry
Migration Analysis

TABLE A.1

COMPARATIVE GAINS AND LOSSES IN EMPLOYMENT, STATES BY MAJOR INDUSTRY GROUPS, 1957-65, 1965-73, AND 1973-79

	Textile Mill Products			Apparel			Lumber & Wood		
	1957-65	1965-73	1973-79	1957-65	1965-73	1973-79	1957-65	1965-73	1973-79
New England:									
Maine	-.168	-.333	.070	-.008	.171	.282	-.189	-.125	.025
New Hampshire	-.193	-.364	-.140	.089	-.062	.058	-.111	-.161	-.029
Vermont	--	--	--	-.452	-.125	.226	-.085	-.366	.280
Massachusetts	.250	-.336	.042	-.158	-.235	-.031	-.067	-.254	.072
Rhode Island	-.236	-.380	-.128	-.169	-.141	.122	--	--	--
Connecticut	-.175	-.200	-.169	-.258	-.282	-.029	--	--	--
Middle Atlantic:									
New York	-.067	-.123	-.230	-.293	-.311	-.080	-.112	-.225	.044
New Jersey	-.205	.000	-.163	-.059	-.173	-.035	-.063	-.357	.412
Pennsylvania	-.093	-.205	-.106	-.026	-.178	-.098	-.051	-.153	.521
East North Central:									
Ohio	.015	-.187	-.304	-.266	-.036	.047	-.007	.113	.198
Indiana	.023	-.070	-.159	-.152	-.041	--	.240	-.125	--
Illinois	-.381	-.369	-.119	-.263	-.300	-.199	-.072	-.217	.016
Michigan	.891	.055	-.561	.716	.084	--	.039	.018	.058
Wisconsin	-.050	-.046	-.293	.006	-.185	.008	-.029	-.113	.308
West North Central:									
Minnesota	--	--	--	--	--	--	-.184	2.68	--
Iowa	--	--	--	-.093	-.036	.143	--	--	--
Missouri	.501	-.360	-.561	-.202	-.065	-.033	.048	-.022	.212
North Dakota	--	--	--	--	--	--	--	--	--
South Dakota	--	--	--	--	--	--	--	--	--
Nebraska	--	--	--	--	--	--	--	--	--
Kansas	--	--	--	.171	.138	-.136	--	--	--
South Atlantic:									
Delaware	-.328	-.341	-.293	-.227	-.486	-.170	--	--	--
Maryland	-.099	-.535	-.009	-.098	-.208	-.068	-.128	-.185	.258
District of Columbia	--	--	--	--	--	--	--	--	--
Virginia	.119	.101	.081	.292	.242	-.046	-.031	-.234	.153
West Virginia	--	--	--	.198	.142	-.107	--	--	--
North Carolina	.142	.089	.004	1.086	.421	.141	-.052	-.220	.249
South Carolina	.109	.039	.024	.527	.084	.110	--	--	--
Georgia	.083	.116	.107	.416	.113	.096	-.098	-.172	.148

	Textile Mill Products			Apparel			Lumber & Wood		
	1957-65	1965-73	1973-79	1957-65	1965-73	1973-79	1957-65	1965-73	1973-79
East South Central:									
Kentucky	.134	1.302	.138	.329	.107	.006	-.020	-.097	.010
Tennessee	.038	.047	-.110	.592	.127	.011	-.063	-.201	.233
Alabama	-.092	.211	.024	.566	.318	.116	-.097	-.059	.159
Mississippi	.284	.131	.078	.301	.187	.035	.093	-.122	.057
West South Central:									
Arkansas	.320	.742	.124	.867	.139	-.075	.102	-.233	-.010
Louisiana	-.045	.515	--	-.220	.543	--	-.126	-.167	-.010
Oklahoma	--	--	--	.449	1.145	.007	.006	.231	.177
Texas	.100	.006	-.117	.381	.515	.102	.009	.164	.431
Mountain:									
Montana	--	--	--	--	--	--	.351	-.033	.114
Idaho	--	--	--	--	--	--	.065	.087	.215
Wyoming	--	--	--	--	--	--	--	--	--
Colorado	--	--	--	--	--	--	--	--	--
New Mexico	--	--	--	--	.577	.059	.111	.192	.599
Arizona	--	--	--	--	--	--	--	--	--
Utah	--	--	--	--	--	--	--	--	--
Nevada	--	--	--	--	--	--	--	--	--
Pacific:									
Washington	--	--	--	--	--	--	.092	-.097	.096
Oregon	.057	-.091	-.037	.029	.035	.152	.089	-.099	.015
California	.557	.819	.197	.028	.309	.336	-.028	-.104	.258

TABLE A.1 (continued)

	Furniture & Fixtures			Paper & Allied Products			Printing & Publishing		
	1957-65	1965-73	1973-79	1957-65	1965-73	1973-79	1957-65	1965-73	1973-79
New England:									
Maine	--	--	--	--	--	--	--	--	--
New Hampshire	.026	-.136	-.164	-.348	.045	-.089	.195	.163	.117
Vermont	.183	.065	.094	.038	-.011	.122	.374	.199	-.029
Massachusetts	-.196	-.426	-.168	-.125	-.179	-.102	-.034	-.110	-.079
Rhode Island	--	--	--	-.023	.105	-.003	.002	-.066	-.005
Connecticut	--	--	--	-.083	-.018	.008	.019	.059	.100
Middle Atlantic:									
New York	-.209	-.372	-.199	-.149	-.289	-.038	-.105	-.226	-.150
New Jersey	-.129	-.055	-.063	-.014	.070	.079	.104	.098	.037
Pennsylvania	-.111	-.148	-.266	-.016	-.043	-.029	-.115	-.051	-.089
East North Central:									
Ohio	-.413	-.158	-.069	-.036	-.048	-.081	-.037	-.113	-.100
Indiana	.021	-.105	-.190	.152	-.054	-.036	.076	.014	.006
Illinois	-.144	-.259	-.236	.078	.090	-.084	-.069	-.089	-.244
Michigan	-.126	-.111	-.012	-.073	-.199	-.098	-.009	.061	-.183
Wisconsin	-.428	.121	.078	-.058	-.026	.086	-.040	.071	.058
West North Central:									
Minnesota	.119	.219	--	1.115	.138	.012	-.013	.041	.186
Iowa	--	--	--	--	.227	-.003	-.037	.045	.109
Missouri	-.329	.314	-.036	-.044	-.016	-.010	.059	-.001	-.042
North Dakota	--	--	--	--	--	--	-.049	.080	.123
South Dakota	--	--	--	--	--	--	-.059	-.009	--
Nebraska	--	--	--	--	--	--	.031	-.015	-.006
Kansas	--	--	--	--	--	--	-.002	.404	.081
South Atlantic:									
Delaware	--	--	--	--	--	--	-.054	-.001	.064
Maryland	-.051	-.272	-.302	.045	.017	-.052	.219	.098	.027
District of Columbia	--	--	--	--	--	--	.093	-.134	-.159
Virginia	.305	.024	-.024	.014	.031	.004	.179	.232	.168
West Virginia	--	--	--	--	--	--	-.126	.055	-.067
North Carolina	.351	.124	.076	.139	.219	.101	.188	.291	.093
South Carolina	.026	.165	-.072	.280	.203	.091	.026	.497	.049
Georgia	-.037	-.019	-.048	.158	.101	.066	.160	.267	.272
Florida	-.051	.284	.023	.017					

TABLE A.1 (continued)

	Furniture & Fixtures			Paper & Allied Products			Printing & Publishing		
	1957-65	1965-73	1973-79	1957-65	1965-73	1973-79	1957-65	1965-73	1973-79
East South Central:									
Kentucky	.104	-.079	-.185	.644	.798	.295	.072	.216	-.020
Tennessee	.658	.041	-.137	.093	.370	.154	.132	.193	.064
Alabama	--	--	--	.266	.240	.071	.101	.251	.010
Mississippi	.829	.633	-.031	-.489	.275	.011	-.042	.212	.459
West South Central:									
Arkansas	.372	.176	-.239	.391	.471	.221	.771	.120	.163
Louisiana	-.284	-.159	-.196	-.243	.012	-.226	-.054	.133	.112
Oklahoma	--	--	--	--	--	--	.007	.174	.057
Texas	.112	.295	-.037	.255	.409	.210	.061	.231	.198
Mountain:									
Montana	--	--	--	--	--	--	-.063	-.016	.099
Idaho	--	--	--	--	.230	.164	--	.199	.388
Wyoming	--	--	--	--	--	--	--	--	--
Colorado	--	--	--	--	--	--	.098	.281	.216
New Mexico	--	--	--	--	--	--	--	--	--
Arizona	--	--	--	--	--	--	.445	.502	.319
Utah	--	--	--	--	--	--	--	--	--
Nevada	--	--	--	--	--	--	--	--	--
Pacific:									
Washington	-.394	.085	-.144	.031	-.209	-.229	-.017	.072	.194
Oregon	.277	.165	-.292	-.064	.191	-.003	-.050	.216	.187
California	-.057	.194	.238	.123	.077	.065	.117	.056	.119

TABLE A.1 (continued)

	Chemicals & Allied Products			Rubber & Misc. Plastics			Leather & Leather Products		
	1957-65	1965-73	1973-79	1957-65	1965-73	1973-79	1957-65	1965-73	1973-79
New England:									
Maine	--	--	--	--	--	--	.344	-.097	.130
New Hampshire	--	--	--	--	--	--	--	--	--
Vermont	--	--	--	--	--	--	--	--	--
Massachusetts	--	--	--	-.238	-.532	-.189	-.186	-.247	-.056
Rhode Island	.146	.331	.074	-.093	-.504	-.270	--	--	--
Connecticut	.079	.046	.046	-.236	-.447	-.335	--	--	--
Middle Atlantic:									
New York	-.157	-.266	-.129	-.093	-.192	-.068	-.129	-.146	-.036
New Jersey	.067	.127	-.035	.034	-.520	-.062	.061	-.022	-.054
Pennsylvania	-.091	-.098	-.028	.079	.009	-.058	.062	-.071	-.130
East North Central:									
Ohio	-.070	.055	.037	-.231	-.302	-.166	-.096	-.018	-.149
Indiana	-.066	-.015	-.058	.095	-.201	-.056	--	--	--
Illinois	-.036	-.029	-.011	.186	-.116	-.153	-.159	-.073	-.373
Michigan	.008	-.169	-.067	--	--	--	--	--	--
Wisconsin	-.176	.328	-.079	-.005	.254	.184	--	--	--
West North Central:									
Minnesota	--	--	--	--	--	--	--	--	--
Iowa	.075	-.061	.143	--	.060	.009	--	--	--
Missouri	.039	-.123	.073	--	--	--	-.173	.079	-.021
North Dakota	--	--	--	--	--	--	--	--	--
South Dakota	--	--	--	--	--	--	--	--	--
Nebraska	.157	-.100	-.027	--	--	--	--	--	--
Kansas	-.092	-.213	.219	--	--	--	--	--	--
South Atlantic:									
Delaware	.080	-.033	-.082	.054	-.046	-.470	-.038	-.304	--
Maryland	.019	-.161	-.224	.059	-.534	-.081	-.180	.152	-.001
District of Columbia	--	--	--	--	--	--	--	--	--
Virginia	.018	-.178	-.164	--	--	--	-.018	.022	.018
West Virginia	-.091	-.242	-.016	--	--	--	--	--	--
North Carolina	.400	.874	-.023	--	--	--	--	--	--
South Carolina	.266	.606	-.025	--	--	--	--	--	--
Georgia	.239	.163	-.031	--	--	--	.310	.104	-.240
Florida	.277	-.048	.210	--	--	--	--	--	--

TABLE A.1 (continued)

	Chemicals & Allied Products			Rubber & Misc. Plastics			Leather & Leather Products		
	1957-65	1965-73	1973-79	1957-65	1965-73	1973-79	1957-65	1965-73	1973-79
East South Central:									
Kentucky	.092	-.055	.052	--	--	--	.253	1.095	-.111
Tennessee	.036	-.004	-.083	.338	.600	.302	.506	.422	-.030
Alabama	.104	.040	.187	-.090	.440	-.035	--	.153	.091
Mississippi	-.436	.203	1.017	--	1.173	-.183	--	--	--
West South Central:									
Arkansas	.068	.016	.362	--	--	--	.922	.449	-.101
Louisiana	-.073	.303	.243	--	--	--	--	--	--
Oklahoma	--	--	--	--	--	--	-.033	1.164	.325
Texas	.071	.104	.180	--	--	--	--	--	--
Mountain:									
Montana	--	--	--	--	--	--	--	--	--
Idaho	--	.242	.264	--	--	--	--	--	--
Wyoming	--	--	--	--	--	--	--	--	--
Colorado	-.166	-.048	1.627	-.246	-.039	--	--	--	--
New Mexico	--	--	--	--	--	--	--	--	--
Arizona	--	--	--	--	--	--	--	--	--
Utah	--	--	--	--	--	--	--	--	--
Nevada	--	--	--	--	--	--	--	--	--
Pacific:									
Washington	-.400	-.496	.385	--	--	--	--	--	--
Oregon	--	--	--	-.032	.401	.167	-.056	.616	.690
California	.146	.023	.121	--	--	--	--	--	--

TABLE A.1 (continued)

	Stone, Glass, & Clay			Primary Metals			Fabricated Metals		
	1957-65	1965-73	1973-79	1957-65	1965-73	1973-79	1957-65	1965-73	1973-79
New England:									
Maine	.011	--	--	--	--	--	--	--	--
New Hampshire	-.084	-.139	.947	.410	.268	.183	.417	.630	--
Vermont	-.046	-.344	-.064	--	--	--	--	--	--
Massachusetts	.260	.062	-.012	-.100	-.086	-.094	-.118	-.116	.195
Rhode Island	--	-.019	.153	-.070	.008	.056	.022	-.161	.001
Connecticut	--	--	--	-.135	-.120	-.072	-.055	-.061	.082
Middle Atlantic:									
New York	-.063	-.209	-.092	-.087	-.088	-.189	-.217	-.294	-.034
New Jersey	.003	-.028	-.124	-.116	-.190	-.245	-.021	-.115	-.062
Pennsylvania	-.180	-.091	-.029	-.086	-.099	-.121	-.172	-.184	.017
East North Central:									
Ohio	-.135	-.115	-.017	-.061	-.015	-.121	-.092	-.082	.027
Indiana	-.055	-.127	.005	.107	.059	-.020	.140	.029	.006
Illinois	-.076	-.144	-.051	.062	-.017	-.118	-.052	-.127	-.098
Michigan	--	--	--	.374	.072	-.161	.401	-.181	.038
Wisconsin	.089	.002	.256	.078	.088	-.062	.104	.034	.223
West North Central:									
Minnesota	-.521	.058	.198	.004	.090	.106	.189	.149	.618
Iowa	.085	-.108	.114	.325	.083	.050	.139	.214	.223
Missouri	-.180	-.268	.182	-.020	.142	.068	.012	-.035	.064
North Dakota	.145	.361	.232	--	--	--	--	--	--
South Dakota	--	--	--	--	--	--	--	--	--
Nebraska	--	--	--	--	--	--	--	--	--
Kansas	.089	-.026	.174	-.076	1.308	.166	.086	.478	.166
South Atlantic:									
Delaware	--	--	--	-.496	.125	-.150	-.256	-.203	.012
Maryland	.138	-.094	-.153	.014	-.157	-.120	--	--	-.182
District of Columbia	--	--	--	--	--	--	--	--	--
Virginia	.319	.034	.049	.390	.269	.256	.155	.479	.148
West Virginia	-.128	-.134	-.206	.122	-.009	-.049	-.069	-.038	-.063
North Carolina	.450	.189	.166	.797	.752	.204	.451	.627	.252
South Carolina	.648	.176	-.039	--	--	--	--	.796	.391
Georgia	.527	.028	.099	.413	.850	.439	.823	.395	.052
Florida	.155	.549	-.093	.509	.673	-.038	.199	.458	.103

TABLE A.1 (continued)

	Stone, Glass, & Clay			Primary Metals			Fabricated Metals		
	1957-65	1965-73	1973-79	1957-65	1965-73	1973-79	1957-65	1965-73	1973-79
East South Central:									
Kentucky	-.037	.317	.203	.282	.536	.144	.081	.169	-.082
Tennessee	.237	.175	-.056	-.083	.070	.122	.157	.202	.107
Alabama	-.043	.005	.136	-.012	.019	-.061	--	--	--
Mississippi	.366	.194	.121	1.725	.623	--	1.607	.425	--
West South Central:									
Arkansas	.324	.186	.029	.102	1.026	.312	.917	1.046	.358
Louisiana	.066	-.153	.242	.143	.556	.192	.400	.041	.473
Oklahoma	.079	.164	.081	.061	.120	.226	.290	.323	.236
Texas	.286	.083	.338	.131	.279	.223	.286	.455	.377
Mountain:									
Montana	--	--	--	-.215	-.088	.004	--	--	--
Idaho	--	.305	.087	--	.071	.076	--	--	1.404
Wyoming	--	--	--	--	--	--	--	1.296	--
Colorado	.310	.450	.291	.023	-.028	--	--	--	--
New Mexico	--	--	--	--	--	--	--	.339	.348
Arizona	--	.981	.255	-.090	.709	.337	.139	.815	--
Utah	--	--	--	--	--	--	--	--	--
Nevada	--	--	--	--	--	--	--	--	--
Pacific:									
Washington	.047	-.065	.200	-.141	.277	-.249	-.005	-.087	.414
Oregon	.225	.017	.172	.255	.404	.283	.148	.265	.396
California	.190	-.039	.098	.039	.097	.009	.079	.025	.251

TABLE A.1 (continued)

	Machinery, Except Electric			Electronic Equipment			Transportation Equipment		
	1957-65	1965-73	1973-79	1957-65	1965-73	1973-79	1957-65	1965-73	1973-79
New England:									
Maine	--	--	--	--	--	--	--	--	--
New Hampshire	--	--	.720	.349	.253	-.086	--	--	--
Vermont	-.259	-.359	-.023	2.705	.545	.380	--	--	--
Massachusetts	-.039	-.199	.132	-.241	-.173	.072	--	--	--
Rhode Island	-.183	-.184	-.286	1.133	-.081	.107	.078	-.183	.728
Connecticut	-.173	-.302	-.143	-.041	-.186	.040	.110	-.203	.061
Middle Atlantic:									
New York	-.143	-.226	-.130	-.178	-.270	-.080	-.137	-.218	-.103
New Jersey	-.095	-.106	-.159	-.281	-.277	-.262	-.303	-.342	-.246
Pennsylvania	-.129	-.112	-.137	-.189	-.170	-.215	.019	.110	.098
East North Central:									
Ohio	-.095	-.059	-.212	-.207	-.242	-.152	-.049	.139	-.081
Indiana	.058	.006	-.123	.101	-.037	-.229	-.060	.148	-.116
Illinois	-.022	-.153	-.190	-.212	-.171	-.278	-.117	.112	-.066
Michigan	.248	-.213	-.157	.082	-.065	-.192	.288	.056	-.092
Wisconsin	.026	-.155	.022	-.092	-.241	.002	.395	-.065	-.103
West North Central:									
Minnesota	.392	.296	.106	.357	.320	-.106	.321	.969	-.127
Iowa	.273	.213	-.011	.158	-.078	-.082	-.386	2.303	.089
Missouri	.125	.030	-.142	--	.194	.016	.390	.021	-.107
North Dakota	--	--	--	--	--	--	--	--	--
South Dakota	--	--	--	--	--	--	--	--	--
Nebraska	--	--	--	--	--	--	--	--	--
Kansas	.385	.672	--	.262	.656	--	-.259	.015	.278
South Atlantic:									
Delaware	--	--	.114	-.136	-.034	.596	-.533	.034	-.244
Maryland	.043	-.104	--	--	--	--	--	--	--
District of Columbia	--	--	--	--	--	--	--	--	--
Virginia	1.068	.321	.048	1.334	.888	-.013	.521	.341	-.113
West Virginia	--	-.066	.173	--	-.423	-.005	--	-.296	.014
North Carolina	.806	.690	.032	.162	.484	-.005	.316	1.861	.013
South Carolina	2.906	.718	.223	--	.624	.129	--	-.064	-.191
	.164	.422	.062	.607	.781	.240	.368		

	Machinery, except Electric			Electronic Equipment			Transportation Equipment		
	1957-65	1965-73	1973-79	1957-65	1965-73	1973-79	1957-65	1965-73	1973-79
East South Central:									
Kentucky	.425	.533	.023	.358	.318	-.180	.238	.719	.177
Tennessee	.137	1.420	.006	.554	.771	-.118	.954	1.013	.092
Alabama	.270	.483	--	.146	.467	--	.006	.206	-.003
Mississippi	1.572	.452	.197	.987	.978	.131	.835	1.272	-.032
West South Central:									
Arkansas	--	1.208	.567	--	1.196	.046	1.192	1.898	-.077
Louisiana	--	-	.254	--	-	.425	.249	.696	.138
Oklahoma	--	.681	.362	--	.767	-.143	-.207	.317	.368
Texas	.134	.469	.562	2.134	.396	.639	-.201	.204	.038
Mountain:									
Montana	--	--	--	--	--	--	--	--	--
Idaho	--	--	3.710	--	--	.471	--	--	--
Wyoming	--	--	--	--	--	--	--	--	1.285
Colorado	.233	1.013	.523	--	1.742	-.172	--	.275	--
New Mexico	--	--	--	--	--	--	--	--	--
Arizona	4.069	.603	--	3.945	.587	--	--	--	--
Utah	.128	.814	--	--	--	--	--	--	--
Nevada	--	--	--	--	--	--	--	--	--
Pacific:									
Washington	--	.249	-.094	--	1.138	.107	.018	-.092	.167
Oregon	.385	.458	.277	1.608	.642	-.372	.913	.919	-.034
California	.233	.306	.255	.436	.095	.154	-.034	-.169	.214

Sources: Calculated from data in U.S. Department of Labor, Bureau of Labor Statistics, Employment and Earnings, States and Areas, 1939-78, 1979 and Supplement to Employment and Earnings, States and Areas 1977-79.

TABLE A.2

VALUES OF INDEPENDENT VARIABLES BY STATE

	Change in Relative Tax Rate[a]			Change in Relative Unionism[b]			RTW Law
	1958-1948	1966-1956	1974-1964	1964-1953	1974-1964	1978-1968	
New England:							
Maine	0.000	0.000	1.186	0.048	-0.086	-0.552	0
New Hampshire	0.000	0.000	1.186	-0.073	-0.105	-0.545	0
Vermont	-0.162	-0.280	0.021	0.054	0.041	-0.654	0
Massachusetts	0.840	-0.380	-0.421	0.025	-0.017	-0.794	0
Rhode Island	-0.033	-0.070	-0.144	0.118	0.082	-0.737	0
Connecticut	-0.121	0.105	0.105	0.102	0.042	-0.741	0
Middle Atlantic:							
New York	-0.215	-0.308	0.150	0.249	0.145	-1.112	0
New Jersey	0.452	0.368	0.494	0.015	-0.018	-0.944	0
Pennsylvania	0.095	-0.336	0.110	0.087	0.119	-1.164	0
East North Central:							
Ohio	0.000	0.000	1.355	0.078	0.023	-1.139	0
Indiana	0.000	0.421	0.008	0.006	0.033	-1.139	0
Illinois	0.000	0.000	0.678	0.083	0.030	-1.134	0
Michigan	0.000	0.000	1.322	0.119	0.018	-1.117	0
Wisconsin	-0.373	-0.392	-0.411	-0.426	-0.036	-1.016	0
West North Central:							
Minnesota	-0.295	0.473	0.158	-0.016	-0.186	-0.956	0
Iowa	-0.210	0.042	0.944	-0.001	0.043	-0.672	1
Missouri	-0.210	-0.112	0.347	0.066	-0.051	-1.137	0
North Dakota	-0.631	-0.336	-0.483	0.023	0.074	-0.596	1
South Dakota	0.000	0.000	0.000	-0.102	0.080	-0.463	1
Nebraska	0.000	0.000	0.466	0.046	-0.074	-0.544	1
Kansas	0.177	0.414	-0.112	-0.102	-0.092	-0.597	1
South Atlantic:							
Delaware	1.292	1.052	-0.029	0.249	-0.046	-0.833	0
Maryland	-0.162	-0.280	-0.063	0.003	0.048	-0.706	0
District of Columbia	0.000	1.052	1.355	0.125	0.048	-0.706	0
Virginia	-0.526	-0.280	-0.233	0.001	-0.008	-0.530	1
West Virginia	0.000	0.000	1.016	0.162	-0.057	-1.319	0
North Carolina	-0.631	-0.336	-0.483	-0.003	0.012	-0.233	1
South Carolina	-0.344	-0.280	-0.233	-0.034	0.054	0.267	1

	Change in Relative Tax Rate[a]			Change in Relative Unionism[b]			RTW Law
	1958-1948	1966-1956	1974-1964	1964-1953	1974-1964	1978-1968	
East South Central:							
Kentucky	0.354	-0.392	-0.766	0.148	0.042	-0.859	0
Tennessee	-0.394	-0.157	0.016	-0.042	0.062	-0.611	1
Alabama	-0.315	0.252	-0.402	-0.129	0.125	-0.619	1
Mississippi	-0.631	-0.968	-0.322	0.006	0.000	-0.435	1
West South Central:							
Arkansas	-0.526	-0.280	-0.233	-0.083	0.064	-0.601	1
Louisiana	-0.421	-0.224	-0.322	0.035	-0.011	-0.573	0
Oklahoma	-0.421	-0.224	-0.322	0.018	0.060	-0.527	0
Texas	0.000	0.000	0.000	-0.018	0.018	-0.442	1
Mountain:							
Montana	0.201	0.305	-0.065	-0.248	-0.212	-1.000	0
Idaho	-0.841	-0.870	-1.635	-0.015	-0.052	-0.615	0
Wyoming	0.000	0.000	0.000	-0.219	0.037	-0.616	1
Colorado	-0.162	-0.280	-0.402	-0.096	-0.034	-0.706	0
New Mexico	-0.210	0.098	0.347	0.055	0.046	-0.420	0
Arizona	-0.526	0.056	0.529	-0.222	-0.016	-0.571	1
Utah	-0.057	0.196	0.016	-0.196	-0.041	-0.592	1
Nevada	0.000	0.000	0.000	0.179	-0.066	-0.934	1
Pacific:							
Washington	0.000	0.000	0.000	-0.143	-0.090	-1.314	0
Oregon	-1.358	-0.870	-0.483	-0.162	-0.147	-1.007	0
California	-0.421	0.091	0.150	0.033	-0.052	-1.022	0

[a] $\left(T_s^1/\bar{T}^1\right) - \left(T_s^0/\bar{T}^0\right)$.

[b] $\left(U_s^1/\bar{U}^1\right) - \left(U_s^0/\bar{U}^0\right)$.

Full Regression Results

TABLE B.1

POOLED REGRESSIONS: ACROSS STATES AND INDUSTRIES
BY PERIOD
(t-values in parentheses)

Variable	1957-79	1957-79	1957-65	1965-73	1973-78
Constant	.038* (3.15)	.051* (2.75)	.029 (1.066)	-.001 (-0.04)	.072* (4.46)
TAX	-.125* (-6.00)	-.118* (-5.54)	-.139* (-2.65)	-.151* (-3.38)	-.103* (-4.75)
UNION	-4.75* (-4.52)	-.460* (-4.37)	-.374 (-1.54)	-.921* (-4.08)	-.423* (-3.63)
RTW	.228* (11.02)	.230* (11.08)	.278* (5.72)	.375* (11.10)	.046** (1.72)
Period II	--	-.001 (-0.04)	--	--	--
Period III	--	-.038 (-1.58)	--	--	--
R^2	.14	.15	.15	.23	.10
F	78.35	47.70	27.20	46.98	16.45
d.f.	1412	1410	456	483	465

Note: Period II $= \begin{cases} 1 \text{ if } SD = 1965\text{-}73 \\ 0 \text{ otherwise} \end{cases}$

Period III $= \begin{cases} 1 \text{ if } SD = 1973\text{-}79 \\ 0 \text{ otherwise} \end{cases}$

*Significant at .01.

**Significant at .10.

Appendix B

TABLE B.2

POOLED REGRESSIONS: ACROSS STATES AND INDUSTRIES
WITH AND WITHOUT INDUSTRY DUMMIES

Variable	Coefficient	t-value	Coefficient	t-value
Constant	.003	(0.09)	.038*	(3.15)
TAX	-.128*	(-6.34)	-.125*	(-6.00)
UNION	-.446*	(-4.38)	-.475*	(-4.52)
RTW	.225*	(11.22)	.228*	(11.02)
Industry:				
Textiles	-.079	(-1.61)	--	--
Apparel	.016	(0.34)	--	--
Lumber	.060	(-1.27)	--	--
Furniture	-.102**	(-2.07)	--	--
Paper	-.023	(-0.48)	--	--
Printing	--	--	--	--
Chemicals	-.029	(-0.62)	--	--
Rubber	-.066	(-1.15)	--	--
Leather	.030	(0.52)	--	--
Stone	-.008	(-0.18)	--	--
Primary Metals	.060	(1.32)	--	--
Fabricated Metals	.123*	(2.66)	--	--
Machinery	.220*	(4.77)	--	--
Electronic Equipment	.237*	(5.10)	--	--
Transportation	.130*	(2.75)	--	--
R^2	.21		.14	
F	21.82		78.35	
d.f.	1398		1412	

*Significant at .01.

**Significant at .05.

TABLE B.3

POOLED REGRESSIONS: CAPITAL/LABOR INTERACTIONS
WITH AND WITHOUT INDUSTRY DUMMIES

Variable	Coefficient	t-value	Coefficient	t-value
A. TAX	$-.166^*$	(-4.47)	$-.167^*$	(-4.35)
(K/L)(TAX)	.024	(1.32)	.026	(1.39)
B. UNION	$-.707^*$	(-3.70)	$-.702^*$	(-3.65)
(K/L)(UNION)	$.159^{***}$	(1.68)	.140	(1.49)
C. RTW	$.303^*$	(8.26)	$.327^*$	(9.87)
(K/L)(RTW)	$-.048^*$	(-2.63)	$-.060^*$	(-3.90)
D. Constant	$-.008$	(0.25)	$.039^*$	(3.19)
E. Industry:				
Textiles	$-.067$	(-1.36)	--	--
Apparel	.009	(0.18)	--	--
Lumber	.050	(-1.08)	--	--
Furniture	$-.105^{**}$	(-2.14)	--	--
Paper	.010	(0.20)	--	--
Printing	--	--	--	--
Chemicals	.017	(.033)	--	--
Rubber	$-.056$	(-0.97)	--	--
Leather	.029	(0.52)	--	--
Stone	.019	(0.40)	--	--
Primary Metals	$.090^{**}$	(1.92)	--	--
Fabricated Metals	$.127^*$	(2.76)	--	--
Machinery	$.222^*$	(4.83)	--	--
Electronic Equipment	$.236^*$	(5.11)	--	--
Transportation	$.131^*$	(2.78)	--	--
R^2	.22		.16	
F	19.43		43.38	
d.f.	1395		1409	

*Significant at .01.

**Significant at .05.

***Significant at .10.

Appendix B

TABLE B.4

POOLED REGRESSIONS: EXPANSION INTERACTIONS
WITH AND WITHOUT INDUSTRY DUMMIES

Variable	Coefficient	t-value	Coefficient	t-value
A. TAX	-.099*	(-4.61)	-.093*	(-4.25)
(EXP)(TAX)	-.739*	(-3.60)	-.804*	(-3.85)
B. UNION	-.317*	(-2.89)	-.346*	(-3.10)
(EXP)(UNION)	-2.549*	(-2.57)	-2.253*	(-2.32)
C. RTW	.187*	(8.59)	.173*	(7.97)
(EXP)(RTW)	.763*	(3.96)	1.107*	(6.48)
D. Constant	-.006	(-0.18)	.035*	(3.03)
E. Industry:				
Textiles	-.047	(-0.96)	--	--
Apparel	.049	(1.05)	--	--
Lumber	-.015	(-0.32)	--	--
Furniture	-.078	(-1.62)	--	--
Paper	-.017	(-0.37)	--	--
Printing	-	-	--	--
Chemicals	-.014	(-0.29)	--	--
Rubber	-.055	(-0.94)	--	--
Leather	.063	(1.08)	--	--
Stone	-.027	(-0.61)	--	--
Primary Metals	.075**	(1.67)	--	--
Fabricated Metals	.122*	(2.71)	--	--
Machinery	.206*	(4.55)	--	--
Electronic Equipment	.198*	(4.28)	--	--
Transportation	.111*	(2.38)	--	--
R^2	.24		.19	
F	21.85		56.01	
d.f.	1395		1409	

*Significant at .01.

**Significant at .10.

Alternative Decomposition Procedure

TO TEST WHETHER the choice of a base affects the conclusions drawn in Chapter 9, we can perform the alternative decomposition by first defining a hypothetical average wage for the South. This is accomplished by assigning to the South the labor force composition of the non-South, that is,

$$\hat{w}^s = \Sigma w_i^s N_i^n / N^n \tag{C.1}$$

where w_i^s represents the average wage for each schooling class in the South and N_i^n / N^n represents the fraction of workers in each schooling class in the non-South. Proceeding along the same lines in the text, a Paasche-type quantity index and a Laspeyres-type wage index can be defined, respectively, as:

$$P_Q = \left(\Sigma w_i^s N_i^s / N^s\right) / \left(\Sigma w_i^s N_i^n / N^n\right) = \overline{w}^s / \hat{w}^s \tag{C.2}$$

and

$$L_w = \Sigma w_i^s N_i^n / \Sigma w_i^{\ n} N_i^n = \hat{w}^s / \overline{w}^n \tag{C.3}$$

The decomposition is derived in the same manner as before and can be expressed as follows:

$$\Delta R = P_Q^0 \left[L_w^1 - L_w^0\right] + L_w^1 \left[P_Q^1 - P_Q^0\right] \tag{C.4}$$

The results of this alternative decomposition for between-cohort changes in the 1960s and 1970s are presented in Tables C.1 and C.2. The within-cohort changes are reported in Tables C.3 and C.4. While the magnitude of the wage and composition effects are obviously not identical to those reported in Chapter 9, the qualitative results are unaltered. Thus, we can conclude that the results derived earlier are not sensitive to choice of a particular base.

Appendix C

TABLE C.1

ALTERNATIVE DECOMPOSITION OF CHANGES IN SOUTH/NON-SOUTH
WEEKLY WAGE RATIOS BETWEEN COHORTS, 1959-69

Age	White Males			Nonwhite Males		
	ΔR	Wage Effect	Composition Effect	ΔR	Wage Effect	Composition Effect
			South/Northeast			
20-24	.013	.012*	.001	.080	.092*	-.012
25-34	-.002	-.006	.004	.072	.065*	.007
35-44	-.013	-.020*	.007	.045	.068*	-.023
45-54	.011	.027*	-.016	.021	.035*	-.014
55-64	-.025	-.014	-.011	-.012	.006	-.018*
			South/North Central			
20-24	.032	.028*	.004	.036	.049*	-.013
25-34	.014	.007	.007	.063	.074*	-.011
35-44	.014	-.005	.019*	.053	.077*	-.024
45-54	.037	.035*	.002	.033	.041*	-.008
55-64	-.007	.018	-.025	-.028	-.006	-.022
			South/West			
20-24	.112	.100*	.012	.112	.164*	-.052
25-34	.058	.053*	.005	.068	.073*	-.005
35-44	.027	.015	.012	.052	.106*	-.054
45-54	.019	.030	-.011	-.047	-.017	-.030*
55-64	-.041	-.014	-.027	.002	.028*	-.026

Source: Calculated from data in U.S. Census of Population, Public Use Sample, 1960 and 1970.

*Dominant effect.

Definitions: Wage effect = $P_Q^0\left(L_w^1 - L_w^0\right)$.

Composition effect = $L_w^1\left(P_Q^1 - P_Q^0\right)$.

TABLE C.2

ALTERNATIVE DECOMPOSITION OF CHANGES IN SOUTH/NON-SOUTH
WEEKLY WAGE RATIOS BETWEEN COHORTS, 1969-78

Age	White Males			Nonwhite Males		
	ΔR	Wage Effect	Composition Effect	ΔR	Wage Effect	Composition Effect
South/Northeast						
20-24	.152	.164*	-.012	.352	.318*	.034
25-34	.018	.020*	-.002	.036	.040*	-.004
35-44	-.022	-.002	-.020*	.182	.121*	.061
45-54	.054	.042*	.012	.112	.087*	.025
55-64	.088	.098*	-.010	-.180	-.143*	-.037
South/North Central						
20-24	.016	.023*	-.007	.147	.110*	.037
25-34	-.007	-.003	-.004	.051	.026	.025
35-44	.004	.009*	-.005	.316	.333*	-.017
45-54	.033	.031*	.002	.104	.086*	.018
55-64	.037	.037*	.000	.065	.105*	-.040
South/West						
20-24	-.061	.076*	.015	.018	.042*	.024
25-34	-.023	-.016	-.007	.054	.030*	.024
35-44	.005	.014*	-.009	.170	.225*	.055
45-54	.008	-.007	.015*	-.031	-.101*	.070
55-64	-.005	.001	-.006*	.071	.038	.033

Source: Calculated from data in U.S. Census of Population, Public Use
Sample, 1960 and 1970.

*Dominant effect.

Definitions: Wage effect = $P_Q^0 \left(L_w^1 - L_w^0 \right)$.

Composition effect = $L_w^1 \left(P_Q^1 - P_Q^0 \right)$.

Appendix C

TABLE C.3

ALTERNATIVE DECOMPOSITION OF CHANGES IN SOUTH/NON-SOUTH
WEEKLY WAGE RATIOS BETWEEN COHORTS, 1959-69

Age in 1969	White Males			Nonwhite Males		
	ΔR	Wage Effect	Composition Effect	ΔR	Wage Effect	Composition Effect
South/Northeast						
35-44	-.010	-.010*	.000	.023	.045*	-.022
45-54	.000	-.001	.001	.021	.019*	.002
55-64	-.004	-.003	-.001	-.004	.004	-.008*
South/North Central						
35-44	.019	.008	.011	.043	.068*	-.025
45-54	.024	.012	.012	.015	.019*	-.004
55-64	-.018	.011*	.007	-.003	.004	-.007*
South/West						
35-44	.039	.046*	-.007	.042	.068*	-.026
45-54	.024	.038*	-.014	-.018	-.004	-.014*
55-64	.005	.006*	-.001	.020	.023*	-.003

Source: Calculated from data in U.S. Census of Population, Public Use
Sample, 1960 and 1970.

*Dominant effect.

Definitions: Wage effect $= P_Q^0\left(L_\omega^1 - L_\omega^0\right).$

Composition effect $= L_\omega^1\left(P_Q^1 - P_Q^0\right).$

TABLE C.4

ALTERNATIVE DECOMPOSITION OF CHANGES IN SOUTH/NON-SOUTH
WEEKLY WAGE RATIOS BETWEEN COHORTS, 1969-78

Age in 1978	White Males			Nonwhite Males		
	ΔR	Wage Effect	Composition Effect	ΔR	Wage Effect	Composition Effect
South/Northeast						
35-44	.002	.020*	-.018	.075	.053*	.022
45-54	.036	.025*	.011	.104	.076*	.028
55-64	.061	.078*	-.017	.002	-.028	.030
South/North Central						
35-44	.013	.017*	-.004	.249	.239*	.010
45-54	.013	.011*	.002	.120	.108*	.012
55-64	.035	.042*	-.007	.130	.123*	.007
South/West						
35-44	.006	.027	-.021	-.044	-.027*	-.017
45-54	-.001	-.010	.009	.183	.149*	.034
55-64	-.035	-.005	-.030*	.056	-.078	.134

Source: Calculated from data in U.S. Bureau of the Census, Current Populations Survey, 1969 and 1978.

*Dominant effect.

Definitions: Wage effect = $P_Q^0\left(L_\omega^1 - L_\omega^0\right)$.

Composition effect = $L_\omega^1\left(P_Q^1 - P_Q^0\right)$.

South/Non-South Wage Ratios and Decomposition by Major Industry Groups, 1959–69

TABLES D.1–D.7 report South/non-South wage ratios in 1959 and 1969 by age for seven major industries. Utilizing the technique developed in Chapter 9, we also decompose the change in these ratios into a wage effect and a composition effect. At this level of aggregation, it is impossible to perform the analysis separately for whites and nonwhites.

The general pattern of South/non-South wage convergence that we observed earlier is also evident once we hold industry composition constant between regions. In addition, wage effects tend to account for most of the change in wage ratios between 1959 and 1969 for each of the seven industries examined.

TABLE D.1

RATIOS OF SOUTH/NON-SOUTH WEEKLY WAGES FOR MALE WORKERS
BY INDUSTRY GROUP, 1959 AND 1969, WITH DECOMPOSITION

Services

Age	1969	1959	ΔR	Wage Effect	Composition Effect
			South/Northeast		
20-24	.900	.732	.167	.143*	.024
25-34	.869	.783	.085	.060*	.025
35-44	.771	.657	.114	.079*	.035
45-54	.750	.644	.112	.126*	-.014
55-64	.749	.688	.061	.072*	-.011
			South/North Central		
20-24	.964	.737	.227	.227*	.000
25-34	.897	.768	.129	.102*	.027
35-44	.825	.713	.112	.101*	.011
45-54	.769	.675	.094	.119*	-.025
55-64	.780	.726	.054	.079*	-.025
			South/West		
20-24	.984	.715	.269	.247*	.022
25-34	.886	.696	.190	.155*	.035
35-44	.776	.623	.152	.143*	.009
45-54	.810	.657	.153	.152*	.001
55-64	.769	.743	.035	.047*	-.012

Source: U.S. Census of Population, Public Use Sample, 1970 and 1970.

*Dominant effect.

Appendix D

TABLE D.2

RATIOS OF SOUTH/NON-SOUTH WEEKLY WAGES FOR MALE WORKERS
BY INDUSTRY GROUP, 1959 AND 1969, WITH DECOMPOSITION

Wholesale and Retail Trade

Age	1969	1959	ΔR	Wage Effect	Composition Effect
			South/Northeast		
20-24	.867	.829	.038	.034*	.004
25-34	.856	.923	.032	.026*	.006
35-44	.866	.849	.017	.012*	.005
45-54	.858	.809	.049	.050*	-.001
55-64	.806	.823	-.017	.005	-.022*
			South/North Central		
20-24	.864	.825	.038	.031*	.007
25-34	.844	.801	.043	.040*	.003
35-44	.838	.826	.011	.008*	.003
45-54	.856	.814	.041	.034*	.007
55-64	.845	.858	-.012	.010	-.022*
			South/West		
20-24	.881	.757	.123	.113*	.010
25-34	.869	.749	.120	.116*	.004
35-44	.884	.798	.086	.074*	.012
45-54	.824	.770	.054	.053*	.001
55-64	.815	.795	.020	.029*	-.009

Source: U.S. Census of Population, Public Use Sample, 1970 and 1970.

*Dominant effect.

TABLE D.3

RATIOS OF SOUTH/NON-SOUTH WEEKLY WAGES FOR MALE WORKERS
BY INDUSTRY GROUP, 1959 AND 1969, WITH DECOMPOSITION

Construction

Age	1969	1959	ΔR	Wage Effect	Composition Effect
			South/Northeast		
20-24	.805	.784	.020	.024*	-.004
25-34	.768	.725	.043	.033*	.010
35-44	.776	.767	.009	.009*	.000
45-54	.772	.745	.027	.036*	-.009
55-64	.746	.705	.041	.041*	.000
			South/North Central		
20-24	.762	.725	.036	.028*	.008
25-34	.746	.705	.041	.030*	.011
35-44	.731	.732	-.001	-.009*	.008
45-54	.754	.750	.004	.019*	-.015
55-64	.746	.737	.008	.008*	.000
			South/West		
20-24	.769	.672	.096	.060*	.036
25-34	.736	.675	.060	.063*	-.003
35-44	.753	.685	.068	.055	.013
45-54	.732	.678	.054	.054*	.000
55-64	.688	.659	.029	.056*	-.027

Source: U.S. Census of Population, Public Use Sample, 1970 and 1970.

*Dominant effect.

Appendix D

TABLE D.4

RATIOS OF SOUTH/NON-SOUTH WEEKLY WAGES FOR MALE WORKERS
BY INDUSTRY GROUP, 1959 AND 1969, WITH DECOMPOSITION

Mining

Age	1969	1959	ΔR	Wage Effect	Composition Effect
South/Northeast					
20-24	.999	.992	.007	.036*	-.029
25-34	.950	1.111	-.160	-.148*	-.012
35-44	.906	.993	-.087	-.061*	-.026
45-54	1.076	.986	.090	-.1.00	.190*
55-64	1.015	.898	.117	-.054	.171*
South/North Central					
20-24	1.116	.827	.289	.244*	.045
25-34	.975	.940	.036	.014	.022*
35-44	1.040	.958	.082	.066*	.016
45-54	1.003	.931	.072	.041*	.029
55-64	1.136	.907	.229	.188*	.041
South/West					
20-24	1.045	.809	.236	.200*	.036
25-34	.932	.896	.035	.041*	-.006
35-44	.917	.862	.055	.028*	.027
45-54	.944	.832	.112	.094*	.018
55-64	.929	.743	.186	.152*	.034

Source: U.S. Census of Population, Public Use Sample, 1970 and 1970.

*Dominant effect.

TABLE D.5

RATIOS OF SOUTH/NON-SOUTH WEEKLY WAGES FOR MALE WORKERS
BY INDUSTRY GROUP, 1959 AND 1969, WITH DECOMPOSITION

Transportation, Communications, and Utilities

Age	1969	1959	ΔR	Wage Effect	Composition Effect
South/Northeast					
20-24	.878	.861	.017	.024*	-.007
25-34	.862	.888	-.026	-.033*	-.007
35-44	.852	.904	-.052	-.059*	.007
45-54	.847	.882	-.035	-.035*	.000
55-64	.884	.930	-.045	-.051*	.006
South/North Central					
20-24	.854	.791	.062	.072*	-.010
25-34	.874	.972	.002	-.007	.009*
35-44	.872	.867	.005	-.008	.013*
45-54	.879	.854	.024	.022*	.002
55-64	.899	.938	-.038	-.033*	-.005
South/West					
20-24	.853	.847	.005	.007*	-.002
25-34	.844	.836	.007	.009*	-.002
35-44	.819	.833	-.013	-.033*	.020
45-54	.791	.846	-.055	-.042*	-.013
55-64	.820	.882	-.062	-.033*	-.029

Source: U.S. Census of Population, Public Use Sample, 1970 and 1970.

*Dominant effect.

Appendix D

TABLE D.6

RATIOS OF SOUTH/NON-SOUTH WEEKLY WAGES FOR MALE WORKERS
BY INDUSTRY GROUP, 1959 AND 1969, WITH DECOMPOSITION

Manufacturing Durables

Age	1969	1959	ΔR	Wage Effect	Composition Effect
		South/Northeast			
20-24	.816	.790	.025	.023*	.002
25-34	.845	.796	.049	.040*	.009
35-44	.810	.815	-.004	.004	-.008*
45-54	.831	.788	.042	.058*	-.016
55-64	.868	.846	.002	.034*	-.012
		South/North Central			
20-24	.772	.752	.020	.021*	-.001
25-34	.825	.789	.035	.024*	.011
35-44	.819	.800	.018	-.003	.021*
45-54	.809	.765	.043	.039*	.004
55-64	.818	.815	.003	.017*	-.014
		South/West			
20-24	.807	.709	.097	.096*	.001
25-34	.800	.730	.070	.054*	.016
35-44	.747	.735	.012	.009*	.003
45-54	.743	.749	-.006	.015*	-.021
55-64	.748	.843	-.095	-.060*	-.035

Source: U.S. Census of Population, Public Use Sample, 1970 and 1970.

*Dominant effect.

TABLE D.7

RATIOS OF SOUTH/NON-SOUTH WEEKLY WAGES FOR MALE WORKERS
BY INDUSTRY GROUP, 1959 AND 1969, WITH DECOMPOSITION

Manufacturing Nondurables

Age	1969	1959	ΔR	Wage Effect	Composition Effect
		South/Northeast			
20-24	.882	.883	-.001	.000	-.001*
25-34	.840	.851	-.011	-.008*	-.003
35-44	.788	.797	-.008	-.014*	.006
45-54	.784	.849	-.065	-.023	-.042*
55-64	.752	.858	-.106	-.092*	-.014
		South/North Central			
20-24	.850	.809	.041	.049*	-.008
25-34	.801	.819	-.017	-.012*	-.005
35-44	.806	.797	.008	-.001	.009*
45-54	.833	.803	.029	.034*	-.005
55-64	.754	.784	-.029	-.022*	-.007
		South/West			
20-24	.867	.768	.099	.086*	.013
25-34	.834	.798	.036	.029*	.007
35-44	.788	.791	-.003	-.002*	-.001
45-54	.795	.793	.002	.013*	-.011
55-64	.750	.821	.071	-.047	.118*

Source: U.S. Census of Population, Public Use Sample, 1970 and 1970.

*Dominant effect.

South/Non-South Annual Earnings Ratios and Decomposition, 1950s

OWING TO A lack of compatible data for weekly wages in the 1950 Census of Population, we were unable to analyze dynamic patterns in South/non-South wage ratios in the 1950s. However, both the 1950 and 1960 Census of Population publish *median annual earnings* for male workers by age and schooling class that can be used to perform the same sort of analysis as those presented in Chapters 8 and 9. These data are published for only two regional breakdowns: South and non-South (North and West). Table E.1 reports the resulting ratios of median annual earnings for males with income in 1949 and 1959. Column 3 gives the gain or loss for each age group between the two census years. With the exception of the 35–44 age group, the overall pattern is one of convergence in regional wage differentials. Some caution should be used in comparing the magnitude of these gains with those for weekly wages in the text. While the gains in the 1950s appear to be greater than those in the 1960s and 1970s, they are merely the result of using annual earnings. If we examine annual earnings for the last two decades (not displayed here), the gains are always smaller in wage than in annual earnings comparisons. Furthermore, the gains in annual earnings for southern workers in the 1960s and 1970s exceed the corresponding gains in the 1950s.

The right half of Table E.1 reports the results of the decomposition of ΔR into wage and composition effects. With one exception (the 25–35 age group), the gains during this period are also primarily attributable to schooling-constant wage effects.

TABLE E.1

RATIOS AND DECOMPOSITION OF SOUTH/NORTH AND WEST ANNUAL EARNINGS FOR AGE GROUPS
IN 1949 AND 1959, ALL RACES

Ratios of Annual Earnings -- All Races				Decomposition of Change in Annual Earnings Ratios			
				Alternative I		Alternative II	
Age	1959	1949	Δ	$L_Q^0\left(P_w^1 - P_w^0\right)$	$P_w^1\left(L_Q^1 - L_Q^0\right)$	$P_Q^0\left(L_w^1 - L_w^0\right)$	$L_w^1\left(P_Q^1 - P_Q^0\right)$
25-34	.788	.767	.021	.006	.015	-.018	.039
35-44	.694	.737	-.043	-.005	.012	-.081	.038
45-54	.745	.704	.041	.036	.005	.024	.017
55-64	.714	.660	.054	.051	.003	.044	.010

Source: U.S. Bureau of the Census, U.S. Census of Population, 1950 and 1960.

Selected Bibliography

Advisory Commission on Intergovernmental Relations. "Interstate Tax and Fiscal Competition." Washington, D.C. (November 1978).
———. "State and Local Tax Differentials and Regional Economic Growth." Washington, D.C. (May 1979).
Aldrich, Mark. "Flexible Exchange Rates, Northern Expansion and the Market for Southern Cotton." *Journal of Economic History* (June 1973): 399–416.
Ashenfelter, Orley. "Racial Discrimination and Trade Unionism." *Journal of Political Economy* (May/June 1972): 435–64.
Ashenfelter, Orley, and John H. Pencavel. "American Trade Union Growth: 1900–1960." *Quarterly Journal of Economics* (August 1969): 435–48.
Barkin, S. *The Decline of the Labor Movement* (Santa Barbara, Calif.: The Fund for the Republic, 1961).
Batra, R., and G. W. Scully. "Technical Progress, Economic Growth, and the North-South Wage Differential." *Journal of Regional Science* (December 1972): 375–86.
Bellante, Don. "The North-South Differential and the Migration of Heterogeneous Labor." *American Economic Review* (March 1979): 166–75.
Bernstein, I. "The Growth of American Unions." *American Economic Review* (June 1954): 300–318.
Bloom, Clark. *State and Local Tax Differentials* (Iowa City: Bureau of Business Research, State University of Iowa, 1955).
Bolton, R. E. *Defense Purchases and Regional Growth* (Washington, D.C.: Brookings Institution, 1966).
Borts, George. "The Equalization of Returns and Regional Economic Growth." *American Economic Review* (June 1960): 319–47.
Borts, George, and Jerome Stein. *Economic Growth in a Free Market* (New York: Columbia University Press, 1964).
Boskin, Michael. "Unions and Relative Real Wages." *American Economic Review* (June 1972): 466–72.
Bradfield, Michael. "Necessary and Sufficient Conditions to Explain Equilibrium Regional Wage Differentials." *Journal of Regional Science* (Vol. 16, No. 2, 1976): 247–55.
Brazer, Harvey. "The Value of Industrial Property as a Subject of Taxation." *Canadian Public Administration* (June 1961): 137–47.
Campbell, A. K. "Taxes and Industrial Location in the New York Metropolitan Region." *National Tax Journal* (September 1958): 198.
Carlton, Dennis. "Why Do Firms Locate Where They Do: An Econometric Model."

In William Wheaton, ed., *Interregional Movements and Regional Growth* (Washington, D.C.: The Urban Institute, 1979), pp. 13–50.

Coelho, P. R., and M. A. Ghali. "The End of the North-South Wage Differential." *American Economic Review* (December 1971): 932–37.

———. "The End of the North-South Wage Differential: Reply." *American Economic Review* (September 1973): 757–62.

Conrad, Alfred, and John Meyer et al. "Slavery as an Obstacle to Economic Growth in the United States." *Journal of Economic History* (December 1967): 518–60.

Creamer, Daniel. "Shifts in Manufacturing Industries." In National Resources Planning Board, *Industrial Location and National Resources* (Washington, D.C.: U.S. Government Printing Office, 1943).

Due, John T. "Studies of State-Local Tax Influences on Location of Industry." *National Tax Journal* (June 1960): 163–73.

Floyd, Joe Summers, Jr. *Effects of Taxation on Industrial Location* (Chapel Hill: University of North Carolina Press, 1952).

Fuchs, Victor. *Changes in the Location of Manufacturing in the United States Since 1929* (New Haven: Yale University Press, 1962).

———. "Hourly Earnings Differentials by Region and Size of City." *Monthly Labor Review* (January 1967): 22–26.

Fuchs, Victor, and Richard Perlman. "Recent Trends in Southern Wage Differentials." *Review of Economics and Statistics* (August 1963): 292–300.

Gallaway, Lowell. "The North-South Wage Differential." *Review of Economics and Statistics* (Auguest 1963): 264–72.

———. "The Economics of the Right-to-Work Controversy." *Southern Economic Journal* (January 1966): 310–16.

Garwood, John. "Taxes and Industrial Location." *National Tax Journal* (December 1952): 365–69.

Glasgow, John. "That Right-to-Work Controversy Again." *Labor Law Journal* (February 1967): 112–15.

Goldfarb, Robert, and Anthony Yezer. "Evaluating Alternative Theories of Intercity and Interregional Wage Differentials." *Journal of Regional Science* (December 1976): 345–63.

Greenwood, Michael. *Migration and Economic Growth in the United States: National, Regional and Metropolitan Perspectives* (New York: Academic Press, 1981).

Hanna, Frank A. *State Income Differentials 1919–1954* (Durham, N.C.: Duke University Press, 1959).

Hanushek, Eric. "Regional Differences in the Structure of Earnings." *Review of Economics and Statistics* (May 1973): 204–13.

———. Alternative Models of Earnings Determination and Labor Market Structure." *Journal of Human Resources* (Spring 1981): 238–59.

Harberger, Arnold. "The Incidence of the Corporate Income Tax." *Journal of Political Economy* (June 1962): 215–40.

Hirschman, A. D. *The Strategy of Economic Development* (New Haven: Yale University Press, 1958).

Hodge, James. "A Study of Regional Investment Decisions." Ph.D. diss., University of Chicago, 1979.

Hoover, Edgar. *The Location of Economic Activity* (New York: McGraw-Hill, 1948).

Johnson, George, and Kenwood Youmans. "Union Relative Wage Effects by Age and Education." *Industrial and Labor Relations Review* (January 1971): 171–79.

Keeble, D. E. "Models of Economic Development." In Richard Chorley and Peter Haggett, eds., *Models in Geography* (London: Methuen & Co. Ltd, 1967), pp. 243–302.

Kuhlman, J. M. "Right-to-Work Laws: The Virginia Experience." *Labor Law Journal* (July 1955): 453–61.

Kuhn, James W. "Right-to-Work Laws—Symbols or Substance?" *Industrial and Labor Relations Review* (July 1961): 587–94.

Ladenson, Mark L. "The End of the North-South Wage Differential: Comment." *American Economic Review* (September 1973): 754–62.

Larson, John. *Taxes and Plant Location in Michigan.* Committee for Economic Development, School of Business Administration, University of Michigan, 1957.

Lebergott, Stanley. *Manpower in Economic Growth: The American Record Since 1800* (New York: McGraw-Hill, 1964).

Lee, Susan, and Peter Passell. *A New Economic View of American History* (New York: W. W. Norton, 1979).

Lewis, H. G. *Unionism and Relative Wages in the United States* (Chicago: The University of Chicago Press, 1963).

Long, Clarence D. *Wages and Earnings in the United States, 1860–1890* (Princeton, N.J.: Princeton University Press, 1960).

Long, Larry, and Kristin A. Hansen. "Trends in Return Migration to the South." *Demography* (November 1975): 601–14.

Lumsden, Keith, and Graig Peterson. "The Effect of Right-to-Work Laws on Unionism in the United States." *Journal of Political Economy* (December 1975): 1237–48.

Marshall, Ray. "Ethnic and Economic Minorities: Unions' Future or Unrecruitable?" *Annals of the American Academy of Political and Social Science* (November 1963).

———. "The Development of Organized Labor." *Monthly Labor Review* (March 1968): 65–73.

McCall, John, and Anthony Pascal, "Agglomeration Economies, Search Costs and Industrial Location." The Rand Corporation Paper Series, P-6348, (June 1979).

McKenzie, Ricard B. *Restrictions on Business Mobility* (Washington, D.C.: American Enterprise Institute for Public Policy Research, 1979).

McLure, Charles E., Jr. "Taxation, Substitution and Industrial Location." *Journal of Political Economy* (January/ February 1970): 112–32.

Meyer, John R. "Regional Economics: A Survey." *American Economic Review* (March 1963): 19–54.

Meyers, Frederic. "Effects of 'Right-to-Work' Laws: A Study of the Texas Act." *Industrial and Labor Relations Review* (October 1955): 77–84.

———. *Right-to-Work in Practice* (New York: The Fund for the Republic, 1959).

Moore, William J. "Membership and Wage Impact of Right-to-Work Laws." *Journal of Labor Research* (Fall 1980): 349–68.

Moore, William J., Robert J. Newman, and R. William Thomas. "Determinants of the Passage of Right-to-Work Laws: An Alternative Interpretation." *Journal of Law and Economics* (April 1974): 197–211.

Moore, William J., and Robert J. Newman. "On the Prospects for American Trade Union Growth: A Cross-Section Analysis." *Review of Economics and Statistics* (November 1975): 435–45.

Moroney, J. R., and J. M. Walker. "A Regional Test of the Heckscher-Ohlin Hypothesis." *Journal of Political Economy* (December 1966): 573–86.

Mueller, E., and J. Morgan. "Location Decisions of Manufacturers." *American Economic Review* (May 1962): 204–17.

Myrdal, G. M. *Economic Theory and Under-Developed Regions* (London: Duckworth, 1957).

Nadworney, Milton. "State 'Right-to-Work' Laws." *Current History* (August 1966): 85–90.

Newman, Robert J. "Industry Migration and Changing Regional Wage Patterns." Ph.D. diss., Department of Economics, UCLA, 1980.

———. "Dynamic Patterns in Regional Wage Differentials." *Southern Economic Journal* (July 1982): 246–54.

———. "Industry Migration and Growth in the South." *Review of Economics and Statistics* (February 1983); 76–86.

North, D. C. "Location Theory and Regional Economic Growth." *Journal of Political Economy* (June 1955): 243–58.

Northrup, Herbert, and Gordon Bloom. *Government and Labor* (Homewood, Ill.: Richard D. Irwin, 1963).

Palomba, Neil, and Catherine Palomba. "Right-to-Work Laws: A Suggested Economic Rationale." *Journal of Law and Economics* (October 1971): 475–84.

Perloff, H. S., Edgar Dunn, Jr., Eric Lampard, and Richard Muth. *Regions, Resources and Economic Growth* (Baltimore: Johns Hopkins University Press, 1960).

Perloff, H. S., and L. Wingo. "Natural Resource Endowment and Regional Economic Growth." In Springler, ed., *Natural Resources and Economic Growth* (Washington, D.C., 1961), pp. 191–212.

Preinreich, G. A. D. "The Economic Life of Industrial Equipment." *Econometrica* (January 1940): 12.

Ransom, Roger, and Richard Sutch. *One Kind of Freedom: The Economic Consequences of Emancipation* (London: Cambridge University Press, 1977).

Reder, Melvin. "Theory of Occupational Wage Differentials." *American Economic Review* (December 1955): 833–52.

———. "Wage Differentials: Theory and Measurement." In *Aspects of labor Economics* National Bureau of Economic Research (Princeton, N.J.: Princeton University Press, 1962), pp. 257–311.

Rees, John. "Regional Industrial Shifts in the U.S. and the Internal Generation of Manufacturing in Growth Centers of the Southwest." In William Wheaton, ed., *Interregional Movements and Regional Growth* (Washington, D.C.: The Urban Institute, 1979), pp. 51–74.

Romans, Thomas, and Ganti Subrahmanyam. "State and Local Taxes, Transfers and Regional Economic Growth." *Southern Economic Journal* (October 1979): 435–44.

Rosen, Sherwin. "Wage-Based Indexes of Urban Quality of Life." In Peter Mieszkowski and M. Straszheim, eds., *Current Issues in Urban Economics* (Baltimore: The Johns Hopkins Press, 1979).

Scully, Gerald. "Interstate Wage Differentials: A Cross Section Analysis." *American Economic Review* (December 1969): 757–73.

———. "The North-South Manufacturing Wage Differential, 1869–1919," *Journal of Regional Science,* no. 2 (1971): 235–52.

Segal, M. "Regional Wage Differentials in Manufacturing in the Postwar Period." *Review of Economics and Statistics* (May 1961): 248–55.

Shister, Joseph. "The Impact of the Taft-Hartley Act on Union Strength and Collective Bargaining." *Industrial and Labor Relations Review* (April 1958): 339–51.

Smith, Vernon. *Investment and Production* (Cambridge: Harvard University Press, 1961).

Soffer, Benson, and Michael Korenich. " 'Right-to-Work' Laws as a Location Factor: The Industrialization Experience of Agricultural States." *Journal of Regional Science* (Winter 1961): 41–56.

Stafford, R. P. "Concentration and Labor Earnings: Comment." *American Economic Review* (March 1958): 174–81.

Sultan, Paul. *Right-to-Work Laws: A Study in Conflict* (Los Angeles: Institute of Industrial Relations, UCLA, 1958).

Terborgh, George. *Dynamic Equipment Policy* (Cambridge: Harvard University Press, 1961).

Thomas, M. D. "Regional Economic Growth and Industrial Development." *Papers of the Regional Science Association, European Congress* (1962), pp. 61–75.

Throop, A. "The Union-Nonunion Wage Differential and Cost-Push Inflation." *American Economic Review* (March 1968): 79–99.

Tiebout, Charles. "Location Theory, Empirical Evidence and Economic Evaluation." *Papers and Proceedings of the Regional Science Association* (1957).

Tollefson, John O., and Joseph A. Pichler. "A Comment on Right-to-Work Laws: A Suggested Economic Rationale." *Journal of Law and Economics* (April 1974): 193–96.

Vernon, R. "International Investment and International Trade in the Product Cycle." *Quarterly Journal of Economics* (May 1966): 190–207.

Weeks, Joseph. *Report on the Statistics of Wages in the Manufacturing Industries with Supplementary Reports on the Average Retail Prices of Necessaries of Life and on Trade Societies, and Strikes and Lockouts* (U.S. Census of Population, 1880).

Weinstein, Bernard, and Robert E. Firestine. *Regional Growth and Decline in the*

United States, The Rise of the Sunbelt and the Decline of the Northeast (New York: Praeger, 1978).

Weiss, Leonard W. "Concentration and Labor Earnings." *American Economic Review* (March 1966): 96–117.

Welch, Finis. "Measurement of the Quality of Schooling." *American Economic Review* (May 1966): 379–92.

Witney, Fred. "The Indiana Right-to-Work Law." *Industrial and Labor Relations Review* (July 1958): 506–17.

Wright, Gavin. "Cotton Competition and the Post Bellum Recovery of the American South." *Journal of Economic History* (September 1974): 610–35.

Yotopoulos, Pan, and Jeffrey Nugent. *Economics of Development, Empirical Investigations* (New York: Harper and Row, 1976).

Index